A
President
in the Family

A
President
in the Family

Thomas Jefferson, Sally Hemings, and Thomas Woodson

BYRON W. WOODSON, SR.

Westport, Connecticut
London

Library of Congress Cataloging-in-Publication Data

Woodson, Byron W.
    A president in the family : Thomas Jefferson, Sally Hemings, and Thomas Woodson /
Byron W. Woodson, Sr.
      p. cm.
    Includes bibliographical references and index.
    ISBN 0–275–97174–0 (alk. paper)
    1. Jefferson, Thomas, 1743–1826—Relations with women. 2. Jefferson, Thomas,
1743–1826—Relations with slaves. 3. Jefferson, Thomas, 1743–1826—Family.
4. Hemings, Sally. 5. Woodson, Thomas, d. 1879. 6. Jefferson family. 7. Woodson family.
8. Hemings family. 9. Monticello (Va.) I. Title.
E332.2.W66 2001
973.4'6'092'2—dc21   00–061169
[B]

British Library Cataloguing in Publication Data is available.

Library of Congress Catalog Card Number: 00–061169
ISBN: 0–275–97174–0

First published in 2001

Praeger Publishers, 88 Post Road West, Westport, CT 06881
An imprint of Greenwood Publishing Group, Inc.
www.praeger.com

Printed in the United States of America

The paper used in this book complies with the
Permanent Paper Standard issued by the National
Information Standards Organization (Z39.48–1984).

10 9 8 7 6 5 4 3 2 1

DEDICATED

to the memory of my mother, Minnie Shumate Woodson, and to
my father, Colonel John S. Woodson, U.S. Army (Ret.);

to the spirits of Martha Wayles Jefferson, Sally Hemings,
Thomas Jefferson, and their descendants;

and to the notion that those joined in bloodline should not
be separated by racial identity.

Contents

Contents

A photo essay follows page 150

Foreword

"It's time you learned the family secret." Those are the words my father, Robert Cooley III, told my brother, sister, and me in 1978 when I was twelve years old. They are the same words his grandfather used in 1949 when Daddy was ten years old. Our "family secret" has been that we are the eighth-generation descendants of Thomas Jefferson and Sally Hemings through their first-born child, Thomas. Why should such an interesting, unique and awe-inspiring fact be withheld or considered a "secret"? Because of our ancestors' desire to protect us from the denigration and skepticism that other people often express when they learn that we descend from the third president of our nation. It is because we are products of Jefferson's "second family" . . . the one he created with his slave, Sally.

We have not always been met with rejection and scorn. There are people like Lucian Truscott IV, a descendant of Thomas Jefferson's "first family." I met Lucian in 1998 in the green room of *The Oprah Winfrey Show*. We were appearing on Oprah's show as representatives of several lines of Jefferson's children who had never before met. It was on Oprah's show that Lucian invited his "black" Jefferson cousins to the next Monticello Association meeting, an annual reunion comprised of descendants of Thomas Jefferson. Lucian continues to work tirelessly to help us gain admission to the association. We have made many national and local media appearances together. One of the most poignant ones was on National Public Radio's *Mark Steiner Show*. A caller asked Lucian why he waited so long to invite us African

American Jefferson descendants to the Monticello Association meetings. It was the first time I found Lucian to be momentarily speechless.

I think the reason he had not invited us previously because it simply had not occurred to him. He, and many of the Thomas-Martha Jefferson descendants, were not aware of our existence. In general, Americans have not learned the whole truth of our nation's history—that which accurately reflects the complexity of white and black Americans' relationships and the significant contributions of African Americans to the greatness of our nation.

The Thomas Jefferson Memorial Foundation, the private organization that owns and operates Monticello, has made tremendous strides in recognizing slaves' contributions to Monticello since Daddy first began taking us there. I can remember when slaves were barely mentioned and the Hemings family was not identified anywhere on the grounds. Tour guides would blush severely from discomfort when Daddy would ask questions like, "Where did Sally Hemings sleep?" They would deny any knowledge of her and try to ignore his subsequent questions. Of course, my siblings and I wanted to melt through the floor. But I did not realize what he was doing until I was much older. Daddy was raising the issue and making the foundation realize that we—TJ-Sally descendants—existed and would not go away, that we could not easily be dismissed.

Daddy grew increasingly impatient with the rejection and denial of the seven Jefferson-Hemings children that some historians, even contemporary historians, perpetuated—regardless of race. He brought national attention to our existence, including an invitation to the White House. In 1998, two weeks before Daddy died very unexpectedly, he said on national television that he wanted to be buried at Monticello alongside his great-great-... grandfather, Thomas Jefferson. The day after he died, I learned that the Monticello Association controlled the burial grounds. The association denied my direct request to bury Daddy at Monticello. Although it is too late for my father, our fight continues to obtain the right for Jefferson's "second family" to be buried beside his obelisk as his "first family" is. I have expressed my own desire to be buried at Monticello alongside my great-great-great-... grandfather. It is symbolic of achieving the equity in rights and privileges long-due our ancestors ... and my Daddy.

Daddy died before the DNA test results were released. However, he was president of the Thomas Woodson Family Association when Dr. Eugene Foster contacted him to request names of living male-line descendants of Thomas Woodson. My father did not reply to Dr. Foster's first letter because of his opposition to such testing. Dr. Foster's second letter expressed impatience and a sense of urgency. Daddy was an attorney, not a researcher like I am. We discussed Dr. Foster's request and our significant concerns with such a volatile medium: Our family's blood. Our biggest concern was that Woodson DNA was being tested against the DNA of Thomas Jefferson's uncle's descendants, not Thomas Jefferson's own DNA. Our family wanted access to half of the DNA samples involved in the study so that our own genetics could conduct independent DNA tests. These assurances were not met and Dr. Foster circumvented my father to obtain blood samples from a handful—out of over 1,000—living Woodson descendants. We still puzzle over the inconclusive results of the DNA testing. Our family has convened a panel of researchers to review the results (without the benefit of the actual blood samples). However, unless and until descendants of Thomas Jefferson's "first family" have to submit to DNA testing to prove their heritage, descendants of Thomas Jefferson's "second family" should not be held to a more stringent standard.

We know who we are. We have 100 percent certainty that our ancestors are Thomas Jefferson and Sally Hemings. We know this because the "secret" has been transmitted from our parents' parents' parents. Similar to how you likely learned who your grandparents and great-grandparents are: You were told. You did not ask for proof via birth certificates or DNA. Skeptics doubt the veracity of our oral history, even when over 1,000 living descendants concur, despite the fact that many of us have never spoken to each other.

Nonetheless, we recognize the need and importance of providing support for our assertion. Our family's struggle to prove our progenitor is fraught with more challenges than most. The DNA testing is one of the most recent challenges, as is the Jefferson Memorial Foundation's lack of recognition of Thomas Woodson as Jefferson's child. The challenges that existed 200 years ago still pose significant impediments to our burden of proof: the illegality of miscegination and public identifying the fathers of slave children, lack of issuance of birth certificates for slaves' children, illegality of slaves being literate, and the conspiracy to "protect" the image of Thomas Jefferson by eradicating evidence of his almost four-decade-long relationship with his paramour and slave, Sally Hemings. Despite these almost insurmountable challenges, my cousin Byron Woodson has composed a research-based, comprehensive and captivating book that provides verifiable support of the Jefferson-Hemings relationship and the five surviving children they bore. It pays homage to our ancestors and is a gift to the American people: To learn the truth about our president in the family.

Michele Cooley-Quille, Ph.D.
Assistant Professor
Johns Hopkins University

Acknowledgments

This book would certainly not have been written or published without large doses of Lauren Trena Woodson's talent, enthusiasm, and determination. My wife was motivated not only by a sense of spousal devotion, but largely by the desire to gain recognition for my mother's genealogical accomplishments. Trena was as stunned as I was that bright summer day in 1984 when we walked into the Woodson cemetery in Jackson County, Ohio, to visit the final resting place of ancestors forgotten long ago. My family line had lost knowledge of the cemetery one hundred years prior to the trip and my mother's discovery. The feeling of that day will never be lost and continues to drive everyone who was there. Trena suggested the book title and performed amazing historical research.

Most writers seek to tell a story or expose a personality. I wanted to be able to thank publicly those who listened and who helped my family pursue its quest. In addition, I also wish to acknowledge those who helped my mother, Minnie S. Woodson, including cousins who sent her genealogies of their family lines, as well as news outlets such as *Ebony* magazine and NBC News who made the public aware of a family history that challenged conventional wisdom.

I thank with warmth and reverence a woman who not only provided me with material pertaining to the arrival of the Woodsons in Ohio in 1821 but who assisted and inspired my mother over twenty-five years ago. This "amateur" historian is Beverly Gray, who hails from Chillicothe, Ohio. Likewise,

Acknowledgments

Lucia "Cinder" Stanton, research historian with the Thomas Jefferson Memorial Foundation, has assisted my family for a number of years and provided material for this book. I met Cinder at a Woodson reunion in Columbus, Ohio, several years after my parents established contact with her. I well remember my first impression of Cinder. As we stood among Woodson relatives at a family reception, I was instantly struck by Cinder's obvious but quiet enjoyment and surmised that she was devouring every morsel of genealogical information and historical implication floating around the room and doing so with a depth of understanding few could hope to match.

Courage has been a considerable component of this journey. Marcia Davis and James L. Mairs have bolstered the family's courage. Ms. Davis, then senior editor at *Emerge*, published my first nationally circulated article in early 1999 at a time when many claimed that "scientific proof" overruled my family's oral history. Mr. Mairs read my book and continued to assist Trena and me and to champion the book's publication. The Race Relations Institute at Fisk University gave impetus to our "No-Book Tour." I am grateful to the institute and to the Kellogg Foundation, which has been its long-term supporter.

Plans for this book emerged abruptly; I had no preparation as a professional writer. Its delivery was aided by Lynette Hazelton, a writer, Barbara Jean Hope, an editor, and Catherine Roberts, a cousin from my mother's side of my family. All these individuals read the book and provided feedback. To my amazement another cousin, Ronald Woodson of Houston, Texas, who had never attended a family reunion, continued research on Thomas Woodson's life, finding documentation going back thirteen years earlier than the oldest documentation my mother was able to find. My cousin Linda Grigsby, one of many soul mates in the family, pushed me on at some very critical moments. The support of Robert Forbes of the Gilder/Lehrman Center at Yale University was more important than he might imagine.

On first encounter, my father, Col. John S. Woodson, U.S. Army (Ret.), is a gregarious and strikingly handsome man. If he grows to like you, you soon discover a very bold and complex man, often brash, demanding, and irreverent amid the ones he loves. You begin to depend on him to add piercing perspective or a fascinating anecdote to every conversation. I repeatedly interviewed Dad while writing Chapters Seven, Eight, and Ten. It is a vast understatement to say that his long, rich, and interesting life has produced a wealth of knowledge and wisdom. How can I limit my gratitude to his help on this book? My brother, Jon S. Woodson, Ph.D., also provided sound advice and encouragement.

Treatment of the Jefferson/Hemings controversy in the press has been checkered; we need to celebrate those who reject the easiest path. *Ebony* magazine has followed the Sally Hemings controversy for decades. When I first spoke to *Ebony* writer Laura Randolph in late 1998, she excitedly explained that she had interviewed my mother and that she knew of Mother's death; emotion poured through the phone line, as if a dam had collapsed. In contrast Warren Fiske of the *Virginia Pilot* came to the controversy without prior knowledge. Yet his grasp of America's attributes and failures allowed him to approach the subject unhampered by the preconceived notions held by many of his journalistic colleagues. Warren, Trena, and I will long remember those initial conversations. I am thoroughly grateful to the *Washington Afro-American Newspaper* and the *Philadelphia New Observer* for their relentless dedication to mission. Kristen Moore of the *Today* show approaches her work with an uncanny humility, which, I imagine, is a rare quality in the world of television. What can I say about Oprah Winfrey that has not been said? I give up. All the superlatives fall short of properly crediting Oprah.

Dr. Bruce Brodie, son of Fawn Brodie, steered me to Newell Bringhurst, who at the time was writing his biography of the outstanding Jefferson biographer. Newell Bringhurst graciously furnished copies of his articles before his book was published. I am in debt to both. The Sally Hemings descendants are also indebted to another Californian, Tina Andrews, screenwriter of the made-for-TV miniseries *Sally Hemings*.

The county and regional historical societies are emerging resources of historical and academic achievement. Only a few years ago such institutions were often no more than collections of dust-covered local newspapers stored in decaying small-town mansions. Aided by the advent of the personal computer, volunteers have indexed vast stores of county marriage, birth, death, and property records, thereby transforming historical societies into user friendly repositories. The Greenbriar Historical Society (West Virginia), the Ross County Historical Society (Ohio), and the Jackson County Historical Society (Ohio) have been important resources for me.

I have enjoyed visits to all these institutions. However, for reasons I cannot begin to describe, every time I enter the John Heinz History Center in downtown Pittsburgh, I am overwhelmed by a sense of spirituality and community. The library staff in the center, operated by the Historical Society of Western Pennsylvania (HSWP), has been not only helpful and friendly, as have all the others, but pleasantly engaging. With boundless gratitude I extend thanks on behalf of the Woodson family to the HSWP for preserving and drawing attention to the work and lives of the Reverend Lewis Woodson, Martin Delany, and John B. Vashon.

Acknowledgments

The Pennsylvania Historical Society (Philadelphia), the Free Library of Philadelphia, the Library of Congress, the Schomberg Library in New York City, and the U.S. Census Bureau site in Philadelphia proved to be immensely valuable resources. I thank David S. Ball of the Union Station Redevelopment Corporation for providing me with history on the station's creation.

I am humbly indebted to editor Heather Ruland Staines, Ph.D., and Praeger Publishers. Heather Staines appreciated the integrity and scope of my family's journey and quest from the outset. While enhancing my manuscript, she protected the continuity of the family legacy as though fondly acquainted with each of my ancestors.

To the many friends and neighbors whom I have not mentioned by name I express my gratitude. Many people offered me advice, information, and perspectives that proved valuable. I cannot list them all, but will mention Carl Word, Ph.D., Maceo Davis, Charlotte Douglass, Esq., and A. Gilbert Douglass, Esq. Any listing of my dear wonderful cousins will be my undoing. I have to suffer the consequences by mentioning only Michele Cooley-Quille, Lucian Truscott IV, Shay Banks-Young, and Julia Westerinen, who have represented the family in such a wonderful manner. I cannot adequately recount the manner in which so many cousins have helped Mother, Trena, and me. I thank my sons, John and Byron, and daughter Kellie for bearing with my single-mindedness during this process.

Introduction

My cousin H. Gregory Cooley, Esq. cried out, "If we had written this book a hundred years ago we would have been lynched." Therein lies the reason why the Hemings/Jefferson paternity controversy has festered for 198 years and remains unsettled. Through this book a descendant of Sally Hemings is, finally, able to tell the family's story without the interference of Jeffersonian historians and architects of racial codification. The publication of this book is in itself an affirmation of partial racial reconciliation in America. Yet the story within reveals the complexity of a house still divided.

Throughout my life my family has been my religion, my raison d'être. When my mother, Minnie S. Woodson, retired in 1972, she engaged in the most remarkable genealogical search, documenting our family's oral history, which identified Thomas Woodson as the oldest son of Thomas Jefferson and Sally Hemings, Jefferson's enslaved concubine. As the family grew through reconnection, so did my awareness of the enormous importance of Mother's product, the *Woodson Family Source Book*. That work is an underpinning for this one.

I don't claim to be the author of this book; I accept authorship as an oversimplification. I did not desire to write this book as much as I inherited the right and the duty to write it, as my mother passed away three years before I began to write. Neither was Minnie S. Woodson the sole motivator. The thoughts, the triumphs, and the pain expressed herein were in large part also inspired by my father, Col. John S. Woodson, U.S. Army (Ret.), my

great-great-grandfather, the great educator, institution-builder, and abolitionist The Reverend Lewis Woodson and his grandfather, Thomas Jefferson,
the great freedom fighter, statesman, and intellect. I am as much humbled as
guided by their enlightenment and wisdom. I wrote as they would have me
write, though I take full responsibility for the transmission. If my wife Trena
and I are to claim any personal accomplishment, it is to have partially and at
least temporarily removed a portion of the wall Jeffersonian historians have
built between Thomas Jefferson and the American people.

The Thomas Jefferson/Sally Hemings controversy has drifted through two
centuries of the American experience. Its heart started to beat when the out-
rageous newsman James Callender reported on September 1, 1802, that Jefferson took a slave named Sally as his concubine and fathered a son by her
named Tom, then twelve years of age, who looked like the president. Callender drowned a year later in three feet of water, but the scandal he created
did not die. It survived and was revived by repeated infusions of oral history
from Sally Hemings' descendants and by the assertions of others, including
the nineteenth-century feminist Frances Wright, who visited Monticello in
1824, and the eminent twentieth-century biographer Fawn Brodie.

The controversy has been declared dead many times. In the nineteenth
century noted Jefferson biographer James Parton confidently attempted to
end the speculation by disclaiming a liaison between Sally Hemings and Thomas Jefferson. In the twentieth century Pulitzer Prize–winner Dumas Malone
of the University of Virginia not only denied the sexual liaison, but lobbied
against the production of a made-for-TV movie about Sally Hemings (one
aired several years after his death). Malone and colleagues banded together
to attack Fawn Brodie's *Thomas Jefferson, an Intimate History*.

Following the broadcast of commercial films that portrayed the reality of
the Jefferson/Hemings liaison, historians from the Thomas Jefferson Memorial Foundation finally acknowledged the liaison. Like their predecessors,
they now consider the controversy resolved. It appears to many that Jeffersonians have surrendered and faced reality.

Publicly, these historians have in part capitulated but have at the same time
fired new rounds at the messengers who dispute the version of this history
now advanced by Jefferson historians. Jeffersonians continue to claim that
Callender's news account of September 1802 is false and that critical aspects
of Brodie's *Thomas Jefferson, an Intimate History* are erroneous. They have
dismissed evidence provided by the descendants of Tom, the first son of
Hemings and Jefferson. The contemporary position of establishment historians is no more rational than those of the past, for example, historian Joseph
Ellis' statement in *The American Sphinx* that "His [Jefferson's] most sensual

statements were aimed at beautiful buildings rather than beautiful women." In *Thomas Jefferson, a Life* historian James Parton concluded that "Jefferson had no more acquaintance with Sally Hemings than the most repulsive of his slaves." Historian John Chester Miller attacked the originator of the scandal in *Wolf by the Ears*, calling Callender "a liar, drunk and whoremonger who never investigated anything."

Contemporary Jefferson historians have abandoned historical evidence to embrace the results of Y-chromosome DNA tests conducted in 1998 even though Dr. Eugene Foster, the organizer of the tests, stated before and after the results were known, "The tests prove nothing." He holds that the test results are evidence but not proof of anything in particular. A DNA sample from Thomas Jefferson was not used. Test results were not released in a scientific journal, as promised, but rather in an extremely politicized manner on the front page of Sunday newspapers, two days before the 1998 congressional elections. The tests, for which I provided a sample, were publicly tied to the Monica Lewinsky scandal by geneticist Eric Lander and historian Joseph Ellis, who suggested that President Clinton's indiscretions should not lead to his impeachment since Jefferson's indiscretions had not impeded his ability to lead the nation. Ellis was a Clinton acquaintance attempting to ward off the president's impeachment.

Jeffersonians such as Dianne Swann-Wright deny any and all gamesmanship as they embrace the "objectivity" of the process. Curiously, newspapers reported the Y-chromosome process as experimental until Jeffersonians assembled their ranks in approval of the test results. The end seemed to justify the means as far as many were concerned.

This book will reveal the lives of the couple who entered the famous sexual liaison and the stage upon which the relationship blossomed. It will explore political and other interests of Jefferson only to set his eminence into the story's context. The amazing history of the Hemings family is recounted, although it deserves much more attention than I can devote to it here. The book exposes the controversy's "fourth heart," which emerged after the death of Fawn Brodie with the public assertion of the oral and documented history of the Woodson family (descendants of Tom, the first son of Jefferson and Hemings).

The object of this book is not to settle the controversy, as Dr. Brodie's book should have, but to return it to a level of serious discussion. To that aim I present my experience as a blood sample donor for the DNA test. The startling trail of genealogical discovery followed in the 1970s by my mother, Minnie S. Woodson, is revealed as vividly as I am capable of presenting it. Those elements are added to the reports of James Callender, published in

1802, and the account of Madison Hemings (another Hemings/Jefferson son), published in 1873.

The book details my genealogy along the Jefferson/Woodson line through each generation. Historical background and context are provided throughout. Establishment historians have ignored the *Woodson Source Book*, which my mother compiled in the late 1970s, but I argue here, compellingly, I think, that the Woodsons did not merely "drop from the sky." The Woodsons present a complete picture of events. Jeffersonians deny that Tom was Thomas Jefferson's son and deny Tom's (Thomas Woodson's) connection to Monticello without presenting a complete account as an alternative.

Nor did Fawn Brodie or James Callender drop from the sky, though Jeffersonians continue to discount their talent, track records, and credibility. I have attempted to provide insight into the lives and characters of Callender and Brodie, while sticking as closely as possible to the Woodson account.

This book reveals the history of the Monticello plantation and continues with the life of the oldest Jefferson/Hemings son, Thomas Woodson. The Woodsons continued the traditions of the Hemings clans, emphasizing education, pride, compassion, and distaste for distinctions based on race. The Reverend Lewis Woodson was a driven man who built institutions to foster stability, opportunity, and achievement in the African American community. One historian, Floyd Miller, called Reverend Woodson the "Father of Black Nationalism"; the appellation certainly recognizes his importance in the struggle to elevate African Americans from degradation to dignity. Reverend Woodson passed the family oral history of the connection to Thomas Jefferson on to his industrious siblings and their families. Nearly 100 years after Reverend Woodson's death in 1878, another Woodson, who married into the family, decided to record the family's genealogy and research its origin. Minnie Woodson's effort was an amazing success. As Mother followed the trail of discovery, her success constantly astounded me and reminded me that my watch was approaching.

In the last year I have met numerous cousins descended from Sally Hemings and Thomas Jefferson, some white and some black. Many have embraced each other, though some are resistant to change. Historians from the Thomas Jefferson Memorial Foundation, Annette Gordon-Reed, and other establishment historians claim that my rather large and assertive Woodson family, which is primarily African American, is mistaken about its roots. In comparison, they recognize Thomas Jefferson as the ancestor of the descendants of Eston Hemings; those descendants are white.

After Fawn Brodie died in 1981 the Woodsons were the only people alive who publicly espoused the reality of the Hemings/Jefferson liaison. Jefferson historians championed the inaccurate history for 150 years. Most prominent Jeffersonians have recently altered their position, but have not adopted the same version as the Woodsons. Is their new version correct, or is the unaltered account of the Woodson and Hemings families the accurate one?

Scandal is not the centerpiece, and certainly not the foundation, from which America can learn and grow. The focus here is the integrity of American history. For if we cannot agree on who we are and where we have been, there is no basis for harmony and only a bleak outlook for the future. The true legacy of the Monticello plantation, presented here, exemplifies the racial interconnections that marked America's origins. If it brings Americans closer to realizing that we are one people, the book will have surpassed its objective.

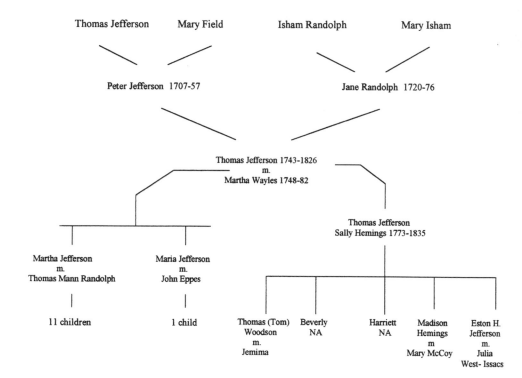

Thomas Jefferson   Mary Field   Isham Randolph   Mary Isham

Peter Jefferson 1707-57   Jane Randolph 1720-76

Thomas Jefferson 1743-1826
m.
Martha Wayles 1748-82

Thomas Jefferson
Sally Hemings 1773-1835

Martha Jefferson
m.
Thomas Mann Randolph

Maria Jefferson
m.
John Eppes

11 children

1 child

Thomas (Tom)
Woodson
m.
Jemima

Beverly
NA

Harriett
NA

Madison
Hemings
m
Mary McCoy

Eston H.
Jefferson
m.
Julia
West- Issacs

CHAPTER ONE

The Fate of Sally Hemings

. . . is quite a child . . . and appears good naturd.
—Abigail Adams describing Sally Hemings to Thomas Jefferson

Despite all that Parisian society had to offer, Thomas Jefferson was lonely. At the end of August 1785, he began a letter to his brother-in-law Francis Eppes with uncustomary abruptness. Francis and Elizabeth Eppes cared for Jefferson's daughter, Polly, while he fulfilled diplomatic missions in France. "I must now repeat my wish to have Polly sent to me next summer." The youngest Jefferson daughter, Lucy, had died of whooping cough at the Eppes' plantation, Eppington, during the fall of 1784. Jefferson's wife, Martha, had died after a prolonged illness two years before then. Thomas Jefferson became frightfully distressed by not having Polly nearby. However, Polly was only seven years old at the time, and Elizabeth Eppes surely considered the child's age as she responded to Jefferson's request that Polly be sent to France. Despite the plea, Polly remained in Virginia with her Aunt Elizabeth, sister of Polly's deceased mother, during the next summer. Jefferson received letters from young Polly avowing her reluctance to leave Eppington for France. She wished to see her father but wished rather that he visit her.[1]

Jefferson traveled from Paris to London in March 1786 in part to secure the release of Americans captured at sea and enslaved by Moroccans while they were held for ransom. The diplomatic mission was ultimately unsuccessful, and the Americans remained in captivity. Thus the threat of Polly's capture at sea by Moroccans or other Barbary Coast pirates injected a cautious tone into Jefferson's quest to have her cross the Atlantic. No doubt Polly Jefferson's voyage to France was also delayed in part by Elizabeth Eppes' attachment to her niece. Elizabeth lost a daughter of her own near the time when Lucy Jefferson died. Elizabeth was certainly torn between concern for Polly's safety, her own feelings for the child, and Jefferson's natural yearning to have his daughter near.[2]

Jefferson missed Polly, yet he had not traveled to France entirely alone. James Hemings and Jefferson's oldest daughter, Martha, sailed with him in July 1784. Twelve-year-old Martha, already tall like her father, was known by a nickname, Patsy.

James was a son of Betty Hemings, a mulatto slave inherited by Jefferson from his deceased father-in-law, John Wayles. Wayles took Betty Hemings, the Hemings family matriarch, as his concubine after his third white wife died eleven months into their marriage. Betty had given birth to children with a black man prior to becoming Wayles' mate, but her youngest six children were the "bright" mulatto offspring of John Wayles. Thus those six children were half brothers and sisters to Jefferson's deceased wife. The Hemings family, although enslaved, was connected in an intimate manner to its owners, as it was impossible to perform the tasks of domestic service unless an atmosphere of trust prevailed. When John Wayles died in 1773, the Hemings family immediately relocated to Monticello, although Betty, who gave birth to Wayles' last child, Sally, in that year, joined her older children some months later. The Hemings family did not own Monticello, but it became their home and they viewed it as such.

When James Hemings came of age he became Jefferson's body servant. Jefferson was assisted by a body servant throughout his life. When he attended the College of William and Mary, Jupiter, a slave inherited from his father, Peter Jefferson, washed Jefferson's clothes, ran errands, attended horses, and performed other domestic duties. When Jefferson traveled to Philadelphia in the fateful year 1776, Robert Hemings, the oldest of John Wayles and Betty Hemings' children, accompanied him. However, upon settling in Paris, Jefferson hired a cadre of French servants and arranged for James to learn the art of French cooking.

Patsy attended a convent school in Paris, the Abbaye Royale de Panthemont, and boarded there. This Catholic school was said to be the most genteel in France and was patronized by the English. Jefferson visited her daily for the first two months. Patsy adjusted to the convent easily: "At present I am charmed by my situation.... I am very happy in the convent." The nuns must have been equally pleased to have Patsy with them. John Adams' daughter, Nabby, described her as "a sweet girl, delicacy and sensibility are read in every feature, and her manners are in union with all that is amiable and lovely."[3]

Travel to Europe was one of Jefferson's boyhood dreams; he had arrived with a sense of destiny. The mission shifted from personal fulfillment more clearly to duty when the aged Benjamin Franklin returned to America and John Adams left Paris for London in 1785. Jefferson then became minister to the French court. This welcomed and anticipated responsibility quieted his impatience but did not fill Jefferson's emotional needs. He had lost his wife; he missed Monticello and Virginia. His assignment in France was a blessing, but it was a sacrifice as well.

ATLANTIC CROSSING

Polly was nearly nine years old when she at last sailed to Europe to be with her father. She, however, never relinquished her desire to stay in Virginia. She did not remember the father who had left for France in 1784; Eppington was the home she knew and loved. The ship on which Polly sailed began its voyage while she was asleep to minimize her distress. Sally Hemings was on board to placate and pacify the child. Jefferson had asked Francis Eppes to send a nanny with Polly and prescribed his choice: "a careful Negro woman Isabell for instance." As Isabell had given birth to a daughter, Edy, in April 1787, Sally Hemings was sent instead.[4]

It is clear why Isabell did not accompany Polly, but the choice of Sally for the voyage is a matter for conjecture. Jefferson's scheme was to send Polly with "some good lady passing from America to France" or as an alternative with a "careful gentleman to superintend . . . a careful negro woman." The gentleman appeared in the person of John Amonit, who sailed to France to receive an inheritance. Elizabeth Eppes and Betty Hemings surely had a large role in the selection of Sally. Betty Hemings may have wanted James to enjoy the companionship of one of his siblings, or she may have wanted Sally to be exposed to the sophistication of the European continent. Then again, Sally Hemings just might have been the most capable candidate, sensible and self-assured beyond her years, and young enough to retain Polly's affection.[5]

Polly and Sally were the only females aboard during the crossing. Sally was worthless as a nanny, according to the captain. Polly became "much attached" to the captain, so reported Abigail Adams, wife of John Adams, who then filled the diplomatic post in London. Mrs. Adams received Polly and Sally upon their arrival in London. She wrote Jefferson on the day of their arrival, telling him of his daughter's disappointment in being passed from one person to another. "An old nurse" had not accompanied Polly, Mrs. Adams informed Jefferson, but a "Girl about 15 or 16 . . . Sister of the Servant you have with you." Sally Hemings was actually fourteen at the time, but she likely looked and acted a bit older.[6]

While waiting for Jefferson to fetch Polly, Mrs. Adams grew very fond of the child. As Polly was motherless, Mrs. Adams' letters to the very absorbed Jefferson contained an appropriate dose of feminine authority. Mrs. Adams passed on to Jefferson Captain Ramsay's assessment that Sally should return to America on his ship, as she would prove to be of little use to her master. Despite the captain's remark, Mrs. Adams deferred to Jefferson's discretion as to the fate of Sally Hemings: "But of this you will be the judge."[7]

Had Sally Hemings returned to Virginia with Captain Ramsay the course of events would have been very different. Sally, certainly, held no desire to return to Virginia with Captain Ramsay. She no doubt was aware of her vulnerability on a ship crossing the Atlantic Ocean with no companion. Sally knew that her grandmother had been the sexual object of a ship's captain who abandoned her and his mulatto child, Sally's mother Betty. Captain Ramsay's criticism of Sally might have been the result of her distrust of him. Aside from her fear of a return voyage, Sally had two other motivations for going on to Paris. One was her duty to care for Polly. Although Sally assuredly recognized the capability of Abigail Adams, she would not have considered her duty fulfilled until Polly was in the direct and permanent care of Thomas Jefferson. Second, Sally no doubt wanted to visit if not permanently join her brother James in Paris, which was not far away. She would have been curious about his life in France. It is also plausible that Captain Ramsay, by attempting to return Sally to Virginia, was following Jefferson's direction as expressed to him by Francis Eppes, but, as was often the case, the Hemings family pursued a different agenda.

Sally was an attractive girl. Though sketchy accounts of her appearance survive, descriptions of very few other slaves and none of the other Hemings daughters have been preserved. If others were available, then comparisons could be made, giving more insight into the degree of Sally's attractiveness. Sally was possibly very beautiful. On the other hand, her looks may have attracted favorable comment because of the attention directed to her by her master. Two accounts survive. Isaac Jefferson, a son of the Monticello slaves Great George and Ursula, described Sally Hemings as "very handsome . . . mighty near white" with "long straight hair down her back." Thomas Jefferson Randolph, Thomas Jefferson's grandson, who only knew Sally Hemings as a middle-aged woman, described her as "light colored and decidedly good looking." Mrs. Adams recorded the only surviving account of Sally's personality: "She . . . appears good naturd."[8]

What part did Jefferson play in Sally's travel from London to Paris? Was he seeking to educate Sally suitably as a servant with the assistance of her brother James? Did Jefferson not trust the intentions of Captain Ramsey, who seemed eager to have Sally return alone to Virginia on his ship? No instruction from Jefferson pertaining to Sally's assignment survives. He was too preoccupied with affairs of state to travel to London to retrieve his own daughter, for which he won no points with Abigail Adams. The fate of Sally Hemings at this time did not register among Jefferson's substantive concerns.

The French servant Petit traveled to London in Jefferson's stead to fetch Polly. Mrs. Adams was deeply affected by Polly's reaction, writing Jefferson as follows:

Upon Petit's arrival, Polly was thrown into all her former distress and, bursting into tears, told me it would be as hard to leave me as it was to leave her Aunt Eppes. She has been so deceived that she will not quit me a moment least [sic] she would be carried away. Though she says she does not remember you, yet she has been taught to consider you with affection and fondness, and depended upon your coming for her. She told me this morning, that as she had left all her friends in Virginia to come over the ocean to see you, she did think you would have taken the pains to come for her, and not to have sent a man whom she can not understand. I express her own words.[9]

Mrs. Adams continued by saying that she would not force Polly into the carriage. She gave Polly her word that Petit would stay put until further word was received from Jefferson. Even John Adams later expressed his displeasure with Jefferson for not personally retrieving Polly. In her letter announcing Polly's arrival in London, Mrs. Adams had held a quite different posture: "As I presume you . . . will not . . . hurry in comeing or sending for her." Mrs. Adams' attitude toward Jefferson's handling of Polly's arrival changed abruptly after Polly's fit of disappointment, signifying Polly's effectiveness in making her feelings known. It is certain that Sally Hemings took note of Polly's assertiveness as well. Polly eventually relented, but we know well of her displeasure.[10]

In France Sally Hemings absorbed a culture much different from that of the Virginia Piedmont (land in Virginia's interior, between the Tidewater area and the western foothills). In the Piedmont, she lived during her early years in a simple cabin along Mulberry Row on the Monticello plantation, tucked safely in the cocoon of the Hemings clan. Life was organized around agricultural production. Paris, many times larger than the largest American city, presented a cornucopia of evolving artistic expression and invention, conditions which set the dawn of the Industrial Revolution apart from life in the late Middle Ages.

Upon arrival in Paris Sally Hemings was no longer legally enslaved, as France had abolished slavery. In time she was made aware of her theoretical freedom. Thomas Jefferson was certainly aware of it. Nonetheless, an alternative to her enslavement was not available to her, as she did not then speak French; she was only fourteen, and a life in France meant separation from the Hemings clan.

Sally Hemings has been described by historians as a body servant to Jefferson's daughters while in Paris, but her duties are really unknown. Her presence in Paris had not been anticipated or planned by Jefferson, who had hired servants long before her arrival. She did receive pay while in Paris. How much time was spent at the convent school, if any, and what work she performed is not known. After her arrival, James Hemings, who had received sporadic gifts from Jefferson since arriving in France, began to receive regular wages. Sally's pay was sporadic, but increased over time. It was not listed with other servants' wages, as James' wages were. What mixture of footloose fancy and call to duty was Sally Hemings' residence in Paris?[11]

While at work or in a social setting, Sally Hemings became acquainted with the friends of Polly and Patsy Jefferson. One friend asked Patsy by letter to pass regards to "Mademoiselle Sally." In a letter to the daughter of Jefferson's stunningly beautiful friend Angelica Schuyler Church, Polly included a notation that Sally likewise sent her regards. Cordiality between Sally and the friends of Patsy and Polly could only mimic fondness between Sally and the Jefferson daughters. Surely friends of the Jefferson girls were not aware that Sally was their aunt. Most likely they had no reason to pry into the relationship or Sally's position in the household.[12]

Polly attended the convent school along with Patsy. Mrs. Adams protested that such a "fine spirit" was contained behind stone walls. Weeks after Polly's arrival, Jefferson began to frequent a monastery on Mount Calvary above the town of Suresnes, only a few miles from Paris. The "hermitage," as he called it, offered guests about forty rooms and a bohemian atmosphere for study and meditation. Guests were encouraged to bring their own servants and would assemble for dinner only. To encourage meditation, guests refrained from talking in the gardens. Jefferson retreated to Mount Calvary, taking his papers along, when some project required his undivided attention or when the compulsion for privacy grew urgent.

JEFFERSON, THE VIRGINIAN

In 1786, the vague authority of the Confederation of American States was threatened by Shays' Rebellion, a revolt of farmers in western Massachusetts who were faced with the loss of their land when they were unable to pay heavy taxes imposed to repay the state's Revolutionary War debt. The revolt was put down by the state militia, but its implications were deeply felt. From Paris Jefferson advised against harsh treatment of the rebels. Enriched by European intellectualism and American experience, Jefferson wrote his friend Edward Carrington from Paris upon learning of events at home:

I am persuaded myself that the good sense of the people will always be found to be the best army. They may be led astray for a moment, but will soon correct themselves. . . . The way to prevent these irregular interpositions of the people is to give them full information of their affairs thro' the channel of the public papers, and to contrive that those papers should penetrate the whole mass of the people. The basis of our governments being the opinion of the people, the very first object should be to keep that right; and were it left for me to decide whether we should have a government without newspapers, or newspapers without a government, I should not hesitate a moment to prefer the latter.[13]

Jefferson hoped that reform would take hold in France, setting the stage for the expansion of democracy across Europe. His liberal French friends, though members of the aristocracy, held similar sentiments. The profound difference in the American and French circumstances eluded them all. American reformers directed the anger of indentured servants and peasant farmers against the English monarchy, then rewarded them with unlimited tracts of land taken from Native Americans. French reformers, themselves part of the social hierarchy, had only that hierarchy to depose.

A year after arriving in Paris, Jefferson moved to the Hotel de Langeac, a house located on the western edge of the city at the intersection of the Champs Elysées and the Rue de Berri. One advantage was a perfect view of the annual Promenade à Longchamp, when the elite of Paris and its workers alike dressed in their finest. The object was to draw attention, to gawk at others, to imbibe, and to maintain a gay spirit for as long a period as possible. The elegant Hotel de Langeac led Jefferson to make comparisons among it, Monticello, and other Parisian residences. In his own words, he was "violently smitten" with a residence constructed during his stay in Paris, the Hotel de Salm. The stately residence was topped by a dome, an unusual feature for that era. Ceilings in public spaces, such as the foyer and parlor, rose to the highest point of the roofline, giving the house a sense of spatial prominence.[14]

Jefferson began to redesign Monticello in his head. Its construction continued in earnest for most of forty years, starting with the South Pavilion, the first brick structure at Monticello, in 1770. The architectural inspiration Jefferson found in Europe led him to demolish much of the original structure and build a larger, more stylish one upon his return.

Jefferson's father-in-law, John Wayles, died a dozen or so years before Jefferson's stint in France, leaving a legacy of large tracts of land, a large number of African American slaves, and considerable debts. Jefferson and his brothers-in-law struggled a lifetime with those debts. Negotiation with creditors was a constant chore. Some land was sold on credit, payable in Virginia's local currency. According to the Treaty of Paris of 1783, debts owed to European creditors were to be repaid in full value of prewar sterling. Since local currency depreciated rapidly, the Wayles heirs had in effect "given away" land and still owed for its purchase. Before the British invasion, Jefferson sold over 5,000 acres of land inherited from Wayles. Compounding the financial malaise, the British army destroyed Jefferson's Elkhill plantation in 1781, taking captive black slaves, some of whom died in captivity. The British also helped themselves to cattle, hogs, and sheep.[15]

Expecting to stay in France a few more years, Jefferson instructed relatives to sell slaves to relieve the debt load. On January 31, 1785, thirty-one of Jefferson's slaves were sold at Elkhill, some to Jefferson's relatives. Harry was sold to Thomas Randolph. Seven slaves were sold to Samuel Woodson, who was related to Jefferson through his aunt Dorothea. Jefferson's mother, Jane, was a daughter of Isham Randolph. Dorothea, Samuel's grandmother, was a daughter of Isham Randolph as well. Thus Samuel Woodson was Thomas Jefferson's first cousin, once removed.[16]

Sending more bad news, Jefferson's brother-in-law soon asked if more land or slaves should be sold or if slaves should be leased to other planters. Jefferson, somewhat mindful of his finances, but also of the welfare of people he owned, chose to lease them. He directed Francis Eppes to condition any lease on the continued payment for any slave who died within the term of the lease, stating, "Otherwise it would be their interest to kill all the old and infirm by hard usage." He indicated unwillingness to sell more slaves, as he would later "try some plan of making their situation happier." Jefferson leased enslaved people for decades, including the time of his presidency. Further, he instructed Eppes to refrain from leasing out Great George, Ursula,

Betty Hemings, or the Hemings youths. Those individuals were to be protected from the uncertain temperament of other planters.[17]

Jefferson owned several plantations, inherited from his father and father-in-law. Before he left for France 129 slaves lived at Monticello. Additional slaves lived and worked at Willis Creek, Poplar Forest, and Elkhill, other Jefferson plantations. He owed 204 slaves in all. In 1784 he was the fifth largest landholder in Albermarle County and possessed the second highest number of slaves.

On the Monticello plantation the Hemings clan, some forty or so in number, lived along Mulberry Row, a stretch of dirt road and mulberry trees on the southern crest of the Monticello mountain within earshot of the mansion. In addition to cabins of various sizes and qualities, storehouses, workshops, and stables were stretched along Mulberry Row. The area functioned as a focal point of plantation life and as a buffer between the fields and the mansion. After John Wayles' death and the move to Monticello, the clan continued to grow in size. Their position as favored house slaves was solidified with the sanction of Martha Wayles Jefferson, the lady of the house and half-sister of six of the Hemings children.

All his life Jefferson struggled with the immorality and the practical aspects of slave ownership. He never saw himself clear of debt, though he often declared it his tormentor. Land sales failed to relieve his financial difficulties. Though he knew the repayment of his debts would give him the flexibility he needed to free his slaves, he spent lavishly on a huge book collection and quantities of the best wines. He was also generous with an ever growing flock of friends, confidants, and admirers, most of whom were highborn.[18]

MRS. COSWAY

In late August 1787, Jefferson's friend Mrs. Cosway returned to Paris, leaving her husband in London. Maria Louisa Catherine Cecilia Hadfield Cosway was a twenty-eight-year-old musician and painter. A year earlier when Jefferson first met this small, fragile, and effervescent woman with blue eyes, a milky complexion, and large golden curls, the tall American was immediately smitten. In the weeks following their first encounter Jefferson and Mrs. Cosway spent a great deal of time together, in spite of the presence of Mr. Cosway. Jefferson later remembered most affectionately the tours of beautiful gardens and the hilly countryside around Paris. For some time, he and Mrs. Cosway seemed to claw at any obstacle standing in the way of their time together. It cannot be known for certain whether or not a sexual encounter arose, but feelings were strong and tender.[19]

While walking along the Seine with Mrs. Cosway one September day in 1786, Jefferson attempted to jump a fence. He fell, fracturing his right wrist. This interrupted six weeks of blissfully exuberant friendship. The Cosways left Paris a few weeks later, during which time Jefferson suffered the novelty of French orthopedics. Jefferson saw little of Mrs. Cosway during those last weeks, yet as soon as she left for London he wrote her a famous twelve-page letter, "My Head and My Heart." Jeffersonian historian Julian Boyd dubbed it "one of the notable love letters of the English language," though it is dishonestly and repeatedly addressed to both Mr. and Mrs. Cosway. The right-handed Jefferson devoted days rather than hours to writing the letter with his left hand.[20]

Jefferson saw little of Mrs. Cosway during her return to Paris in the fall of 1787. When he did, she was amid an entourage of admirers. Letters between these friends turned to the reluctant reality that the romantic attraction between them would never be fully actualized. Jefferson had written to her the previous November asking about the prospect of her return to Paris, to which she replied, "[In London] pleasures come in search of me." Instead of going to London to see his friend, Jefferson traveled to northern Italy.[21]

Sally Hemings no doubt witnessed some of the attentions Jefferson granted the fairer sex. She doubted, however, that much would become of the friendships he maintained with veteran ladies of the salon, whom he met through Benjamin Franklin and the Marquis de Lafayette or even the younger acquaintances of these women. Sally had been present during the sad scene between Thomas and Martha Jefferson just before she was "torn from him by death." Along with her mother, Betty, three of her sisters, and the slave Ursula, Sally heard Jefferson promise his wife "never to marry again."[22]

While abroad, Jefferson journeyed through an impressive slice of western Europe. The mission of these travels was artistic, architectural, commercial, agricultural, historical, and positively educational. Instead of one grand tour, he took a series of four trips attached in some fashion to diplomatic business. Jefferson's notations, written along the way, cover a wide variety of topics. He recorded the details of Parmesan cheese production as well as the enduring integrity of Roman architectural remnants. One journey followed a trip to Amsterdam, where he and Adams went to borrow funds for the United States. At The Hague Jefferson viewed the outstanding collection of Flemish and Dutch paintings. He enjoyed shopping, but the flatness of the land and the urban orientation of the culture did not encourage him to stay.

Without Adams, who returned to England, Jefferson went off on a long journey southward through the Rhine River Valley. Near Frankfurt he visited an old acquaintance, Baron Geismar. Major Geismar was a Hessian officer captured at Saratoga and held for some time by the Americans in the Charlottesville area. Most captives were housed in barracks, but some officers, including Geismar, rented houses. Jefferson had befriended Major Geismar and even made an attempt to secure his freedom.[23]

In 1788 Major Geismar was attached to the garrison at Hanau, a town on the Main River east of Frankfurt, and Jefferson had renewed their friendship by letter after arriving in France. For four days Jefferson and Geismar visited wineries, Frankfurt, and notable landmarks. In Hochheim, Jefferson ordered one hundred vine cuttings for delivery to Paris. Near Rudesheim, he bought several types of wine and more cuttings. He and Major Geismar tasted several wines in this area, known for its Riesling.

Jefferson continued toward the headwaters of the Rhine through the cities of Heidelberg and Karlsruhe. His notes reflect an unusually fresh awareness:

The women here . . . do all sorts of work. While one considers them as useful and rational companions, one cannot forget that they are also objects of our pleasures. Nor can they ever forget it. While employed in drudgery some tag of ribbon, some ring or bit of bracelet, earbob or necklace, or something of that kind will shew that the desire of pleasing is never suspended in them. . . . They are formed by nature for attentions and not for hard labour.[24]

The word "mulatto" appears in the journal from this trip much more often than in previous writings. He used the word eight times in describing the soils of the Rhine Valley. In the journals of his trip through southern France, made before Sally Hemings' arrival, he used the word only once. Perhaps Sally Hemings was then a fixture in his thoughts. Jefferson returned to Paris from the Rhineland through the Alsace, Lorraine, and Champagne regions of France.[25]

SALLY HEMINGS IN PARIS

Evidence indicates that after Jefferson's return from the Rhine Valley excursion in mid-1788 Sally Hemings drew more of his attention. In the spring of 1789, Jefferson began to spend significantly on Sally's clothing. On April 6 he spent 96 francs on her clothing, followed by another 72 francs on April 16. In the next few weeks additional clothing was purchased for 50 francs, prompting two more notations, "clothes for servants" and "pd. making clothes for Sally." Compared to Sally's wages of 24 francs a month, these expenditures seem substantial. Compared to the cost of Patsy's clothing and accessories and the frequent allowances to Patsy, which often amounted to 200 francs or more, the expenditure on Sally's clothing was modest. Yet the purchases did reflect a specific attention on Jefferson's part to Sally's needs and/or desires.[26]

The strangest notation was an expenditure on April 29, 1789, for Sally's boarding for five weeks. Since Jefferson paid many bills after some delay, the timing of her boarding cannot be determined. Why was Sally placed in a boarding home, and when?

There are no notations on clothing for James, but a Monsieur Perrault received payment to teach him French. Apparently, lessons did not always progress smoothly, as Monsieur Perrault complained about James' quick temper. Jefferson was keenly aware of James' thin skin and at times found his servant's demeanor somewhat amusing. Not long after they arrived in France, Jefferson wrote to Betty Hemings through a Monticello gardener, assuring her of her son's well-being, adding, "He has forgot how to speak English, and has not learnt to speak French." James eventually earned the title "chef de cuisine" after apprenticeship in the kitchens of the Prince de Conde. When he returned to Monticello, he worked as its chef and trained a younger brother.[27]

In 1788 Jefferson returned to some of the same gardens and parks he had visited with Maria Cosway, traveling to Marly and St. Germain on September 28. In autumn, the serenity of these arboretums is blessed with a faithful and delightful climate; frequent drizzle teases the dominant sunshine, which intermittently pierces treetops above with the occasional sparkle of a star. It was uncharacteristic for Jefferson to retrace steps without an assigned purpose, for which none is apparent. Characteristically, he would have educated and tantalized someone with this beauty, but there is no record of a companion.[28]

Sally Hemings learned social graces and gained an education under Jefferson's watchful eye. Theirs transcended the typical servant/master relationship. It is doubtful that she attempted to emulate the sophistication of Mrs. Cosway or other ladies of the salon. Her model was more likely someone like Polly, who was quite charming but demanded a degree of independence and expected reward for her devotion. The attention paid to Sally began with her usefulness but doubtlessly transformed into something like an experiment, as did many of Jefferson's interests. The days spent creating a web of fantasy with Maria Cosway were past; the attention he paid to Sally Hemings brought certain complexities into play as well, but they were complexities of a far different and less mystical nature.

LAFAYETTE, JEFFERSON, AND A NEW REVOLUTION

Jefferson and John Adams failed to negotiate commercial treaties with England, so Jefferson concentrated on improving trade with France. Tobacco was the first order of business. As a matter of convenience the French government ceded the collection of import duties to a chartered monopoly, Farmers-General. Compounding the noncompetitiveness of the situation, the Farmers-General arranged for supply by granting a three-year exclusive contract to American financier Robert Morris. Jefferson approached the French foreign minister to argue that the monopoly was "contrary to the spirit of trade." The Marquis de Lafayette, whom Jefferson first met in Virginia during the Revolutionary War, helped to win the foreign minister's cooperation in weakening Morris' monopoly to the advantage of Virginia tobacco growers and French consumers. Attentive to the needs of other American states, Jefferson helped South Carolina rice growers and the New England whaling industry. Street lamps in Paris and Marseilles were lit with whale oil from New England. This success strengthened the Jefferson/Lafayette friendship.[29]

Marie Joseph Paul Yves Roch Gilbert du Motier, Marquis de Lafayette, was a hero of the American Revolution, a man of action. He was also a visionary whose nation remained divided by feudal order into aristocrats, dilettantes, and fancy ladies on the one hand and multitudes of wretchedly poor and illiterate peasants on the other. Jefferson described the population from which disgruntled French mobs would grow as follows: "Of twenty millions of people supposed to be in France . . . there are nineteen millions more wretched, more accursed in every circumstance of human existence than the most conspicuously wretched individual of the whole United States."[30]

The French monarchy spent excessively on foreign wars, including the American Revolution, causing a financial crisis and civil unrest. A chamber of government representing commoners bargained for increased powers in exchange for higher taxes. Lafayette became the pivotal political leader and agreed to draft a constitution, wisely enlisting Thomas Jefferson's assistance. Lafayette exiled himself to his rural manor while preparing a draft constitution; his shield from interruptions was so great that his wife Adrienne could only contact him through Jefferson. In early July 1789 Lafayette introduced his declaration and constitution to the French National Assembly.[31]

Despite the effort to manage a peaceful revolution, violence broke out in the streets of Paris. On July 14, a mob stormed the Bastille, an old high-walled prison and barracks. When the garrison offered an inspection to a few members of the mob to prove that it was not preparing an offensive, the gates were rushed. The mob overran and slaughtered the garrison. The heads of two commanders were placed on stakes and then paraded through Paris. Such grotesque acts were often repeated in the months and years to come.

Horrified, the National Assembly commissioned Lafayette as commander-in-chief of a newly formed National Guard and vice president of the Assembly. In the ensuing weeks violence took an increasingly macabre character, mixing hatred, entertainment, gruesomeness, and death. Neither the National Assembly nor the monarchy was in full control. The king's veto power was a prime issue of contention. Lafayette imposed on Jefferson and invited key Assembly members to Jefferson's home, the Hotel de Langeac, to discuss the situation over dinner. During the meeting Jefferson steered the dialogue to zones of comfort. The king would lose the power to dissolve the Assembly. He would retain the veto, but, without the ability to administer taxes, his power was dependent. These were Jefferson's recommendations.

Yet Louis XVI refused the Declaration of Rights! On October 5, 1789, a mob gathered at the barracks of the National Guard. The mob wished Lafayette to accompany them to Versailles to confront the king. Lafayette argued for calm, but his troops began to side with the people. "Strange that Lafayette should wish to command the people, when it is the people['s right] to command Lafayette." With that sentiment, they marched through the night in the cold and drizzle to Versailles with Lafayette an effectual prisoner at the head of his troops. Some citizens called for the queen's liver and others for her thighs. Women appeared to be in the majority, though many men were dressed as women, as the king's army had been instructed not to fire upon women.[32]

At Versailles, Lafayette assured the president of the Assembly that he would protect Louis XVI and Marie Antoinette. He dismissed the Hessians and Swiss guards, offering his guard for royal protection. Very early in the morning Lafayette roused the queen, bringing her to a balcony for the mob to see. He warned her not to shrink. When he bowed to kiss her hand silence reigned. Somewhere in the mob a murmur started, rippling into a clamor. "Vive le général! Vive la reine!" The citizens spared the lives of the king and queen, yet had not gained a greater voice in government; they insisted that the king and queen return with them to Paris. The royals settled into the Tuileries Palace, where the monarchs were virtual prisoners. Months later, Louis XVI sanctioned a constitution, but the thirst for freedom was not wholly satisfied.[33]

HOMEBOUND

After living in Paris for nearly five years, Jefferson planned to return home to Virginia. The United States of America had been formed during his absence, though through frequent correspondence with James Madison he influenced the drafting of the Constitution. Freedoms of a more personal dimension now demanded attention.

At seventeen, Patsy struggled with the choice between the burdens of her birthright and her spiritual needs. Patsy was not a timid person. Nonetheless she was appalled by the turmoil into which her father repeatedly threw himself, and likewise frightened by memories of her mother's death and the deaths of siblings. Patsy considered becoming a nun. Her inclination may have been a catalyst for her father's decision to return home. American slavery also troubled Patsy. She wrote a friend in May 1787, "I wish with all my soul the poor negroes were all freed. It grieves my heart." With the streets of Paris taken over by mob rule and America shaken by Shays' Rebellion, Patsy's inclination to avoid the secular world is understandable. Her father removed Patsy and Polly from the Abbaye Royale de Panthemont in April 1789, anticipating their return to America.[34]

Jefferson also had to consider the fate of James and Sally Hemings. Sally was by then pregnant with Jefferson's child. He was infatuated with the young beauty, who brought with her reflections of life at his beloved Monticello. He attracted her compassion as a widower whose womanly comfort had been torn from him by death. Sally's own father, John Wayles, lost three wives. Just as her vibrant father had turned to his mulatto slave, Sally knew that Jefferson's thirst for love and masculine validation had not ended. Such tradition was not openly acknowledged by whites, yet blacks could not avoid sight of its effects. Blacks had no world of fantasy in which to hide.[35]

Sally and James understood that French law afforded them freedom. They loathed returning to slavery in Virginia, though each burned with desire to return to the cocoon of the Hemings clan. James worked at the Hotel de Langeac alongside free men and received wages as they did, making a life in Paris at least conceivable. Jefferson promised to free James upon his return after James had trained another. This was actually achieved, but not without considerable delay. Jefferson promised Sally that her children, including the one growing in her body, would be freed at the age of twenty-one.[36]

After considerable preparation, as Jefferson had acquired quantities of books, household items, and furniture, he and his entourage left Paris on September 26, 1789, reaching Le Havre two days later. Jefferson was busy with matters of transport and baggage arrangements while his dear friend Lafayette was engrossed in some of the most extraordinary events in French history.

Jefferson and his family sailed first to Britain aboard the packet *Anna* in order to secure passage there to the newly formed United States of America. No doubt James saw the greatest of ironies in the short but momentous sail to Britain. Near the end of the Revolutionary War the Jefferson and Hemings families had spent six months constantly running from the British advance. Some members of the Hemings family and a few other Monticello slaves were actually captured in Richmond, where Jefferson was situated as Governor, and taken behind British lines at Yorktown. James well remembered the chilly January day when he and his brother Robert briskly drove a carriage westward out of Richmond, carrying Martha Jefferson and her three daughters to safe haven. Not a decade had passed; he was sailing toward Britain. Oh, how times had changed!

While in Britain, Jefferson learned of more stormy events taking place in France. His first inclination was to deny the credibility of English newspaper reports. Later, he revised his denial, maintaining that the macabre events were justified by the result, never acknowledging their inhumanity. It was not until October 22 that his entourage, which had come to France in two parts, left as one, sailing for Virginia aboard the American ship *Clermont*.[37]

Thomas Jefferson, Patsy, Polly, Sally Hemings, and James Hemings were the only passengers. Beyond the nervousness felt on an ocean crossing, a confident exhilaration prevailed. Patsy knew that a lifetime of duty, reward, and honor was her destiny. As her father carried on with his mission, she would dignify whatever requests he made of her. Polly planned to immerse herself in the warm affections of Eppington, the Eppes plantation. She daydreamed of James River plantations and wished that she could introduce her friends from the convent school to her aunts, uncles, and cousins at Eppington.

James had learned new skills in France as well as a new language. Freedom was now his great prospect. Sally yearned for her mother's touch and lovingly wise words. Mentally, she was already telling her sisters and brothers of fine Parisian clothing, the elaborate pretentions of the bourgeoisie, and danger in the streets. Like most enslaved women, she could not expect marriage, but Jefferson had promised to free her children. She knew his baby would receive special treatment though she could not envision the child's adult life. Jefferson's dreams continued to reshape realities with far-reaching effect. Americans had achieved a massive transformation. Jefferson's role then evolved from freedom fighter to protector of freedoms secured.

NOTES

1. Julian Boyd, *The Papers of Thomas Jefferson*, vol. 7 (Princeton: Princeton University Press, 1950–), 451: letter from Thomas Jefferson to Francis Eppes dated 8/3/1785.

2. William H. Adams, *The Paris Years of Thomas Jefferson* (New Haven: Yale University Press, 1997), 203: danger at sea.

3. Fawn M. Brodie, *Thomas Jefferson, an Intimate History* (New York: W. W. Norton, 1974), 187.

4. Boyd, *The Papers of Thomas Jefferson*, vol. 7, 451: quote regarding Isabell; Robert C. Baron, ed., *The Garden and Farm Books of Thomas Jefferson* (Golden: Fulcrum, 1987), 244: birth of Edy.

5. Edwin M. Betts and James A. Bear, eds., *The Family Letters of Thomas Jefferson* (Charlottesville: University Press of Virginia, 1986), 38: role of John Amonit.

6. Lester J. Cappon, ed., *Adams-Jefferson Letters*, vol. 1 (Chapel Hill: University of North Carolina Press, 1959), 178: letter from Abigail Adams to Thomas Jefferson dated 6/26/1787.

7. Ibid., 179: letter from Abigail Adams to Thomas Jefferson dated 6/27/1787.

8. James A. Bear, ed., *Jefferson at Monticello* (Charlottesville: University Press of Virginia, 1967), 4: Isaac Jefferson quote; Brodie, *Thomas Jefferson*, 216: Thomas Jefferson Randolph quote; Boyd, *The Papers of Thomas Jefferson*, vol. 6, 503.

9. Brodie, *Thomas Jefferson*, 218.

10. Cappon, *Adams-Jefferson Letters*, vol. 1, 178.

11. James A. Bear and Lucia C. Stanton, eds., *Jefferson's Memorandum Books*, vol. 1 (Princeton: Princeton University Press, 1997), 720–31: payments to Sally Hemings.

12. Annette Gordon-Reed, *Thomas Jefferson and Sally Hemings: An American Controversy* (Charlottesville: University Press of Virginia, 1997), 178: Sally Hemings' relations with friends of Martha (Patsy) and Mary (Polly) Jefferson.

13. Merrill Peterson, *The Portable Thomas Jefferson* (New York: Viking Press, 1975), 414.

14. Jack McLaughlin, *Jefferson and Monticello* (New York: Henry Holt, 1988), 211: "violently smitten."

15. Herbert E. Sloan, *Principle and Interest: Thomas Jefferson and the Problem of Debt* (Oxford: Oxford University Press, 1995), 16: currency imbalance; Dumas Malone, *Jefferson and the Rights of Man* (Boston: Little, Brown, 1951).

16. Lucia C. Stanton, *Slavery at Monticello* (Charlottlesville: Thomas Jefferson Memorial Foundation, 1996), 6: sale of slaves.

17. Brodie, *Thomas Jefferson*, 220.

18. Sloan, *Principle and Interest*, 3.

19. Brodie, *Thomas Jefferson*, 200; Malone, *Jefferson and the Rights of Man*, 71.

20. George Green Shackelford, *Thomas Jefferson's Travels in Europe, 1784–1789* (Baltimore: Johns Hopkins University Press, 1995), 70.

21. Ibid., 73.

22. Brodie, *Thomas Jefferson*, 167: promise not to marry again.

23. Shackelford, *Jefferson's Travels in Europe*, 145.

24. Brodie, *Thomas Jefferson*, 230.

25. Ibid., 229: use of the word "mulatto."

26. Bear and Stanton, *Jefferson's Memorandum Books*, vol. 1, 720–31.

27. Ibid., vol. 1, 220, 233.

28. Ibid., vol. 1, 715.

29. Adams, *Paris Years of Thomas Jefferson*, 186.

30. Willard Sterne Randall, *Thomas Jefferson, a Life* (New York: Holt, 1993), 385.

31. Sabra Holbrook, *Lafayette, the Man in the Middle* (New York: Atheneum, 1977), 76–79.

32. Ibid., 93.

33. Ibid., 5.

34. Brodie, *Thomas Jefferson*, 236: Patsy's desire to become a nun and "grieves my heart" quote.

35. Ibid., 472: Sally Hemings' pregnancy from Madison Hemings' remembrances.

36. Ibid., 473.

37. Bear and Stanton, *Jefferson's Memorandum Books*, vol. 1, 742, 746.

CHAPTER TWO

Monticello

Make no little plans, they have no magic to stir men's blood.
—Daniel H. Burnham, 1907

The *Clermont* sailed homeward with favorable winds. Five Virginians and an unborn child were the only passengers. The first course was more southerly than westerly, to avoid the flow of the oncoming Gulf Stream. At sea, Jefferson planned for a temporary return to Monticello. He hoped to discover agreeable situations for his daughters there, ideally a husband for Patsy and a school for Polly. Accustomed to Parisian sophistication and enraptured with a new revolution, Jefferson considered his diplomacy and unofficial counsel to French revolutionaries as the most useful application of his talents.

Nearing port, a gale roughened the waters and ripped through the *Clermont*'s topsails as she beat to windward. Thirty days out of England, the *Clermont* reached Norfolk, her home port, on November 23, 1789. After the passengers disembarked, fire erupted, threatening Jefferson's valuables, but the blaze was extinguished in time to save them. The ship suffered extensive damage.[1]

Two days after landing, Jefferson learned of his nomination as secretary of state by President George Washington and his subsequent confirmation by the Senate. He had not sought the position, yet, as a former governor,

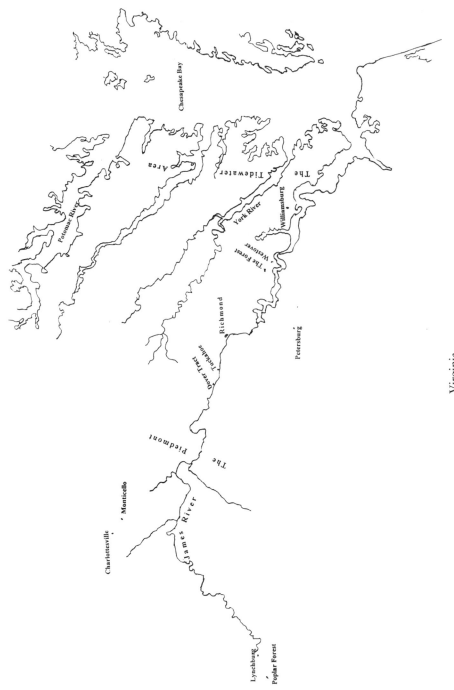

Virginia.

former congressman, seasoned diplomat, and famous patriot, he was well suited indeed. John Jay moved to the Supreme Court, Franklin was too old to carry such a responsibility, and Adams was to become vice president; Washington's choice was all but obvious. Nonetheless, Jefferson did not immediately accept the position.[2]

Jefferson wrote to William Short in Paris predicting his "plunge into the forests of Albemarle." Away from Monticello for seven years, he held no illusions about the condition of the plantation and the house. In his absence, some of his slaves and his extensive land holdings had been sold, and other slaves had been leased out. On his return he resumed the role of on-site owner and master of several families of African Americans whose numbers had not dwindled through sale, as natural increase kept their ranks from diminishing.[3]

Jefferson made his way slowly and grudgingly to Monticello, crossing the James River by boat to Hampton, making visits to Williamsburg and Carter's Grove, the home of his friend Colonel Nathaniel Burwell. He called on politicians in Richmond, gathering the latest political news, then visited the Randolphs at Tuckahoe. Crossing the James again to visit the Eppeses at Eppington, Polly was reunited with Elizabeth Eppes and Tabitha Skipworth, her aunts, half-sisters of her deceased mother. Polly now insisted on being called Maria, a derivation of her given name, Mary. Crossing the James for the third and last time at Goochland Courthouse on December 20, the Jefferson entourage arrived at Monticello on the twenty-third.

As the team strained to pull the fully loaded phaeton up the "little mountain," slaves collected around it. Slaves from Monticello and Jefferson's other nearby plantations were granted a day of leisure for celebration. The ever-growing Hemings clan was prominent among them. During much shouting and cheering, they stopped the carriage and, despite Jefferson's embarrassed protest, unhitched the horses and insisted on pulling the carriage up the winding mountain road themselves. Patsy described the startling scene:

Such a scene I never witnessed in my life. . . . The shouting, etc. had been sufficiently obstreperous before, but the moment [we] arrived at the top, it reached the climax. When the door of the carriage was opened, they received him in their arms and bore him to the house, crowding around and kissing his hands and feet—some blubbering and crying—others laughing. It seemed impossible to satisfy their anxiety to touch and kiss the very earth which bore him.[4]

Most of Monticello's slaves were elated with Jefferson's return, as it meant that rations would be dispensed by plan, rather than by whim, and the overseers were sure to be less harsh. Some slaves were just happy to have a day of leisure, others ecstatic to see James and Sally, and still others speculated that the master's return would speed the return of those leased to other farms. Family members gathered bits of information about Jefferson's promise to free James and of Sally's pregnancy. Furthermore, most imagined that a display of affection might gain favor with the two young Jefferson women, who would inevitably become their owners. Moreover, Jefferson was an American hero, and the assemblage of African Americans who labored long and hard on Virginia soil was beginning to feel that anything American was as much theirs as anyone else's.

Weeks later, Jefferson wrote President Washington and accepted the cabinet post. Nine days later, on February 23, 1790, Patsy married Thomas Mann Randolph, Jr., at Monticello in a small ceremony. The marriage neatly accommodated Jefferson's designs. Patsy was thereafter known as Martha or Mrs. Randolph, though her father continued to use her childhood nickname.

Jefferson was pleased by the marriage. Randolph was a tall man, a desired attribute since Martha, like her father, was tall. In the years to follow, Jefferson was very supportive of his son-in-law. Though Randolph was described by some as impetuous and moody, Jefferson referred to him in the most complimentary fashion. The proud patrician gave the newlyweds 1,000 acres of woodland and twenty-five slaves, deeding the land to Martha and her heirs. In January 1792, Martha gave birth to the first of twelve children, Anne.

Thomas Mann Randolph, Sr., granted the 950-acre Varina plantation, located southeast of Richmond, to his newly married son. Though Jefferson implored the couple to live close to Monticello, the land he granted them was part of his Bedford acreage, ninety miles from Monticello. Mortgages on his Albemarle County land prevented him from giving them property nearby. Martha and Randolph later bought Edgehill, a plantation near Monticello, and Randolph obligingly became the intermittent master of Monticello, as well as master of his own plantations. The abiding bonds between Martha and her possessive father were not disturbed by her marriage; Jefferson remained the center of her life.

As Washington's secretary of state, Jefferson had responsibility for a wide range of matters, both foreign and domestic. He left for New York City on March 1, leaving twelve-year-old Maria with Martha. James Hemings accompanied Jefferson to Richmond, where he settled and rearranged debts, then on to Alexandria, where Robert Hemings met them with Jefferson's phaeton, an open-air carriage common to the period. Snow prevented travel in the phaeton, so it was sent to New York over water, while Jefferson and his servants traveled by public coach. While passing through Philadelphia, Jefferson visited Benjamin Franklin's bedside a month before the sage's death.[5]

CABINET RIVALRY

The Washington administration converged on New York, powerful political figures of the time who, united in the struggle for independence, established a new democratic government. Jefferson, Adams, Hamilton, and Madison acted in accord, while Washington judged occasional disputes. When President Washington's second term arrived, the competitive political process fully emerged.

The French Revolution was one source of discord. Those who coalesced as the Federalist Party viewed the bloody revolution as anarchic and unprincipled. Jefferson and his disciples, known as Republicans, believed that the chaos would yield a purer state of democracy than that achieved in America. When Thomas Paine's *The Rights of Man* was published in 1791, lines of political demarcation were drawn. Jefferson received the treatise with ebullience; John Quincy Adams, the vice president's son, also a Federalist, sharply criticized Paine's writings. Unfortunate personal conflict between Jefferson and John Adams evolved from opposing valuations of Paine's writings. Disagreements between Jefferson, the secretary of state, and Hamilton, the secretary of the treasury, likewise were carved into the political landscape.

Reduction of the national debt was also a primary point of contention between Jefferson and Hamilton. In January 1790, Hamilton made the first of several well-conceived reports to Congress regarding the debt, which then stood at $54,124,464, mostly accumulated during the Revolutionary War. Veterans, veterans' widows, and farmers were among the creditors. Increasingly, debts in the form of notes were held by speculators, who purchased them at a discount. Including state debts, the total was approximately $70 million.[6]

Hamilton argued for the full face value repayment of debts. He called for custom duties and excise taxes, a national bank, and the expansion of domestic manufacturing. He sought to use the federal debt to create a pool of capital as the basis of circulating a medium of currency, as hard currency was scarce. James Madison, aligned with Jefferson and other Republicans, was opposed to an overpowering federal government, which they feared would be the outcome of Hamilton's plans. Instead Republicans proposed a complicated plan, designed to prevent the establishment of a permanent federal debt. Madison suggested sale of federal land west of the Allegheny Mountains to eliminate the debt. Hamilton won supporters in the North, particularly among speculators who stood to reap large profits when the war debt was satisfied. Southern states had previously repaid most of their debt, while northern states had not, thus Southerners opposed federal assumption of state debt. In 1791, the Bank of the United States was chartered. Hamilton's vision was realized. Though Jefferson served successfully as secretary of state, Hamilton's light burned brighter.

Thomas Jefferson was separated from Maria Cosway by an ocean; Sally Hemings was home on Mulberry Row. Patsy was married to a Virginia planter. Alone on Manhattan Island, he wrote his daughter Maria in April 1790:

Where are you, my dear Maria? How do you do? Write me a letter by the first post and answer me all these questions. . . . Be good my dear as I have always found you, never be angry with any body, nor speak harm of them, try to let everybody's faults be forgotten, as you would wish yours to be; take more pleasure in giving what is best to another than in having it yourself, and then all the world will love you and I more than all the world. If your sister is with you kiss her. . . . What would you do without them, and with such a vagrant for a father, say to both of them a thousand affectionate things for me: and Adieu my dear Maria.[7]

Jefferson would have taken Maria to live in New York, but she preferred not to make the journey. The fissure between them had been created when he left for Paris in 1784, leaving Maria parentless; she bonded thereafter with her aunt. When the federal government moved to Philadelphia in late 1790, Jefferson happily assumed more permanent accommodations there, leaving behind the "indifferent" house he had rented in New York. At great expense, books and other acquisitions were shipped from Le Havre to Philadelphia; he rented a house on High (now Market) Street from Thomas Leiper, a merchant. Maria finally came to live with her father in Philadelphia in late 1791. She attended Mrs. Pine's school and became fondly acquainted with Martha Washington's granddaughter, Nellie Custis. Her cousin Jack Eppes also lived with Jefferson during this time; thus Maria was able to enjoy his company during holidays.[8]

MULBERRY ROW

After four years as secretary of state Jefferson resigned and retired to Monticello in January 1794. At fifty-one years of age he thought his life was near its end. His father had lived fifty years; his father-in-law, John Wayles, died at the age of fifty-eight; and his mother, Jane Randolph Jefferson, lived to

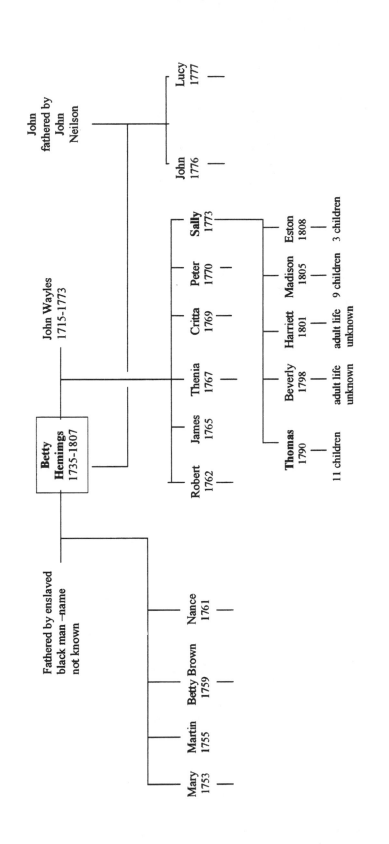

the age of fifty-six. Jefferson wrote to President Washington in July 1793, "I am every day convinced that neither my talents, tone of mind, nor time of life fit me for public life," but his self-doubt failed to convince Washington.

Though he commonly made similar comments during this time, rivals thought the retirement was a ploy. Sally Hemings gave birth to a boy shortly after returning to Monticello from France, though the date is not known. Thomas, as the boy was named, was four years old when Jefferson left the Washington administration. He most likely began to meet people outside of the Mulberry Row compound. Jefferson knew the risk of scandal and was then more attuned to such risks. Withdrawing from political life, he assumed the life of a Virginia aristocrat.

The matriarch, Betty Hemings, born in 1735, was fifty-five when her grandson Thomas was born. Betty's mother, an African woman whose name is lost to history, was raped by Captain Hemings during her passage from Africa to Virginia. The African woman and her child, Betty, were owned by John Wayles, who refused Captain Hemings' offer to purchase his child. Wayles was curious to see what kind of person the light-skinned child would become. The child, Betty, grew to maturity on Wayles' plantation, The Forest, located on the James River south of Richmond.

Isaac, a son of Great George and Ursula, described Betty Hemings as a "bright mulatto woman." Several of Betty's children were known to be of light complexion. Mulatto families served as house servants on many large plantations; the children in these families were most often offspring of the master. The practice sometimes compounded until the new generation looked white enough to pass, leaving to establish themselves in white society. Betty bore six children by a black man before bearing Wayles six mulatto children after his three white wives consecutively died. The fate of the father of the first six children is unknown; emasculation of black men was the rule, not the exception.

Of course, John Wayles did not marry his slave, Betty Hemings. Even if he had been so inclined, Virginia law prevented marriage between the black and white races. A marriage certificate does not exist, nor do birth certificates. Madison Hemings, a son of Sally Hemings born in 1805, asserted that John Wayles was his mother's father. The Wayles/Hemings liaison is now accepted by most historians, but not by all. Willard Sterne Randall maintains that we do not know who fathered Betty Hemings' children. He dismisses Madison Hemings' statement but presents no historical evidence to the contrary. Additional documentation affirms the Wayles/Hemings liaison, including a letter dated December 20, 1802, which Thomas Gibbons, a Federalist lawyer, wrote to an associate, Jonathan Dayton:

You ask, are the heirs apparent to our throne flat nosed, thick lipped and tawney? That Jefferson lives in open defiance of all decent rule, with a Mulatto slave his property named Sally, is as correct as truth itself, and that his children, to wit, Tom, Beverly and Hariot are flat nosed, thick lipped and tawney I can have no doubt, tho I have never seen any of them. And what adds to the monstrous disgrace of this amorous encounter is first that she is half sister to his first wife, and secondly that she is the most abandoned prostitute of her color. Pampered into a lascivious course of life, with the benefits of a French Education, she is more lecherous than the other beasts of the Monticellian Mountain.[9]

This letter was written before Madison Hemings was born; it is extremely unlikely that he ever read it, as he moved to rural Ohio in 1838. Gibbons' language may be considered harsh, yet it is typical of nineteenth-century attitudes toward African Americans.

As a boy, Thomas (Tom) lived among the close-knit Hemings clan. Among his aunts and uncles were Mary, Martin, Bett, and Nance, Betty Hemings' oldest children. The oldest, Mary, born in 1753, was a house servant who bore six children; it seems all were fathered by white men, though the father of the oldest children is uncertain. One of Mary's sons, called Joe Fossett, was the only one of her children to remain at Monticello during Tom's residence. Mary had been leased to Charlottesville merchant Thomas Bell during Jefferson's years in Paris. Upon his return, Jefferson acceded to her wish to be sold to Bell. Mary and Thomas Bell lived as husband and wife, and their mulatto children were given the Bell surname.

Martin, Betty's next oldest child at Monticello, performed some of the menial tasks of the plantation house. Bett, often known as Bett Brown, produced eight children; her son Burwell eventually became Jefferson's body servant. No references to Nance appear in Jefferson family letters; she was not a house servant. She worked in the Mulberry Row weaver's cottage for a time and labored in other Monticello enterprises at other times.

Though plantation tradition, individual overseers, and Jefferson himself made distinctions between enslaved people based on skin color, the Hemings clan was a creation of Betty Hemings, who recognized no such distinction among her offspring or her grandchildren. The six children Betty Hemings bore as John Wayles' concubine were adults by the time Tom began to move around Mulberry Row on his own accord. These five aunts and uncles were Robert, James, Thenia, Critta, and Peter. The children's maternal grandmother was the only African grandparent. Having one African grandparent and three white grandparents, the children were quadroons, a term commonly used in the eighteenth century. Robert, born in 1762, briefly worked as Jefferson's body servant, but usually maintained the horses and phaetons. He often transported Jefferson's numerous houseguests around Virginia for entertainment; Robert was, no doubt, one of America's first tour guides. James, three years younger than Robert, served Jefferson's constant requirements after Martha Wayles Jefferson's death. After traveling to Europe with Jefferson, James continued at his side and served as his cook when Jefferson joined the federal government in New York and Philadelphia. In a letter to an acquaintance in 1821, Jefferson cited Peter, Wayles' youngest son, as "a servant of great intelligence and diligence." Martha Wayles Jefferson taught him to brew beer, and his older brother, James, later taught him French cooking.[10]

Thenia, born in 1767, was sold to James Monroe in 1794 along with her five daughters. Critta was the closest in age of Sally's older sisters. The sisters must have been very attached to one another; references in the *Farm Book* and Jefferson family letters often paired the two names. Critta bore a son, Jamie, who "ran" from Monticello at age seventeen. He was not pursued.[11]

Sally was the youngest of the six children of Betty Hemings and John Wayles. Betty Hemings bore two more children after moving to Monticello. John was born in 1776 and Lucy was born a year later. The paternity of these children is unknown.

Betty Hemings created an unusual family. The Hemingses were slaves, but their lives were unlike the slave life most often visualized by twenty-first-century Americans. A white overseer did not govern their lives. Some family members never worked in the fields; others did so sparingly. To the extent that they received direction from anyone other than Thomas Jefferson, the black overseer, Great George, usually organized their work until his death in 1799. The white overseer, Edmund Bacon, who worked at Monticello from 1806 to 1823, reported, "They were old family servants and great favorites. . . . I was instructed to take no control of them."[12]

The Hemings family grew vegetables, not only for their consumption but to earn cash. Among the dozen children and twenty grandchildren of Betty Hemings at Monticello, only two, Wormley Hughes and Joe Fossett, joined with spouses from other Monticello slave families. Two of Betty Hemings' grandchildren, Burwell, a son of Bett Brown, and Critta, daughter of Nance, married. (This Critta was named after her aunt, a daughter of Betty.) This union emulated the Jefferson pattern and that of other prominent Virginia families who married cousins. Inward-directed tendencies of the clan were certainly encouraged by Betty Hemings, whose realm on Mulberry Row lasted thirty-two years. She left an indelible mark on the top of the little mountain.[13]

Disgusted with his abiding slavery to debt, Jefferson planned to make his landholdings more profitable upon his return to Virginia. After selling substantial tracts of land near the James River in Goochland and Cumberland Counties, he still held 11,000 acres in Albemarle and Bedford Counties upon which several farms operated. Jefferson sought greater productivity and put more land into wheat production and less into tobacco, and designed elaborate crop rotations. None of these efforts achieved the desired results.

Construction at Monticello became a focus of contemplation, frustration, and gratification, starting in the fall of 1790 when Jefferson instructed his steward, Nicholas Lewis, to build a washhouse and two meat houses with clapboard covers. The work was performed by enslaved carpenters. In 1794, a larger project emerged. Haunted and tantalized by visions formed in Paris of a domed house, cast in Palladian style, which offered ample living space but the understatement of a single story, Jefferson began construction, eventually doubling the size of his mansion.[14]

Some materials were assembled in 1794, but little tangible progress was made, as another project took precedence. In the search for greater and more stable income, slave labor was redirected from agriculture to a nail production venture. In the first year, Jefferson's supervision was close; he weighed nail-rod in the morning and nails in the evening, meticulously measuring the waste and efficiency of each worker. The nailery's profitability started according to plan, but fluctuated in time with managerial changes, the availability and price of nailrod, theft, and the variability of account collections. Evidence recorded by Jefferson himself indicates that the Hemings family on occasion abused the nailery by "mismanagement" of its cash flow.

Boys were trained to use tools and molds purchased for nail production. They were physically suited for the work, as it was not unusually strenuous and did not demand a high level of skill. Yet the work was monotonous, and boys defy boredom as wild horses defy capture. Close supervision and repressive measures were used, though some boys performed well without the use of force. Joe Fossett and Burwell were among the most efficient workers and were rewarded with more training and better positions over time. Bonuses in the form of cash or extra clothing (often dress clothing) rewarded exceptional production, a clear break from plantation traditions.[15]

FREEDOM ON THE HORIZON

Jefferson rewarded diligence, but he was reluctant to reward it with freedom. He promised James Hemings freedom while in Paris but later delayed its realization. James' patience increasingly wore thin. While in Philadelphia in September 1793, James extracted a written promise that Jefferson would free him on February 5, 1795, after James had taught his brother Peter the art of French cooking. The written promise bore no legal significance, as James Hemings would not have been recognized by any court; however, James drew further assurance from his master's capitulation.

Gaining freedom in late February 1795, James traveled to Philadelphia and then on to Paris to find work. However, mixing into French society proved difficult for James, and he subsequently returned to Philadelphia in 1797. From the onset James' life in freedom was bound to fall short of his expectations, as America was saturated with enmity against African Americans. Though he was skilled, literate, and multilingual, only menial jobs were open to him even in the North. He would never receive full pay for his skills. Tens of thousands of free African Americans lived in the South at the time, but under precarious conditions. They were often abused, as they had no civil rights; they could not testify in court against whites. They could not use courts to collect money due them or use the law for protection from assault, rape, or murder. Some free African Americans were taken captive and sold in the Deep South, a wicked yet profitable enterprise.[16]

James' dreams and ambitions gave confidence to others. His older brother, Robert Hemings, bought his freedom in 1795, after Jefferson's written promise to free James but before he was actually freed. Robert fell in love with an enslaved woman from Richmond who bore his child. Her owner agreed to advance money to Hemings for him to purchase her freedom. Jefferson agreed to the transaction, which allowed Robert to marry and live in Richmond. Robert Hemings was overwhelmingly appreciative of Jefferson's consent. Martha wrote her father, describing an encounter with Robert:

I saw Bob frequently while in Richmond. He expressed great uneasiness at having quitted you in the manner he did and repeatedly declared that he would never have left *you* to live with any person but his wife. He appeared to be so much affected at having deserved your anger that I could not refuse my intercession when so warmly solicited towards obtaining your forgiveness. The poor creature seems so deeply impressed with a sense of his ingratitude as to be rendered quite unhappy by it but he could not prevail upon himself to give up his wife and child.[17]

Despite the close relationship with the Jeffersons, the Hemings family was fully cognizant of its enslavement. Deploying his charisma, Jefferson willed peace and tranquility upon the mountaintop, yet the sense of duality never left these relations. Intimacy and friction coexisted. Intimacy grew from familiarity and interdependence; friction was born of the unseemly tradition of one person owning another. Freedom was the mantra. Hemings men sought and anticipated freedom. Hemings women yearned for freedom for their children, caring not whether those children lived as black or white. The Hemings clan bore the burdens of these circumstances, making the best of them.

A few other slaves at Monticello were rewarded for their diligence and skill. Great George and Ursula's children included Isaac and Smith George, also called Little George. While serving as secretary of state, Jefferson took Isaac to Philadelphia to apprentice as a tinner. Isaac lived there for four years, then returned to Monticello, where he manufactured tin utensils, also working in and managing the nailery at times. A photograph of Isaac survives, showing a man of dark complexion. The comparatively favorable treatment accorded this family was based on skill and disposition, not white parentage. Smith George, a blacksmith, also worked in the nailery.[18]

Great George held the position of overseer from 1797 to his death two years later. Jefferson's son-in-law, Thomas Mann Randolph, who referred to Great George as George the Ruler, advised Jefferson of his competence: "George I am sure could not stoop to my authority and I hope and believe he pushes your interests as well as I could." Smith George and Great George were both literate. Decades before, it was on Martha Wayles Jefferson's insistence that her husband purchased Ursula; Jefferson complained much later of paying a dear price for her, but it is apparent that her family added much to the Monticello plantation.[19]

Jupiter, who was the same age as Jefferson, carved a notable presence in his owner's life beginning with his service as body servant when Jefferson attended the College of William and Mary. Jefferson inherited Jupiter from his father, Peter Jefferson. Despite early closeness, Jefferson leased Jupiter out during his time in France. Later, Jupiter was given the pitiless task of quarrying limestone for the construction of Monticello. At times, Jupiter was a recalcitrant worker, possibly a reaction to the favored treatment the Hemings family received. Jupiter no doubt considered them newcomers. It seems Jupiter received no favoritism. Jefferson rewarded and punished to further performance and conformity, but, if there was a bias, it favored the enslaved people his deceased wife had cared about most, the Hemings family and Ursula and Great George.

The Monticello plantation lost a significant share of its eighteenth-century character when Ursula, Great George, Smith George, and Jupiter all died of the same disease in 1799 and 1800. Such a momentous loss must have caused residents of the plantation to contemplate their circumstances. Had they lost neighbors? Had they lost friends? Or had they lost members of their own family? Thomas Jefferson repeatedly referred to all residents of Monticello as his family. He entitled a 1776 plantation census "The Number of Souls in My Family." Later making reference to illness vexing the plantation, he noted the number of sick "in our family, both in doors and out." Friedrich Engels explained the origins of this word usage. "This expression (familia) was invented by the Romans in order to designate a new social organism that the head of which had a wife, children and a number of slaves under his paternal authority and according to Roman law, the right of life and death over all of them." The English did not create a separate word to describe what twenty-first-century Americans know as the nuclear family. Jefferson often used the word in the same manner as the Romans.[20]

Some slaves adamantly resisted the intrusions of slavery upon their freedom and dignity and evaded abuse. Sandy, a carpenter and shoemaker, took a white horse and shoemaking tools and "ran" in 1769. Jefferson placed an advertisement in the *Virginia Gazette* to assist in his recapture. Sandy was recaptured and sold in 1773, as Jefferson decided that his "government" of Sandy was not possible. As an institution, slavery could not be sustained without violence, the threat of it, and recapture of those who escaped. As a slaveowner, Jefferson employed the required traditions.[21]

Sandy escaped before the Revolutionary War. Another slave, Jamie Hubbard, lived a generation later. His experience indicates that the repressive traditions of slavery at Monticello remained unaltered while Jefferson occupied the President's House (as the White House was then known). Jamie was a son of Cate, another slave Jefferson inherited from his father; Jamie's father was also named Jamie Hubbard. Jamie's twelve siblings lived and worked at Jefferson's Bedford plantation.

When Jefferson started his nail-making operation, Jamie was brought to Monticello. The lad did not adapt to the confinement of the nailery, the repetitiveness of the work, or the dormitory-style sheds; he ran off to Fairfax County. After his apprehension and return to Monticello, Jamie was caught stealing nails but expressed great remorse. Jefferson refrained from having him beaten and gave him a "heap of good advice," according to overseer Edmund Bacon. Several years later, Jamie ran off again and was again recaptured. Brought back in irons and severely flogged in front of the other nailers, Jamie ran a third time. Jefferson, then convinced Jamie would never be a tractable slave unless still harsher measures were used, sold him in absentia. The buyer was Reuben Perry, a carpenter, who paid for Jamie with work on Poplar Forest, the house then under construction at the Bedford plantation.[22]

Floggings and the sale of slaves to far-off places were practices Jefferson embraced when he deemed them necessary, yet his inclinations were more humane than those held by the overseers. One overseer at Bedford complained of slaves running away to Monticello for a hearing with Jefferson. Jefferson's *Notes on the State of Virginia* is widely quoted for its degrading comments about enslaved black people, but his appraisal of white overseers was far from gracious. He described them as "the most abject, degraded and unprincipled race, always cap in hand to the Dons who employed them, and furnishing materials for the exercise of their pride, insolence and spirit of domination."[23]

Between the enslaved individuals who obligingly gave too much of their soul and sweat for no gain and those who resisted the repression of slavery at every turn was the majority. Most slaves accommodated their captivity and rewarded their owners to stave off abuse and neglect; the tremendous wealth and power of America would otherwise not have been produced. Some slaves required only sufficient food and a sturdy cabin to make them acquiescent; other sought to reunite torn families or dreamed of freedom. Different conditions and times, as well as human emotions, compelled them to cope with slavery in ways unique to each individual.

Sally Hemings bore no children in 1791, 1792, 1793, or 1794, when her youthful beauty would have been at its height. Her sexual desires would have been most potent, but she was abandoned. This was the time of life, seventeen to twenty-two, when women were most likely to bear children. Sally did not. The course of events directed Jefferson's talents to high office in New York and Philadelphia. Sally Hemings, meanwhile, took on no lovers. Jefferson was away from Monticello for eleven months in 1791, nine months in 1792, and eleven months in 1793. These absences spent in service to the new nation allowed him to place his fatherhood of Sally's mulatto son as far from his thoughts as possible.

For 150 years, historians attempting to deny the liaison of Sally Hemings and Thomas Jefferson claimed that two of Jefferson's nephews, Samuel and Peter Carr, fathered Hemings' children. There is no evidence that Samuel Carr spent any time at all at Monticello during the appropriate years. However, young Peter Carr, who, aided by Jefferson's mentoring, became a lawyer, spent considerable time at Monticello in 1791, 1792, and 1793. In *Fame and the Founding Fathers* Douglass Adair claimed that the greatest love of all time raged between Sally Hemings and Peter Carr, but, oddly, Sally produced no children. When she did finally bear more children, Peter Carr was married and owned slaves of his own. Insistent upon protecting Jefferson the icon, historians such as Andrew Burstein in *The Inner Jefferson* and John Chester Miller in *Wolf by the Ears* maintained this ruse nearly to the end of the twentieth century.

Sometime during 1795 Jefferson constructed a roll of the persons enslaved at Monticello and his other plantations. He had done this before, usually when he had time on his hands. The records were entered in the *Farm Book*, written in his own hand. The last such roll was recorded in 1783, when he operated three plantations in addition to Monticello—Poplar Forest, Wills Creek, and Elkhill. Jefferson listed 204 slaves then. Betty Hemings' name appeared first on the register, which included the year of birth for most but not all slaves. That list was made after Jefferson returned to Monticello from an aborted trip to France. While he waited for the actual duty in France to materialize he performed what he called these and other "unremitting duties." Before 1795 Jefferson sold the Wills Creek and Elkhill plantations and many slaves who lived there, but the roll had not fallen much because of natural increase. This time Jefferson refined the entry by placing names in male and female columns and by year of birth, so the oldest were listed first and the youngest at the bottom.

REKINDLED INTIMACY

Evidence of rekindled intimacy between Sally Hemings and Thomas Jefferson appeared about a year after his 1794 retirement to Monticello. Harriet, the first of Sally Hemings' children to be conceived after her return from France, was born on October 5, 1795. The whimsy of Sally's youth surely returned as she regained Jefferson's attention.

Thomas (Tom) attracted considerable attention on the Monticello plantation as the firstborn; when Harriet was born, he was five years old. Sally's large family doted upon Tom, resulting in his self-assurance and possibly a streak of cockiness. Unaware of the contradictions, complexities, and eventual instability of his situation, Tom grew into a proud, handsome, and self-reliant young man. His early years were also much influenced by Betty Hemings, whose spirit touched every child near her.

During the summer of 1796, two Frenchmen visited Monticello and recorded observations of its plantation life. The Duc de la Rochefoucauld-Liancourt wrote of seeing "particularly at Mr. Jefferson's, slaves who have neither in their color nor features a single trace of their origin, but they are sons of slave mothers and consequently slaves." The Comte de Volney observed slave children "as white as I am." Though miscegenation was a widespread but unacknowledged feature of Virginia plantation life, the repeated crossover by white men mating with black women, who progressively lost African characteristics with each generation of mixing, was most pronounced at Monticello.[24]

These accounts are quite specific. Rochefoucauld-Liancourt identified the children as males. Volney's account leaves no doubt as to the appearance of the boys; not "yellow children" but children, whom he compared to himself. Though Bett Brown's sons Burwell, Wormley, and Edwin were probably light-skinned, they could not have looked entirely white; the only "sons" fitting this description would have been Tom and Jamie, Critta's son, and it took the presence of both to cause Rochefoucauld-Liancourt to use the plural.

During the years that Jefferson lived as a Virginia planter, he failed to reduce the debt that caused him so much concern. Neither did he gain confidence in his former political colleagues. He longed to gain control of the new capital to prevent the errant measures of Federalists from wasting the success of the American Revolution.

Republican congressman James Madison and Jefferson devised strategies to place themselves at the head of the government. They predicted that the administration that followed Washington's term would be doomed, as expectations were unreasonably high and political fracturing was bound to become wider. Madison and Jefferson, then, were not distraught when Jefferson lost the election of 1796 to Adams by a margin of three votes. Following the practice of the times, Jefferson, as runner-up, became vice-president. Adams distrusted the British and was not warm to many of Secretary of the Treasury Hamilton's proactive governmental programs. Adams' moderation drew some Virginians into the Federalist ranks. Through inactivity, Jefferson avoided the scorn of Federalists; through his distance from Adams, he maintained favor with Republicans.

Jeffersonians have produced a half-dozen books covering Jefferson's relatively unproductive mission to France (1784–89), some of which concentrate on pure adventure, his travels through Europe. Yet the first six years following his return to America would comprise the most pivotal portion of his life. Jefferson resigned from the weighty post of secretary of state during the embryonic years of our government in part disillusioned, but also wiser as to the opportunities and pitfalls of partisan politics. He awakened to the reality of his longevity and came to terms, as much as he ever would, with his affections for Sally Hemings. He planned to capture the President's House (as the White House was then known) and contemplated the immortality of his legacy.

In February 1797 Thomas Jefferson reentered public life as vice president of the United States in the administration of John Adams, but he returned to Monticello after a mere two weeks in Philadelphia. After another brief trip to Philadelphia, he again returned to Monticello in July 1797. Sally Hemings became pregnant within a month of his return. This travel was quite an ordeal and would not have been undertaken had the desire to attend to loved ones at home, the call to duty in Philadelphia, or both pressed forcefully upon Thomas Jefferson.

According to *Jefferson's Memorandum Books*, journals he kept for over fifty years, he again left Monticello in early December 1797. Two-year-old Harriet died days after his departure. During Harriet's illness, a young slave, Edy, was assigned to help Sally care for the children. Domestic help for a slave was not merely rare; it was unique. When Edy returned to her mother, Isabell, another helper, Aggey, was summoned in her place.[25]

Sally bore a son, Beverly, on April 1, 1798. While serving as vice president, Jefferson made frequent trips between Monticello and Philadelphia. He was not only devoted to Sally Hemings but spent a good deal of energy to be with or near her. After four years of abandonment, she undoubtedly felt wanted and needed once again. Betty Hemings, who no doubt viewed the estrangement as a setback to her grand design, welcomed the rekindled fire as a return to the natural order.

Beverly is a name handed down in the Randolph family. William Randolph, one of Jefferson's maternal relatives, married his cousin Elizabeth Randolph and produced a son, Beverly Randolph, who was a friend of Jefferson's. Harriet was also a name used by the Randolph family. The names of Sally's children are connected to the Randolph clan, not to the burgeoning Hemings clan. Sally knew some of the Randolphs; however she did not know them well. Of course the name of the firstborn, Thomas, has an obvious origin. It is probable that the boy was commonly called Tom on the plantation, but his father named him and called him Thomas. Sally did not name her children, as she would have used names common within the Hemings family. The father, Thomas Jefferson, named the children.

In 1801, James Hemings returned to Monticello to work for a short time. His return must have been disappointing, as his freedom had little meaning at Monticello. After leaving once again, he committed suicide. Thomas Jefferson described this as a "tragical end." Why was freedom such a failure for James? Did he fail at freedom, did freedom fail him, or was it ever possible for him to be truly free?[26]

Maria, Jefferson's younger daughter, married her cousin John Wayles Eppes in October 1797. The marriage was anticipated; the couple knew each other from their earliest memories. Unlike her older sister, Maria freed herself of her father's possessive grip by moving to Eppington, a substantial distance from Monticello. Maria had spent part of her childhood at Eppington and probably considered it her destiny to live there. She remained a loving daughter, writing her father often and visiting whenever possible. Maria's husband became a congressman. She gave birth to a son; however, both she and her son suffered periodically from frighteningly poor health.

The Adams administration (1797–1801) was fraught with turbulence. The French began to confiscate cargoes of American ships upon the high seas, a conflict remembered as the Quasi Wars. As a consequence the Alien and Sedition Acts were adopted to quell activities of suspected subversive elements, including French immigrants. The acts granted the federal government powers which threatened to undermine individual rights, and they eventually stirred more turbulence than they quelled.

Jefferson returned home again on March 8, 1799. Sally Hemings conceived for a fourth time within a month of his arrival. During this stay, reconstruction and expansion of Monticello greatly accelerated. In July 1798, a carpenter, James Dinsmore, had come to Monticello from Philadelphia. Dinsmore was literate, skilled, creative, and well organized. His competency allowed work on the expansion of Monticello to continue even when Jefferson was not at home.[27]

Sally Hemings' youngest brother, John Hemings, who was born after the family moved to Monticello, apprenticed with Dinsmore, becoming a talented carpenter/joiner. During the summer of 1799, a roof was finally installed over the north end of the house, which had been exposed to the elements for two winters. Thomas (Tom) in turn learned carpentry skills from John Hemings. John was a very willing instructor.

In December 1799, Sally gave birth to an unnamed daughter who died in infancy. Jefferson left Monticello on December 21 for Philadelphia. George Washington died during this time, but Jefferson bypassed Mount Vernon, Washington's plantation. Jupiter traveled with Jefferson but soon became ill. Jefferson insisted several times, unsuccessfully, that Jupiter return home for medical care. When Jupiter finally accepted the seriousness of his condition, his health was appalling. Only then was Jefferson able to convince Jupiter to return to Monticello. He died shortly thereafter. Thomas Jefferson and Jupiter had been born at Shadwell in the same year and had known each other from the earliest years. Jefferson expressed his dismay at this loss in a letter to his daughter, Martha (the nickname, Patsy, was dropped when Martha married). Following Jupiter's death John Hemings traveled with Jefferson and served his personal needs. Thomas accompanied the pair on one trip as a companion to both men. Jefferson's notes show that he gave the boy small sums of spending money. The boy was probably of some help to them, but they no doubt spent more time doting upon him.[28]

While in Philadelphia, Jefferson began preparation for a presidential bid by heavily supporting Republican newspapers and pamphleteers. Vicious attacks against the opposite party were a common thread of Republican and Federalist newspapers. Jefferson paid pamphleteer James Callender $50 in September 1799 through his cousin George Jefferson, a Richmond merchant. In January 1800, $113 was paid to Tenche Coxe, another Republican writer. The payments represented substantial sums in the currency of that time.[29]

Enthusiastic as ever about the political opportunities that lay ahead and also about his family situation and experimentation at Monticello, Jefferson returned home again in May 1800 and stayed until November 24, 1800. The grateful planter described the wheat crop of 1800 as the heaviest ever. In May 1801, Sally gave birth to the only daughter who would live to maturity. Like the two-year-old who had died in December 1797, she was named Harriet. This newborn shared her mother's home with two brothers.

Monticello overseer Edmund Bacon declared decades later that this Harriet was not the daughter of Thomas Jefferson. He told historian Hamilton Pierson, "She was not his [Jefferson's] daughter; she was ——'s daughter. I know that. I have seen him come out of her mother's room." When Bacon's statement was published in 1862 by Charles Scribner, the father's name was omitted. Bacon said that he had seen the individual in question emerge from Sally Hemings' room upon his arrival early in the morning at the top of the mountain. However, Bacon did not begin to work at Monticello until September 29, 1806. He could not have known about the comings and goings of Sally Hemings or her visitors in the fall of 1800, because he was not at Monticello at the time. Even when he began to oversee farming at Monticello, he did not live at the top of the mountain and did not visit it daily. Bacon apparently thought that his statement would be believed when he spoke with Pierson in Kentucky approximately thirty-five years after Thomas Jefferson's death. Little did he know how closely Jefferson's life would be studied.[30]

In November 1800, voters cast their ballots for electors in each state, who in turn voted for presidential candidates. The vote by the electoral college on December 3, 1800, gave Jefferson's Republican Party victory over the Federalists; however, Jefferson and fellow Republican Aaron Burr received the same number of electoral votes. The responsibility of breaking the tie fell to the House of Representatives, which cast thirty-six ballots before the tie was broken and Thomas Jefferson was elected the third president of the United States. On March 4, 1801, he was inaugurated in Washington, D.C., as the federal city had been established there in June 1800. Jefferson and Madison had read the political tea leaves correctly.

Thomas Jefferson excelled in the duties of the presidency. He ended the Quasi Wars, protected American shipping in the Mediterranean, and later purchased the vast Louisiana Territory. Yet he remained powerless to construct a new future for himself, one which would satisfy his vision and self-image. Vestiges of slaveowning plantation society engrossed him; debt, lifestyle, and a continuing hunger for power restricted his options.

The liaison of Sally Hemings and Thomas Jefferson was neither idyllic nor fraught with emotional pain. It was not a marriage, but it mirrored marriage in its buoyancy, overcoming anxiety and vacillation, while attraction, seduction, and temptation pulled the couple together. The liaison was complicated by Jefferson's intermittent resolve to discontinue it, his many other interests, political and otherwise, as well as Sally's aversion to continuing life as a slave and her dreams of freedom for her children. Certainly a predictable and dependable relationship developed over time. The Hemings family history of compounded miscegenation and Jefferson's determination to keep the liaison out of the public domain further ruffled the tranquility for which both yearned. Hemings was attracted to Jefferson's power, intellect, handsome and powerful physique, and the charismatic but aloof personality which has eluded comprehension for over 200 years. Hemings offered beauty, charm, and continuity to a long life riddled with the loss of loved ones. If the relationship had inflicted deep emotional pain upon Sally Hemings, the pain would have been reflected in the lives of her children. It was not.

SLAVE INSURRECTION

During the Revolutionary War and the British invasion of Virginia, thousands of blacks escaped slavery. The loss of labor caused white Virginians great concern. However, the American and French victory at Yorktown saved Virginia planters from further loss. A few blacks who joined the British were eventually transported to Africa; yet most blacks who ran to the British encampments fared poorly, dying of disease and starvation. Separately, Toussaint-Louverture, a black slave, led a successful revolt in Haiti in 1791. The effect of these events on black Americans was significant and lasting.

More and more black slaves came to view insurrection and violence as a way to break the bonds of captivity. In northern white communities the roots of the antislavery movement began to take hold. Pennsylvania adopted gradual abolition of slavery in 1780. When Jefferson finished his second term as president, 430,000 blacks lived in Virginia, including 30,000 who were free. Southern whites vehemently protested the existence of free blacks in their states. They were quick to ferret out connections between insurrection attempts and the activities of free blacks.

The population of free blacks grew faster than the overall black population, but it remained small, as it grew from a very small base. In 1800, an uprising was planned by a Richmond blacksmith, Gabriel Prosser, and his brother Martin, a preacher. The insurrection was quelled in its infancy; nonetheless, it caused great concern among slaveowners. The frequency of insurrections did increase, but most were stopped early as the slaveholders devised an effective intelligence system.[31]

Indentured servitude among whites ended at this time. Pennsylvania abolished such servitude in 1780 along with the enslavement of blacks. Other states, even southern states, also put an end to the practice. Whites could no longer be bound to service in factories or on plantations, even for a finite period of time. Enslaved black Americans were further influenced by this emancipation. Until this point there had always been clusters of whites in the neighborhood whose freedom was restricted. Enslaved blacks yearned for the freedom indentured whites gained.[32]

Many Southerners did view slavery as a curse. Leading southern politicians proposed plans for gradual emancipation and relocation of blacks; yet these plans and proposals died in conversation. Northern states abolished slavery, typically through gradual abolition, a system designed to ensure that newborns would live in freedom. Out of fear, southern states created laws that increasingly restricted and degraded African Americans. For the next twenty years, enslavement became more ruthless in character, continuing to mock the principles of the Declaration of Independence until the Civil War would provide relief.

Relations at Monticello grew more tense and unsettled as well. In a letter to her father dated April 21, 1802, Maria Jefferson Eppes wrote from her plantation at Eppington, "My dear Papa I shall write again by Crity when she goes up. I hope you had no objection to her spending this winter with me. She was willing to leave home for a time after the fracas which happen'd there and is now anxious to return." Critta, sister of Sally Hemings, had left Monticello for Eppington before November 6, 1801, according to another letter. We are left to ponder the nature of the "fracas." Thomas Jefferson was then president of the United States, but Monticello was not immune to turbulence. The American Revolution secured liberty and privileges for white Americans, who had suffered under a nearly feudalistic social order, while it raised expectations among blacks.[33]

NOTES

1. Fawn M. Brodie, *Thomas Jefferson, an Intimate History* (New York: W. W. Norton, 1974), 247.

2. Dumas Malone, *Jefferson and the Rights of Man* (Boston: Little, Brown, 1951), 244.

3. Brodie, *Thomas Jefferson*, 247. The "plunge" is mentioned in a letter to William Short, a former aide, who remained in Paris, in Julian Boyd, *The Papers of Thomas Jefferson*, vol. 16 (Princeton: Princeton University Press, 1950–), 28.

4. Jack McLaughlin, *Jefferson and Monticello* (New York: Henry Holt, 1988), 240; Brodie, *Thomas Jefferson*, 248; from George Tucker, *The Life of Thomas Jefferson, Third President of the United States* (Philadelphia: Care, Lea & Blanchard, 1837), 301–2.

5. James A. Bear and Lucia C. Stanton, eds., *Jefferson's Memorandum Books*, vol. 1 (Princeton: Princeton University Press, 1997), 750: Jefferson leaves for New York.

6. Robert A. Rutland, *James Madison* (New York: Macmillan, 1987), 78: from Harold C. Syrett and Jacob E. Cooke, eds., *The Papers of Alexander Hamilton*, vol. 6, 77.

7. Edwin M. Betts and James A. Bear, eds., *The Family Letters of Thomas Jefferson* (Charlottesville: University Press of Virginia, 1986), 52.

8. Bear and Stanton, *Jefferson's Memorandum Books*, vol. 1, 755: "indifferent house" (see notes), and 770: rental of house from Leiper (see notes).

9. Letter from Thomas Gibbons to Jonathan Dayton, December 20, 1802, Clements Library, University of Michigan; provided by Lucia C. Stanton of the Thomas Jefferson Memorial Foundation.

10. Bear and Stanton, *Jefferson's Memorandum Books*, vol. 2, 912: description of Peter.

11. Ibid., vol. 2, 922: Thenia (see notes).

12. James A. Bear, ed., *Jefferson at Monticello* (Charlottesville: University Press of Virginia, 1967), 99–100.

13. Bear and Stanton, *Jefferson's Memorandum Books*, vol. 2, 957: marriage of Burwell and Critta.

14. McLaughlin, *Jefferson and Monticello*, 246.

15. Lucia C. Stanton, *Slavery at Monticello* (Charlottesville: Thomas Jefferson Memorial Foundation, 1996), 23.

16. Brodie, *Thomas Jefferson*, 290: travels of James Hemings.

17. Ibid: from Betts and Bear, *Family Letters*, 131.

18. McLaughlin, *Jefferson and Monticello*, 104.

19. Ibid., 104, 143.

20. Stanton, *Slavery of Monticello*, 13: Jefferson notations and Engels explanation; Barbara Chase-Riboud, *Sally Hemings* (New York: Ballantine, 1994), 256.

21. McLaughlin, *Jefferson and Monticello*, 126.

22. Ibid., 115–16.

23. Ibid., 127.

24. Stanton, *Slavery at Monticello*, 20.

25. Annette Gordon-Reed, *Thomas Jefferson and Sally Hemings: An American Controversy* (Charlottesville: University Press of Virginia, 1997), 195.

26. Brodie, *Thomas Jefferson*, 376.

27. McLaughlin, *Jefferson and Monticello*, 270; Betts and Bear, *Family Letters*, 176: progress on Monticello construction.

28. Gordon-Reed, *Thomas Jefferson and Sally Hemings*, 195: birth and death of child.

29. Bear and Stanton, *Jefferson's Memorandum Books*, vol. 2, 1012: payment to Coxe.

30. Bear, *Jefferson at Monticello*, 102: alleged visitor to Sally Hemings' room.

31. Michael Durey, *With the Hammer of Truth: James Thomson Callender* (Charlottesville: University Press of Virginia, 1990), 137–38: Gabriel's insurrection.

32. Bear and Stanton, *Jefferson's Memorandum Books*, vol. 1, 346, 468. Thomas Walker, an indentured servant at Monticello, gained his freedom in 1778.

33. Betts and Bear, *Family Letters*, 224.

CHAPTER THREE

James T. Callender with the Hammer of Truth

He is unfit to be a friend of virtue who cannot defend her dignity, who dares not execute her vengeance.

—James Callender[1]

On September 1, 1802, the *Richmond Recorder* printed an article by James Thomson Callender that set 200 years of scandal and controversy into motion. Callender wrote in part:

It is well known that the man, Whom is delighteth the people to honor, keeps and for many years has kept, as his concubine, one of his slaves. Her name is Sally. The name of her eldest son is Tom. His features are said to bear a striking though sable resemblance to those of the President himself. The boy is ten or twelve years of age.[2]

Before this article was published, only hints of Jefferson's tryst with an unnamed slave had appeared in print. Callender's was a direct, full-blown accusation; the scandalous report spread throughout the nation. What impelled Callender to incriminate a sitting president while others contented themselves with innuendo? Callender had been jailed for sedition in 1800. Did this father of four sons wish to return to jail? Was he jealous, resentful, or deranged? What compelled Callender to start swinging the hammer of truth?

For 199 years vilification of Callender was one of the primary tactics used by historians intent on denying the sexual liaison between Sally Hemings and Thomas Jefferson. Callender was easily criticized. He was certainly a "notorious scandalmonger," as the famous Jefferson biographer Dumas Malone noted. He was a heavy drinker and not a responsible provider for his wife and children. He was known to brutally criticize persons who were once his friends and patrons. Were his writings untruthful and baseless? Did he slander the president? Would he write anything that a few dollars would bring? Was he a genius, as Thomas Jefferson once noted?[3]

EDINBURGH ORIGINS

James Thomson Callender was born in Scotland, most likely in 1758. Little is known of his early life. Scotland had a comparatively advanced educational system. Callender may not have been able to afford a university education; however, lectures at the University of Edinburgh were often open to the public. He loved literature, but writers who lacked wealthy patrons found their path a difficult one. Patrons were acquired through social contact, and Callendar lacked the appropriate social rank.

In 1782, Callender obtained employment in the Sasine office in Edinburgh, equivalent to the Recorder of Deeds in most of today's communities. As subclerk he was paid fourpence a page, which gave him a meager income.

Callender's interests reached beyond the routine and mind-numbing work of the Sasine office. He anonymously published two pamphlets, mixing personal and literary criticism. The target of Callender's satire was the eminent English writer, poet, and critic Samuel Johnson. During and after Johnson's travels to Scotland in 1773, he disparaged Scottish culture and Presbyterian preferences. What Scots detested most was Johnson's pensioner status, granted after he suffered a mental breakdown, as Scots resented taxes paid to the British government and, particularly, misuse of the money. Johnson's pension was a sore spot. Beyond appealing to Scottish sensibilities, Callender's pamphlets promoted patriotic principles, subtly supporting the cause of the American Revolution and stirrings of Scottish nationalism. Callender's *Deformities of Samuel Johnson* was so well received that a second edition was printed. The pamphlets extended Callender's realm beyond the drudgery of the Sasine office. Success inspired more writing.[4]

The Sasine office remained Callender's primary means of support. The keeper of the Sasines at the time was Andrew Stuart, Member of Parliament. The chief clerk, Andrew Steele, actually managed the office, continuing a tradition of graft involving inflated fees skimmed off by managers. The practice incensed Callender. Steele soon found himself challenged by Callender's crusade to end such corruption in the office. In 1785, Callender openly protested the practice of double bookkeeping. Steele had not created this practice, but continued it upon his appointment as chief clerk. Steele was a haughty individual and lacked the finesse to keep the racket going without raising resentment. Stuart and an aide were investigated, but were exonerated. Undaunted, Steele discovered new ways of maximizing personal profit.

After a short respite, harmony in the office broke down. Callender now blatantly accused Steele of pilferage. Callender demanded a raise for the clerks and threatened to publicize the offenses of the office if the raise was not granted. He again miscalculated. Within months he was dismissed from the office, losing a means of supporting his family.[5]

Not long after Callender left the Sasine office in 1790, his poetry caught the attention of Francis Garden, Lord Gardenstone. Gardenstone was an eccentric unmarried judge noted for local government reform. He was also a literary patron. Gardenstone secured a position for Callender as messenger for a lawyer, James Balfour. The position allowed Callender time to write, and he often published under the pseudonym "Timothy Thunderfoot." Gardenstone wrote also; some work was probably jointly produced. Still, Callender's patron was a social maverick, limiting Callender's ability to become better connected to the social and political establishment.

In 1789 brewer Hugh Bell employed Callender to produce *An Impartial Account of the Excise*, to expose corruption and the uneven application of the excise tax in Scotland. Callender named offending officials and provided detailed evidence of corruption. Grateful brewers subsequently offered money for a second pamphlet. Callender next began writing a series of eight letters, *The Political Progress of Britain*, to be published in a magazine, the *Bee*. The letters anonymously enumerated the wars with Holland, France, and Spain, civil wars in Ireland and Scotland, and numerous wars and conquests in Asia and the New World. They advocated breakup of the British Empire. As demand for the writings grew, second and third editions were printed. The government increasingly sought to identify the author. While the work was not the most openly seditious writing of the time, its impact was the sharpest.[6]

Under pressure from the deputy sheriff of Edinburgh, Gardenstone incriminated Callender, who failed to appear in court on January 28, 1793. He fled to America for fear of reprisal, landing on the shores of the Delaware River in May 1793 and making his way to Philadelphia, then the capital of the United States of America.

COMING TO AMERICA

Philadelphia was the largest city in the country at a time when no American city was very large. The first U.S. Census, taken in 1790, found a population of 44,000 there. The ranks of artisans, craftsmen, builders, and lawyers were growing, but not without interruptions. In the year of Callender's arrival, a yellow fever epidemic killed dozens of residents and disrupted operations of the new government.

As President George Washington began his second term in office, the two-party system began to evolve. In the summer of 1793, Alexander Hamilton and James Madison, who collaborated on *The Federalist Papers*, which supported the adoption of the Constitution, wrote a series of letters published in Philadelphia newspapers. Each man then revealed opposing ideological positions. Madison's views paralleled those of Thomas Jefferson, who was in France at the time.

After doing some freelance writing, Callender began as a congressional reporter for the *Federal Gazette*, which soon after changed its name to the *Philadelphia Gazette*. Having found a measure of stability, he brought his wife and children to Philadelphia, where another son, Thomas, was born.

The Fourth Congress convened in 1795 with a Republican majority. The two-party system had now fully emerged. When the Republicans hired a stenographer and filled other positions from their ranks, Callender became embroiled in an exchange of accusations. As a result the *Philadelphia Gazette*'s owner fired Callender. Shaken by this loss, he left Philadelphia in search of work, but soon returned there to join militant Republican propagandists. In 1797, Callender published *The History of the United States for the Year 1796*, employing his signature style of searing satire and nasty personal attack. With this propaganda Callender created a major public scandal. Alexander Hamilton was forced to acknowledge an affair with a married woman, but he denied financial impropriety involving his duties. Explaining his innocence (except for adultery), Hamilton claimed that the husband of his paramour had blackmailed him. Callender used further documents to cast suspicion on Hamilton's explanations. Callender's effectiveness caused Hamilton to call for a duel with James Monroe, which was averted by the intervention of none other than Aaron Burr![7]

The successful attack on Hamilton, the ideological leader of the Federalists, was complete fulfillment for a political propagandist. Callender, however, was freelancing when his attack hit target. Federalists counterattacked with a vengeance. An assassin twice visited Callender's home when he was absent. He fell into a state of abject poverty. Federalist rivals wrote about him scornfully; William Corbett cited him as a "little mangy Scotsman" who "loves grog, wears a shabby dress . . . and goes along working his shoulders up and down with evident signs of anger against fleas and lice." Callender's critics highlighted his inadequate support of his children and wife, who was then ill.[8]

FOREVER DEFIANT

The Federalist president John Adams was also stung by the propagandist's efforts. Federalists controlled the majority of banks, which began to deny financial support to Republican newspapers and printing shops. Thomas Jefferson, who was then secretary of state, encouraged Callender through veiled payments to criticize the Federalists. Secrecy was essential, because any knowledge of Jefferson's payments to Callender while the latter maligned George Washington, John Adams, and Alexander Hamilton would have dangerous political consequences for Jefferson. Callender's wife died during this time.

In 1798, the Alien and Sedition Acts became law. Sedition statutes empowered the government to imprison journalists who criticized government policies, Callender's raison d'être. He was rightly worried about being charged under the new law, but characteristically did nothing to mend his habits.

In May 1798, Callender protested libel charges against Federalist writer William Corbett, who was brought before Republican judge Thomas McKean in the Pennsylvania courts. Callender turned his pen against the judge. For Callender, the sanctity of the free press stood above partisanship; however, Republicans, including men he thought of as his friends, ostracized him for criticizing a fellow Republican. Hitting a new low point, Callender left Philadelphia for Virginia in the summer of 1798, leaving his four sons with a former landlord, Thomas Leiper.[9]

RICHMOND—BATTLE OF THE PRESSES

After spending some time in northern Virginia, Callender obtained a position with the *Richmond Examiner*, a newspaper owned by John Dixon and Meriwether Jones, a friend of Thomas Jefferson. On arrival in Richmond, Callender moved into Jones' home and soon was engaged in Jefferson's presidential campaign against the incumbent, John Adams. Callender attacked Adams in *The Prospect Before Us*, effectively whipping up suspicion of Federalist incumbents. Again, Callender exploited minor issues with scathing effectiveness.

Federalists sought to convict Callender under the new sedition statutes and to remove him from the campaign. On May 24, 1800, a Richmond grand jury indicted Callender. Prosecutors claimed he had incited the American people to hate their president by printing and publishing false, scandalous, and malicious statements. On a previous occasion, Callender had fled when faced with arrest. Now he stood his ground.

The agent of Federalist persecution was Supreme Court Justice Samuel Chase, a signer of the Declaration of Independence, an unsuccessful land speculator, and a former Anti-Federalist. His intent on arrival in Richmond on May 21, 1800, was to exploit the potential of the Sedition Act. The trial was a purely political affair. Upon hearing of Callender's arrest, Chase vented, "It is a pity you have not hanged the rascal." Historian Charles Jellison summed up the depth of this iniquity: "Few more unsavory and generally obnoxious figures than James Thomson Callender have ever set foot on American soil, but even he deserved something better than he received from American justice." Callender was thus a victim of the embryonic government's abuse of power. For Republicans, Callender's misfortune presented an opportunity. If Callender could be billed as a martyr, his persecution could be used as a platform for Jefferson's election as president. Neither Jefferson nor James Monroe, then governor of Virginia, missed the opportunity. The zealous little Scot, fined and jailed by his enemies and hailed as a martyr by his aristocratic friends, was handed a nine-month sentence.[10]

A treacherous place, the old Richmond jail tested the faculty of self-preservation. During Callender's incarceration, the insurgents who planned Gabriel's Insurrection were captured and placed in the Richmond jail. After arriving in Virginia, Callender began to favor the institution of slavery, though, like many Southerners, he deplored the original establishment of slavery in the Virginia colony. At the time, half the population of Virginia was black. Callender dismissed the expatriation of blacks to Africa as impractical, favoring moving them into the West to decrease their proportion of the state's population. Unlike many Southerners, he was not paternalistic. He found blacks physically repulsive, feared them, and blamed them for the commonplace sexual relations between white men and black slave women. Since his acquaintance with the insurgents, who were ready to kill to obtain freedom, occurred while he himself was jailed, Callender's attitudes toward blacks were sharpened. He favored hanging the "African speculators in fire and blood."[11]

OUT OF JAIL

Callender's imprisonment ended in March 1801, along with Adam's presidency. The Alien and Sedition Acts expired. President Jefferson pardoned Callender, who had by then already served his full term. The pardon erased the conviction. James Monroe, Meriwether Jones, George Wythe, and other grateful Republicans had visited Callender in jail. By Callender's own account, he played a crucial role in Thomas Jefferson's election and rightfully sought the position of postmaster in Richmond, but Jefferson denied it to him. Though he certainly benefited from Callender's past allegiance and had solicited his assistance, Jefferson was wary of the feisty newsman. Callender interpreted this rejection as another affront by an ungrateful, corrupt aristocrat to his commonplace upbringing. This was a pattern well established in Callender's life; its root is unknown, but it no doubt emanated from slights inflicted during his childhood.

In the summer of 1801, a new newspaper, the *Richmond Recorder*, owned by Henry Pace, began publication. Callender obtained a job there and was soon joint editor. The *Recorder* was not a partisan paper, and the position freed Callender from political debt. He was without a patron or mentor. He was essentially free to choose one of two courses: to find less volatile material to cover and enjoy the peace he claimed to yearn for, or to let the spirit of his resentment and Puritanism run its course.

Before long, Callender fell into a muckraking duel with Meriwether Jones as a result of insults exchanged regarding misdeeds of Jones' brother, Skelton Jones. In May 1802, Callender, who had once lived with Meriwether Jones, exposed the latter's lavish treatment of a slave mistress whom he kept in a Richmond apartment. Callender quoted Jones as boasting that "he had never had any pleasure, but in a certain kind of woman; that it was the custom of his family to be fond of the other colour." Jones was stricken. The story was true. He was helpless and defenseless.[12]

Callender then grew bolder. He asserted that Thomas Jefferson had paid him to produce *The Prospect Before Us*. When Jones claimed that the money was given in charity, Callender quoted from a letter written by Jefferson, and he claimed to possess more letters. When Jones denied the existence of the letters, Callender printed them in full. The battle of the presses had escalated into total war among journalists and politicians in Virginia.

In August 1802, William Duane, a Philadelphian, used his *Aurora* to lob some muck back in Callender's direction. He asserted that before her death Callender's wife had been "overwhelmed by a created [venereal] disease, on a loathsome bed, with a number of children, all in a state next to famishing

... while Callender [was] having his usual pint of brandy at breakfast." When copies of the Philadelphia newspaper arrived in Richmond, Callender was stricken with rage. Information he planned to use against Jefferson during the next election became the instrument of counterattack.[13]

SCANDAL OF TWO CENTURIES

In September 1802, the *Recorder* printed clear and direct assertions of Thomas Jefferson's sexual liaison with Sally Hemings. Callender was not the first to allude to Jefferson's liaison with a black mistress. In July 1802, the *Port Folio*, a literary sheet printed in Philadelphia, published an anonymous ballad that hinted at the president's sexual activity. Still, the publication that has received the most attention for nearly 200 years is the one printed on September 1, 1802, quoted at the outset of this chapter.

It is critical to note that, on September 22, Callender corrected an error in his shocking exposé, not then a month old. He wrote, "The negro wench did not go to France in the same vessel with the president. Mr. Jefferson sailed first, with his elder daughter. The younger Miss Jefferson went afterwards, in another vessel, with the black wench as her waiting maid." This clearly reflects Callender's reverence for accuracy. The mistake was not of major consequence, but the correction was prompt; acceptance of responsibility and candor on this point affirm Callender's professional integrity.[14]

Callender proclaimed Jefferson to be the father of Sally's son Tom (Thomas), a boy of twelve. According to Virginius Dabney's *The Jefferson Scandals*, twentieth-century commentators such as Garry Wills and Merrill Peterson denied that Tom ever existed and claimed that Callender fabricated his existence. Yet these historians failed to explain why at the time no one challenged Callender's creation of an allegedly fictional boy. After all, the subject here was the president of the United States, and Callender's accusation spread nationwide! Yet none of the 1 million Virginians then living denied Tom's existence.[15]

After Callender's allegations appeared, others investigated them. In December 1802, the *Recorder* reprinted an article from the *Fredrick-town Herald* confirming Callender's allegation. The reprint reads as follows:

Other information assures us, that Mr. Jefferson's Sally and their children are real persons, and that the woman has a room to herself at Monticello in the character of seamstress to the family, if not as housekeeper, that she is an industrious and orderly creature in her behavior, but that her intimacy with her master is well known, and that on this account, she is treated by the rest of the house as one much above the level of his other servants. Her son, who Callender calls President Tom, we are also assured, bears a strong likeness to Mr. Jefferson. We make bold to these circumstances of confirmation, because although the subject is a delicate one, we can not see why we are to affect any great squeamishness against speaking plainly of what we consider an undoubted fact interesting to the public.[16]

Callender dared the president to deny the assertion that he had fathered Tom as well as Sally's younger children. Jefferson did not respond to Callender's allegations. He had witnessed Callender's attacks on Alexander Hamilton in prior years, and Hamilton's denial only worsened his predicament. Each denial allowed Callender to expose a new lie. The president remained silent, while his supporters smeared Callender's name with labels: drunk, blackmailer, whoremonger, and so on. Scandalmonger became one of the nicer appellations. Jeffersonians (but not Jefferson) denied that Tom was the president's son, but they could not and did not deny any other details of Callender's exposé. Callender meanwhile was far from inactive. He raked over another scandal, born long before he came to America, the Walker affair, wherein Jefferson was accused of making a pass at the wife of an Albermarle County neighbor of notable social rank. The neighbor wished the scandal dead; but, with it in the open again, he demanded satisfaction, adding to Jefferson's burden.

Subscriptions to the *Recorder* grew with the scandals. By December, 1,000 copies were purchased weekly—a several-fold increase in demand. Callender, recognizing the increase in circulation, asked Pace for a share of the profits. Pace refused. In the coming months Callender wrote only sporadically for the paper.

Harry Croswell's *New York Wasp*, published in Hudson, twenty-five miles south of Albany, reprinted an anti-Jefferson barb on September 9, 1802. The original article had appeared in the *New York Evening Post*, owned by Alexander Hamilton. In part the article read, "Jefferson paid Callender for calling Washington a traitor, a robber, and a perjurer—for calling Adams, a hoary headed incendiary; and for most grossly slandering the private characters of men, who, he well knew were virtuous." On January 10, 1803, New York Attorney General Ambrose Spencer obtained two indictments against Croswell. It was now Jefferson's turn to use the criminal "justice" system for partisan gain, though he had campaigned against such shockingly undemocratic abuses by the Federalists. During this time Jefferson wrote in a letter, "I have therefore thought that a few prosecutions of the most prominent offenders would have a wholesome effect in restoring the integrity of the presses. Not a general prosecution as that would look like a persecution, but a selected one."[17]

The People vs. Croswell was another political battleground. Each side brought to bear the best legal talent it could muster. Croswell was found guilty of libel. According to instructions that the Republican judge Morgan Lewis delivered to the jury, it mattered not if the material Croswell printed were true; it only mattered that Croswell was the printer of the material and that President Jefferson was injured. Defense counsel then motioned to the full bench for a new trial based on their position that the judge's instructions were inconsistent with New York law. The full bench included Judge Lewis and two Federalist judges. Not surprisingly, a new trial was granted.

Federalists, in order to free Croswell, planned to prove that Jefferson indeed paid Callender to slander Adams, Washington, and Hamilton. Hamilton, who was then directly involved with the Croswell case, wrote his friend William Rawle of Philadelphia on June 26, 1803, to secure advice. Rawle had handled a case where testimony of an absent witness was obtained by deposition. Depositions were uncommon at the outset of the nineteenth century. Hamilton sought to use the same maneuver in defense of Croswell. The absent witness was to be James Thomson Callender. Hamilton hoped to have Callender confirm payments by Jefferson for the scandalous attacks on Federalists. Callender had already published this information in the *Richmond Recorder*.[18]

SUDDEN DEATH

It came as a shocking blow to the defense team of Harry Croswell when Callender drowned in the James River on Sunday, July 17, 1803. His body was reportedly seen floating in only three feet of water. A doctor "tried every method to restore him to life," but to no avail. A coroner's inquest hurriedly recorded the death as accidental drowning while drunk. Callender was buried the same day in a local churchyard. Richmond was rampant with rumors of foul play. Many took it for granted that Callender's sudden demise had been hastily arranged.[19]

Callender had too many enemies to track. However, a letter to Callender from Meriwether Jones in November 1802 is of special import. "The James River you tell us, has suffered to cleanse your body, is there any menstrum capable of cleansing your mind. . . . Oh! could a dose of James River, like Lethe, have blessed you with forgetfulness, for once you would have neglected your whiskey." Unfortunately, the river, aided or unaided, was responsible for more than Callender's forgetfulness.[20]

Callender's death certainly did not end the virulence of partisan politics. Yet, stung by the rumors about Callender's death, as well as by the death of Alexander Hamilton in a duel the following year, the furious nature of political rivalry in the early years of partisanship was quelled. Jefferson never instigated another libel prosecution. Croswell received a new trial after the New York legislature passed a statute ensuring that truth could be used as a defense in a libel trial.[21]

The maligning of James Thomson Callender began, certainly, well before his death; his manner seemed to attract it. Afterwards, the maligning drastically distorted all record of Callender's difficult character and life. An effort to sort through the tangle of misrepresentations and distortions did not begin until fairly recently, and Callender-bashing continues to be a favored tactic among Jeffersonian historians. Though most of them now acknowledge the Jefferson/Hemings liaison which Callender exposed, they nevertheless maintain that Tom was not Jefferson's son. These historians fail to provide an alternate identity for Tom, declaring that his existence or nonexistence has attracted attention beyond its importance. They foist a new version of events upon the unwitting public with an incomplete account, relying, as did their predecessors, on the weight of their credentials rather than the application of logic.

Callender's maligning has emphasized three points. First, he is often labeled a "pen for hire" who lacked professional integrity. Second, his sharp words are often considered too brutal to carry any truth. Third, the misfortunes of his private life are used to impugn his professionalism.

AWESOME AUSSIE

With the publication in 1990 of *With the Hammer of Truth*, a biography of James Thomson Callender, an Australian historian, Michael Durey, made a valuable contribution to American history. Durey chronicled and assessed the life of this fascinating man who added to the most volatile and philosophically rich political struggle in our history. Durey approached the subject with courage, untangling misapprehensions and historical shams. No American historian has ever approached Callender with the objectivity Durey summoned. Durey found Callender to be professionally ethical and reliable. He found that the streak of Puritanism held firmer ground in Callender's constitution than any affection for alcohol.

James Callender shook the pretenses of Monticello. At the time, the attack was far less effective than attacks on Hamilton's career and Adams' presidency. Sexual relations between slaveowners and female slaves were common, but taboo masked the practice, and rarely was it broken. It took a unique man and unique circumstances to produce the scandal and controversy, which has bridged two centuries.

NOTES

1. Michael Durey, *With the Hammer of Truth: James Thomson Callender* (Charlottesville: University Press of Virginia, 1990), 9.

2. Quoted in Fawn M. Brodie, *Thomas Jefferson, an Intimate History* (New York: W. W. Norton, 1974), 349.

3. Dumas Malone, *Jefferson and His Time*, vol. 1, *Jefferson, the Virginian* (Boston: Little, Brown, 1948), 448. Malone branded Callender "the notorious scandalmonger."

4. Durey, *With the Hammer of Truth*, 4: Callender's livelihood.

5. Ibid., 16.

6. Ibid., 33–36.

7. Robert A. Hendrickson, *The Rise and Fall of Alexander Hamilton* (New York: Van Nostrand Reinhold, 1981), 478: role of Aaron Burr.

8. Durey, *With the Hammer of Truth*, 103.

9. Ibid., 109.

10. Ibid., 127.

11. Ibid., 138.

12. Ibid., 154.

13. Ibid., 157.

14. Brodie, *Thomas Jefferson*, 349.

15. Virginius Dabney, *The Jefferson Scandals* (New York: Dodd, Mead, 1981), 47.

16. Durey, *With the Hammer of Truth*, 159: Dec. 8, 1802, *Richmond Recorder*.

17. Hendrickson, *The Rise and Fall of Alexander Hamilton*, 577: letter from Thomas Jefferson to McKean.

18. Ibid., 579: letter from Hamilton to William Rawle.

19. Brodie, *Thomas Jefferson*, 374.

20. Ibid., 356.

21. Hendrickson, *The Rise and Fall of Alexander Hamilton*, 583. Croswell received a new trial.

CHAPTER FOUR

Tom Is Banished

You may write me down in history
With your bitter, twisted lies
You may trod me in the very dirt
But still, like dust, I'll rise.

—Maya Angelou, "Still I Rise"

According to oral history handed down in Thomas' (Tom's) family for 130 years, "When Thomas was about twelve years old he had a dispute with his father and was sent to the farm of John Woodson." The Woodson family interpretation of this oral history and events holds that public disclosure of the liaison between Sally Hemings and Thomas Jefferson was inevitable, that in some way Thomas had a hand in the disclosure, and that Thomas was indignant toward the idea that he did anything wrong. The family lost knowledge of James Callender's blistering news reports, if indeed it ever had known about them. Callender knew not of Thomas' departure; if he had, he would surely have reported it. The precise time of Thomas' banishment cannot be determined, but it certainly coincided closely with Callender's scandal mongering.[1]

Thomas' eventual freedom was anticipated, as Thomas Jefferson promised Sally he would free her children, but not banishment at so young an age. Whether or not the banishment was intended to be permanent, there is no

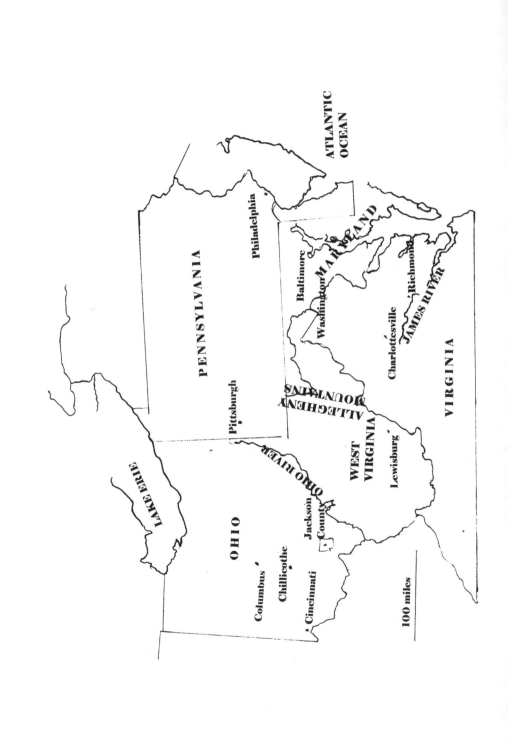

record of Thomas ever returning to Monticello to live or for a visit. Thomas may have boasted about his lineage while living at Monticello, prompting Callender's investigation, but Jefferson did not act out of vengeance. The president was attempting to ameliorate a menacing political problem. It is most plausible that Jefferson's intent was a temporary banishment, a cooling-off period of sorts, but Thomas was angered by it and undaunted by the prospect of losing his mother's immediate attention and support. Most important, Thomas quickly began to focus on his freedom, defined in the broadest possible sense.

Even though sexual relations between owners and slaves were commonplace, Callender's challenge to Jefferson's authority was unprecedented. As a result Thomas' childhood was severed, as if floodwaters had swept him away from his family. In retrospect, the predicament could have been easily anticipated. Thomas' presence at Monticello could not be finessed forever. As the oldest child, and for years the only child, he drew attention. When Callender released his news report Beverly was four years of age and sister Harriet was just one year old. Thomas was the only child old enough to have learned about and understood that he was Thomas Jefferson's son.

Two men named John Woodson, father (b. 1730) and son, were related to Thomas Jefferson through the elder Woodson's wife, Dorothea. Dorothea and Thomas Jefferson's mother, Jane, were both daughters of Isham Randolph. The older Woodson was Jefferson's uncle and the younger his first cousin. John and Dorothea's other children included Jane, Josiah, Elizabeth, Nannie, Isham, Martha, and others who were all Jefferson's first cousins. This branch of the extended Woodson family lived in Goochland County about twenty-five miles southeast of Monticello in the direction of Richmond. The Woodson family traces its American roots to yet another John Woodson who came to Virginia in 1619 and established a plantation, Flower Dew Hundred, on the lower washes of the James River.[2]

Members of this family served as officers in the Revolutionary War, as county sheriffs, and as members of the House of Burgesses during the colonial era. Jefferson's uncle served as a colonel in the Revolutionary War and submitted reports to him while Jefferson served as governor of Virginia. The Woodsons were not as aristocratic as the Randolphs and the Lees. Members of both of those families signed the Declaration of Independence. The Woodsons were more typical of the larger, landowning, slaveowning class of Virginia gentry. Like the Randolphs and many families of elevated status, the Woodsons often married relatives. Two of the elder John Woodson's children married other Woodsons.

Although the elder John Woodson was dead by the time Tom left Monticello, his primary residence at Dover Tract still retained the designation "John Woodson's farm." The names of prominent men outlived them, particularly while their widows remained alive, as was the case here. Dorothea was alive when Thomas left Monticello. Dover Tract was less than two miles from Tuckahoe, a Randolph plantation where Jefferson had spent a large portion of his adolescence. Jefferson knew the area and its people as well as he knew his own Albermarle County neighborhood. He traveled through the area innumerable times as a small boy while living at Tuckahoe, later while attending William and Mary, and still later as a member of the House of Burgesses and as governor of Virginia. Jefferson often traded with members of the Woodson family, including Woodsons not as closely related who lived in Albermarle County.

Yet another John Woodson, cousin of the Woodsons of Dover Tract, operated a ferry on the James River under the regulation of the Commonwealth of Virginia, which set rates charged by ferry operators. A half-dozen Woodsons operated ferries on the James River. This John Woodson owned land on both sides of the river where the Willis River (or Creek) empties into the James River. The land on the south shore of the river was in Cumberland County. The ferry operation was only a few miles from Dungeness, the Randolph plantation where Jane Randolph Jefferson, the president's mother, was raised.[3]

Thomas' whereabouts during the first two years following his departure from Monticello are not documented. This is not surprising. Thomas' banishment from Monticello was for an entirely clandestine purpose. His life was closely tied to the Woodson family in those years.

TOM MEETS JEMIMA

Jemima, the woman Thomas would soon marry and would remain with for sixty-three years, lived near John Woodson's ferry in her childhood. She was enslaved on the farm of Drury Woodson (b. 1722), who lived in Cumberland County on the opposite side of the James River from Monticello and Dover Tract. Her mother, Hannah, and her sister, Fanny, were also slaves there. Jemima was the younger child, but seven years older than Thomas. Drury Woodson made a will dated May 7, 1788, and died in October that same year. Hannah, Fanny, and Jemima (Mima in the will) were left to Drury Woodson's heirs, his wife and children. Drury owned a total of eighteen slaves at his death. Daughters Elizabeth, who married Charles Gilliam, and Martha, who married Peyton Riddle, were among the heirs. Elizabeth and

Martha each inherited one of Hannah's daughters, Fanny and Jemima, respectively.[4]

Drury Woodson's will also cited a small debt owed to a John Woodson; Drury Woodson did not have a son named John. This establishes contact between Drury and a John Woodson, probably the ferry owner. Most likely the several Woodsons who owned ferries linked the entire Woodson family as a result of frequent use of their ferries. The notation signifies a business relationship and occasional contact, and establishes a point of contact through which Thomas may have met Jemima.

Immediately after the Louisiana Purchase (1803), descendants of the elder John Woodson of Dover Tract and Drury Woodson of Cumberland County traveled over the Allegheny Mountains to settle in Kentucky. Dorothea Woodson, the widow of the elder John, died in 1803. Josiah (b. 1758), the oldest son of John Woodson, inherited Dover Tract. Josiah's oldest daughters left for Kentucky in 1804. The younger John Woodson (of Dover Tract) left in 1805 for Woodford County, Kentucky, where he settled. Evidence indicates that a John Woodson helped Thomas move west; most likely it was this John Woodson, as the other men who shared that name remained in the Piedmont.

The history of Drury Woodson's family's movement west is more complex. Daughter Elizabeth moved to Kentucky with her husband, Charles Gilliam. It appears that Martha's husband, Peyton Riddle, died on the westward trek. Martha Woodson Riddle returned to Piedmont Virginia as a widow. The lives of the slaves Drury and John Woodson (the elder) had owned became destabilized; nonetheless, as Americans, they yearned for westward movement as well.[5]

Westward movement intensified in 1803 and would remain a defining part of American life for decades. Correspondingly, a small portion of the slave population was manumitted by owners who sought a different life in the West. Many but not all whites who moved to Kentucky abandoned the tradition of slavery and the pressure of debt. They farmed in Kentucky without the assistance of slaves. A large number of enslaved people were sold as a result and transported to the cotton fields of the Deep South. Some slaves benefited from western movement, but many more fell deeper into the den of iniquity.

MIGRATION TO GREENBRIAR COUNTY

Precisely how and where Thomas and Jemima met is not known. They may have met in the vicinity of John Woodson's ferry or further west, after each migrated to Greenbriar County. Regardless of how they met, we know that the union, which lasted sixty-three years, started soon after Thomas was sent to the Woodsons' farm. The union was the definitive juncture in the lives of Thomas and Jemima and the origin of a legacy that has thrived through several generations.

Banished from the comforting embrace of the Hemings clan on Mulberry Row, Thomas (Tom) now found a new clan, one not then as large but certainly as strongly bonded. Jemima, Hannah, and Fanny became his family. Tall, handsome, and self-assured, Thomas adopted Woodson as his surname and began to assume adult roles. Whether by luck, fate, or compatibility, the attachment was exceedingly propitious. Jemima was steadfast, pious, and loving. Hannah seemed to possess some of the qualities of Tom's grandmother, Betty Hemings. Hannah may very well have played a key role in the union of young Thomas and the older but unattached Jemima. As if that were not enough, Jemima's sister Fanny was just as eager to face life's challenges and reap its rewards as Thomas. They both seemed to evoke an indomitable spirit. Thomas and Jemima's first child, their son Lewis, was born in January 1806 in Greenbriar County, Virginia.[6]

The Greenbriar County deed of a property sold by Robert Renick to James Kincaid places "Tom Woodsen" on an adjoining property in 1807. The land is located on Brushy Ridge, just east of Sinking Creek, four miles from the county seat of Lewisburg. Greenbriar County, located just west of the Allegheny Mountains, became part of West Virginia during the Civil War but was part of Virginia when Thomas migrated there. Lewis Woodson's birth establishes the family in Greenbriar County in early 1806. John Woodson's trek to Kentucky suggests that Thomas was there in 1805. Fanny was manumitted in Greenbriar County in 1803 and Hannah was manumitted there in 1805. These points suggest that Thomas and Jemima both had moved to Greenbriar County by 1805 and that Tom spent less than two years on the Piedmont after leaving Monticello. Thomas, Jemima, Hannah, and Fanny may not have moved west as one group, but the time frame was fairly tight.[7]

The manumission of Fanny and Hannah is documented, but the nature of the manumission is not. Did they buy their freedom? Did someone purchase freedom for them? If so, who? Manumission papers were not filed for Jemima, but she lived as a free person. Hannah's family gained freedom, a family, and a homestead. This was all extremely fortuitous. There is no documentary evidence that these events were arranged or aided, but if they were not arranged (in part), then Thomas Jefferson, his mulatto son Thomas (Tom) and Thomas' newfound family all happened upon good fortune at the same time by chance.

The citation of the name "Tom Woodsen" in Greenbriar County in 1807 is particularly telling. Callender recorded the presence of a boy named Tom (Thomas) at Monticello; President Thomas Jefferson's son Tom carried that name to Greenbriar County and assumed the Woodson surname. He was the only Woodsen or Woodson in the county then and the only Woodson male adult (all children there were his own) in the county in 1820 according to the U.S. Census. The U.S. Census of 1810 was lost or destroyed. The 1820 census reflects the formalization of his given name, then changed to Thomas. Tom is not unknown as a given name. An individual would have to have some motivation to change his name from Tom to Thomas, and Tom (Thomas Woodson) certainly had a motive. Having relocated, started a family, and matured, he became comfortable using his given name.

Greenbriar County is a rugged but alluring land of hills and flats, spotted with an occasional fragment of the Allegheny Mountain chain. The Greenbriar River carries off the flow of streams, which meander around the bases of heavily wooded mountains and ridges. Thomas and Jemima settled about four miles west of Lewisburg, on a rise called Brushy Ridge. The site was adjacent to the Midland Trail, a dirt road leading from Virginia to the Ohio River. Like the Cumberland Trail to the south and the National Road to the north, the Midland Trail was a major westward migration route. It seems Tom was more of a cattle grazer than a dirt farmer. Thomas Woodson became the quintessential American in many respects. His family sprang to life just as the nation's population was exploding. He resettled just west of the Allegheny Mountains, at a time when it was almost un-American to stay put. He focused on the practicalities of life. Yet, one characteristic set Thomas Woodson apart from the mainstream. By marrying Jemima, a woman far too dark to consider passing in white society, he chose to live as an African American.

With a complexion light enough to be taken for white, Thomas Woodson experienced and witnessed many of the horrors and contradictions of racial taboos. Situations that were black and white for others were much more complex for mulattos. The nature of Thomas' freedom in Greenbriar County was not an anomaly, although he was not a free man by Virginia law. He looked like a white man, and in truth a former slave who looked white could choose to be free and white.

STRADDLING BLACK AND WHITE

The following tale taken from Virginia court records imparts a lesson about race as Thomas Woodson must have experienced it:

A mulatto named William Hayden was apprehended in the county of Prince William and committed to the jail of the said county, and advertised as the law in such cases directs, and was by order of the county court advertised for sale., and no person having claimed him, and he not having proved his freedom, he was offered at public auction for sale . . . when one Robert Lipscomb, being a bidder and making the highest bid became the purchaser of the said Hayden, as agent . . . Lipscomb informed your petitioner, that his principal would pay the purchase money in a few days. The said Hayden was returned to the jail to await the arrival of the trader, who in a short time came and being requested, refuse to pay the amount which he had authorized the said Lipscomb to bid. Your petitioner afterwards sent the said Hayden to the town of Fredericksburg. And the City of Richmond, by one Col. James Ferrell, of Prince William (who had a number of slaves to be offered for sale) to be sold if the amount could be obtained for him equal to the said Lipscomb's bid. The said Hayden was offered for sale to sundry persons in Fredericksburg by Ferrell and myself, he was also offered in Richmond by Ferrell and myself, all of who refused to purchase him at any price, on account of his color. All alleging he was to [too] white. The said Ferrell returned him to your petitioner in the town of Brentsville, when he offered him for sale on a court day, several traders were present, all of whom refused to make a bid for him, all alledging that his color was too light and that he could by reason thereof, too easily escape from slavery and pass as a white man, and while your petitioner was endeavoring to sell the said Hayden, he made his escape, and altogether your petitioner has made every exertion to regain possession of him, he had not been able.[8]

State laws gave whites more rights and protections than nonwhites; thus it was necessary to fit everyone into a racial grouping. The terms varied among states in legal definition. The Virginia law of 1785 declared that "every person, who has one quarter or more of Negro blood shall be deemed a mulatto, and the word Negro in any section of this or any other statue shall be construed to mean mulatto as well as Negro." North Carolina took a very different approach, stipulating that "all persons descended from Negro ancestors, though one ancestor of each generation may have been a white person, shall be deemed free negroes and persons of mixed blood." It was the only state to consider all persons with some African ancestry as Negro. As slaves, African Americans were denied surnames and prohibited from learning to read or write, in part to disconnect them from their genealogy. If they were inclined to prove their lineage in order to live as part of white society, they were unable to do so; yet, if they looked white enough to pass, moved to another locale, and/or kept a low profile, they could pass.[9]

As time went on, the number of quadroon and octoroon children increased. No state enacted a statute that defined white persons as those whose ancestors were entirely white! Courts were often called on to determine the race of a person and regularly did so based upon inspection. Whites no doubt expected those mulattos who looked white to live as white persons. Otherwise the system of racial discrimination would deteriorate. If some individuals looked white but acknowledged their African heritage, then how could whites that did not have or acknowledge African ancestry expect society to recognize their alleged racial purity? Mulattos often migrated for precisely this reason.[10]

The following amusing account reflects the absurdity that mulattos found in the caste system that still prevailed in the early nineteenth century:

In the summer of 1838, the monotony of Memphis was relieved by the sudden appearance of Monsieur Dukay, an individual of foreign aspect, peculiarly French in his accent and the color of his cuticle. . . . Agreeable in conversation and prepossessing in manner, he was not long in making himself the center of a social circle. The ladies smiled delightedly in his presence, and through the long summer months no party or fashionable assemblage was complete without Monsieur Dukay. He sang charmingly in French. But his greatest attraction was the possession of two sugar plantations in Louisiana. On the upper plantation, he claimed an annual production of four hundred hogheads, and six hundred on the lower plantation. This was enough to sweeten his society, and give a saccharine tinge to his general conversation. The merchants, too, were happy to make his acquaintance. He talked eloquently of finance. But all things have an end, and it became necessary in the course of events for Monsieur Dukay to depart, and on the event of this interesting occasion, he deplored with tearful eyes the necessity that compelled him to return to his plantations. . . . From a friend in the grocery line, he purchased a bill of supplies for the upper plantation, giving in payment a draft on his New Orleans merchant. From a "old dear friend" he obtained, in similar manner, a fine riding horse, saddle and bridle; and from a bosom friend and companion he reluctantly consented to receive a diamond ring for his only sister. Months passed away, and no tidings came from the elegant Frenchman. The drafts were duly returned for non-acceptance. . . . But, during the ensuing winter, a gentleman with whom he had been intimate, happened in New Orleans and found "Mon cher Dukay" manipulating in the capacity of a quadroon barber.[11]

Though miscegenation was condemned by so-called decent society, the practice persisted from the early years of the Virginia colony. In 1662, the Virginia Assembly broke tradition with English law, declaring, "Whereas some doubts have arisen whether children got by an English man upon a Negro woman shall be slave or free, Be it enacted . . . that all children born in this country shall be bond or free only according to the condition of the mother." Not only did this act break with English legal tradition, whereby paternity defined the status of an offspring, it broke with the tradition of Roman law—a tradition over 1,000 years old.[12]

The French retained Roman tradition. Consequently, in Louisiana, mixed-race offspring were usually acknowledged and treated well by their fathers. Slaveholders in colonial Virginia and other southern areas rigidly followed taboos that prevented discussion of the origin of mixed-race children. Mary Boykin Chesnut wrote of this condition:

God forgive us but ours is a monstrous system, a wrong and an iniquity! Like the patriarchs of old, our men live all in one house with their wives and concubines; and the mulattoes one sees in every family partly resemble the white children. Any lady is ready to tell you who is the father of all the mulatto children in everybody else's household but her own. Those, she seems to think, drop from the clouds.[13]

What did Thomas Jefferson think about this monstrous system? Leaving in-depth analysis of this difficult question to historians, the following Jefferson quotation conveys a great deal about his perspective toward slavery: "We have the wolf by the ears; and we can neither hold him, nor safely let him go. Justice is in one scale, and self-preservation in the other."[14]

How did Jefferson regard the standing of his mulatto children vis-à-vis southern society, whose racial schism was its defining characteristic? An acquaintance, Francis C. Gray, asked a related question in 1815: "When does a black man become white?" Jefferson's response is intriguing. "You asked me in conversation, what constituted a mulatto by our law. . . . Our canon considers two crosses with the pure white, and a third with any degree of mixture, however small, as clearing the issue of negro blood."[15]

Let us express the pure blood of the white in the capital letters of the printed alphabet, the pure blood of the negro in the small letters of the printed alphabet, and any given mixture of either, by way of abridgment in MS. letters.

Let the first crossing be of a, pure negro, with A, pure white. The unit of blood of the issue being composed of the half of that of each parent will be $a/2 + A/2$. Call it, for abbreviation, h (half blood).

Let the second crossing be of h and B, the blood of the issue will be $h/2 + B/2$, or substituting for $h/2$ its equivalent, it will be $a/4 + A/4 + B/2$, call it q (quarteroon) being $1/4$ negro blood.

Let the third crossing be of q and C, their offspring will be $q/2 + C/2 = a/8 + A/8 + B/4 + C/2$, call this e (eighth), who having less than $1/4$ of a, or of pure negro blood, to wit $1/8$ only, is no longer a mulatto, so that a third cross clears the blood.

From these elements let us examine their compounds. For example, let h and q

cohabit, their issue will be $^b/_2 + {}^q/_2 = {}^a/_4 + {}^a/_8 + {}^A/_8 + {}^B/_4 = {}^{3a}/_8 + {}^{3A}/_8 + {}^B/_4$, wherein we find ⅜ of *a*, or negro blood.

Let *h* and *e* cohabit, their issue will be $^h/_2 + {}^e/_2 = {}^a/_4 + {}^A/_4 + {}^a/_{16} + {}^A/_{16} + {}^B/_8 + {}^C/_4$ wherein ⁵⁄₁₆ *a* makes still a mullato.

Let *q* and *e* cohabit, the half of the blood of each will be $^q/_2 + {}^e/_2 = {}^a/_8 + {}^A/_8 + {}^B/_4 + {}^a/_{16} + {}^B/_8 + {}^C/_4 = {}^{3a}/_{16} + {}^{3B}/_8 + {}^C/_4$, wherein ³⁄₁₆ *a* is no longer a mulatto, and thus may every compound be noted and summed, the sum of the fractions composing the blood of the issue being always equal to unit.[16]

By Jefferson's definition, therefore, the five living children he and Sally Hemings produced were white. He spoke of "clearing the issue of negro blood," viewing the amalgamation as the elimination of Negro heritage. Jefferson viewed his miscegenation not in terms of an increase in the mulatto population, but in terms of the erasure of Negro blood from the veins of the children he fathered by Sally Hemings. The twist was that Tom took an African American wife. Given that experience, would Jefferson then prearrange marriages for the other children?

A GOOD LIFE WEST OF THE MOUNTAINS

Native Americans never populated Greenbriar County heavily. Shawnee living in the Scioto River Valley in what is now Ohio considered white settlement west of the Allegheny Mountains a threat, predicting that once over the mountains, whites would continue to move westward. Shawnee sent raiding parties to Greenbriar County in the early 1760s and successfully dislodged white settlers, who then organized retaliatory incursions into Ohio. After more bloodshed, a "treaty" was made in 1765. No doubt both parties violated the treaty, but the prevailing result was continued white migration westward. In May 1778, whites, aided by at least one very effective African American rifleman, fought off Shawnee warriors in the vicinity of Brushy Ridge. According to John Stuart, who fought there, it was the last time Native Americans invaded Greenbriar County "in large party."[17]

Westward migration flowed along the Midland Trail at a relentless pace. The English, Scots, Welsh, and Germans sailed in a steady procession to American shores. Young Americans who were born on the eastern shores walked, rode, and pushed west. Anxieties of the past were lost in the task of clearing land, clothing babies, digging wells, and building shelter. Free colored who were manumitted or had escaped found their way west also. No longer were northern states and Canada the only options. Slavery was outlawed in the Northwest Territories by the Ordinance of 1787; as a consequence, Ohio was slave-free when it was admitted as the seventeenth state in 1803.

Both Fanny and Hannah were manumitted by Samuel Price, a local man.[18] Hannah established a household on Price land as a "free colored" person, as free blacks were then known. There seemed to be a bond between Hannah and the Price family, but its precise nature is lost to history. Fanny bought land in the county in her own name, as her husband, Lewis Leach, remained a slave there. Several families who lived in the vicinity of Thomas Woodson's farm on Brushy Ridge stayed in the area for several generations. The Hugart family built a grist mill; branches of the Renick family raised cattle on several farms in the county.

Jemima Woodson gave birth to another son, George, in 1808. Fanny's family grew also; she soon named a son Thomas—certainly a reciprocation since Jemima's first son, Lewis, took the name of Fanny's husband. A new generation sprang forth in hearty fashion. Whether it was the mountain spring water, the excitement of westward movement, release from the iniquitous vise of slavery, or the strength of their family bond, something allowed them to flourish.

SALLY HEMINGS BEARS MORE
OF THE PRESIDENT'S CHILDREN

Sally Hemings lost Thomas to the scandal that exposed his paternity, but she held onto her two younger children, Beverly and Harriet, who remained at Monticello. Beverly was the older of the two; Harriet was born two months after Jefferson became president. During this time Sally moved to a room among newly completed the South Dependencies, a row of rooms built into the hillside, a level below the mansion. The Dependencies were connected to the mansion by an all-weather passageway. Most of the rooms that comprised the South Dependencies, however, were not residencies; among them were the kitchen and the smoke house. Terraces above extended over the entrances to the Dependencies reaching brick columns for support. This provided a cover above the entrances but no hindrance to the lawn immediately forward, which no doubt provided the perfect setting for child's play.

Hemings gave birth to no children in 1802 or in the two years after the scandal that rendered her liaison with Jefferson a political liability. The president traveled to Virginia, arriving on April 4, 1804, because his daughter Maria Jefferson Eppes was very ill. When Maria had been too young to travel with him to France, Jefferson worried about his child, separated by an ocean; now he was worried by her fragility. She had given birth to a daughter,

Martha, on February 15. Maria's husband, Congressman John Eppes, left the capital prior to Jefferson to be at Maria's side. He found the baby in satisfactory health, but Maria was weak and nauseous, resembling her own mother's frail condition upon giving birth. The anxious vigil ended when Maria died on April 17. Jefferson was stricken. For weeks his letters avoided direct admission of his loss.[19]

While Jefferson was at Monticello, Sally Hemings conceived again. Jefferson left Monticello on May 11, 1804. James Madison Hemings was born on January 19, 1805. Madison's birth says a great deal about the liaison of Sally Hemings and Thomas Jefferson. He no doubt held no forethought of a tryst with Hemings during this trip to Virginia. One can only imagine the emptiness in his heart and conclude that he found Sally Hemings' love irresistible and sustaining.[20]

While serving as president, Jefferson usually returned to Monticello every summer for a few months. In 1807, he stayed at Monticello from the beginning of August until October 3. Sally Hemings' last child was born May 21, 1808. His name, Eston, was very uncommon. Yet the name appeared in the Randolph family tree, as had the names of Sally's other children, Thomas, Harriet, and Beverly. Madison, named for the president's closest political protégé, was the exception.[21]

Thomas Jefferson was sixty-five years old when Eston Hemings was born. This was an advanced age to father children in the early eighteenth century; of course most men of his age lacked a sexual partner young enough to bear children. Actually, it was relatively uncommon to live to the age of sixty-five. At the time, life expectancy was about forty-five years of age, though many of Jefferson's aristocratic friends lived longer. Jefferson gave little indication that age was taking a toll on him. He did have arthritis and occasionally suffered from headaches throughout his life; serious illnesses were, however, rare. Jefferson lived eighteen years beyond Eston's birth. He rode horseback until the year of his death. Sally Hemings was thirty-five when she gave birth to Eston; no record of the state of her health survives, though it is known she remained attractive into middle age. She was nearing the end of her childbearing capability. Even if sexual expression ended at this time, intimacy between Thomas Jefferson and Sally Hemings continued.

The liaison of Thomas Jefferson and Sally Hemings was the culmination of three successive generations of extramarital miscegenation in the Hemings family. The rape of Betty Hemings' mother by Captain Hemings, John Wayles' claim of sexual privilege with Betty, and the intimacy of Jefferson and Sally Hemings each exhibited stark differences, yet all intrinsically grew from racial and sexual domination. Captain Hemings abandoned his child, Betty

Hemings, and her mother. The exploitation was raw and abrupt, typical of the behavior that accompanied military conquests throughout the ages, as armies burned villages, torturing and raping conquered people to subjugate them or killing them to acquire land.

Betty Hemings lived on John Wayles' plantation from birth. Wayles did not sexually exploit her until after his three white wives had died. He extended his sexual life; Betty gained social status and material comforts. Betty filled an important role in the scheme of Wayles' plantation enterprises. Wayles, an ambitious planter and large landowner, was not born a member of one of Virginia's leading families. He borrowed and married into wealth. He did not have a living son. There was little incentive for him late in life to forego natural urges and emotional attachment only to keep up appearances. Betty did not have the choice of denying Wayles; yet, had she been given a choice, the outcome may have been the same. The union of Betty Hemings and John Wayles was a case of mutual accommodation. The biggest loser was Betty's former mate, the father of her first six children.

In contrast, the union of Thomas Jefferson and Sally Hemings was less deliberate. Jefferson, a forty-six-year-old statesman, probably did not plan to consort with a sixteen-year-old girl. Yet, in the whirlwind of the Parisian panorama, intimacy ripened and blossomed. Despite Jefferson's attempts to ignore, deny, or disavow his attraction to her, it reasserted its magnetism years later. Hemings, whether in Paris or at Monticello, had no pretensions of arranging a life for herself outside of that which might be planned and permitted by her master. Since Sally's mother had become the consort of her master, Sally Hemings saw no shame in the liaison. She embraced no lovers during Jefferson's long absences from Monticello in the early 1790s. During the years Jefferson served as secretary of state, he was successful in disavowing his desire for Hemings. However, for a few years, from 1795 to 1801, interruptions were put at bay and attraction ascended the scale to devotion. As Jefferson grew older, many old friends died; his circle of political contacts and friendships remained large, but his intimate circle tightened. Sally Hemings and his daughter Martha became the centers of his emotional world. The relationships were obviously vastly different; but Jefferson's need for each was great.

THE JEFFERSON PRESIDENCY

The presidency and Jefferson's glorification were sources of strain, mixed emotion, and suspicions within the family. The Jeffersons were mortals, but the exaltation aimed at Thomas Jefferson possessed a quality of divinity and imperishability. Though Martha loved her father deeply and grasped the range and uniqueness of his talent, she also disliked having to share him with so many people and responsibilities. Jefferson was in the nation's new capital, Washington, when he learned of his first presidential electoral victory. Martha waited two months after the election to write her father. She mentioned nothing of his election then, nor in subsequent letters.

Both of Jefferson's sons-in-law were elected to Congress. Initially both lived at the President's House, as the White House was then called. Martha's husband, Thomas Mann Randolph, stormed out of the President's House one day in February 1807 in a rage emanating from a conflict with his brother-in-law, John Eppes. Randolph wrote a bitter letter to Jefferson, accusing him of favoritism. Jefferson did everything he could think of to assuage Randolph's bitter feelings, but Randolph elected to remain in a boarding house rather than return to the President's House. This was not the first evidence of Randolph's erratic behavior, and it would not be the last. About this time, Jefferson decided that his daughter should move to Monticello with him after his retirement.

Martha's move to Monticello would not be a matter of small consequence. She and Randolph had eight children at the time. Three more would be born at Monticello. Randolph sometimes mistreated his wife and assaulted his sons, particularly the oldest. Jefferson was aware of the consequences of the arrangement before the Randolphs joined him. Jefferson also knew of his son-in-law's weak finances and realized that the Randolphs' residence would be problematic. Jefferson would forfeit quiet enjoyment of his cherished Monticello in exchange for the opportunity to impose his calming presence upon the family for his daughter's sake. He felt that the arrangement was his duty and his right.

In the meantime, the business of government consumed most of Jefferson's time. In the early days of his first term, he received reports of Spain's intention to relinquish the Louisiana Territory to France. Jefferson promptly moved to block the transfer through diplomacy. He advised the American envoy in Paris that, if France occupied New Orleans, "from that moment we must marry ourselves to the British fleet and nation." Spain was not a threat to American expansion into the Mississippi Valley, but Jefferson viewed France's presence cautiously.[22]

Extending their power and influence, the French had established New Orleans in 1718, gaining control of the Mississippi River and access to the vast Mississippi River Valley. At the end of the French and Indian War in 1763, France lost the Louisiana Territory to Spain. However, the French-speaking people of Louisiana remained. Though the French regained the territory in the secret Treaty of San Ildefonso in 1800, they did not garrison it. In 1801, Haitian slaves led by Toussaint-Louverture revolted successfully. The French army, sent in 1802 to suppress the revolt, succumbed to yellow fever. The Haitian colony had been France's primary outpost in the region. France had little use for Louisiana unless it controlled Haiti. Jefferson was now anxious to determine the intentions of France, which undoubtedly had changed during the course of these events.

Jefferson dispatched James Monroe to Europe as a special envoy. Samuel du Pont, a close friend, informed Jefferson that France was willing to negotiate for the sale of the Louisiana Territory. On April 11, 1803, Talleyrand, the French foreign minister, summoned American diplomat Robert R. Livingston to ask him if the United States would be interested in purchasing the Louisiana Territory, as Napoleon had abandoned plans to reconquer Haiti. On the verge of renewed warfare with Britain, Napoleon valued money more than the distant territory. James Monroe arrived in Paris with a fresh knowledge of Jefferson's ambitions. On April 30, Monroe and Livingston initialed an agreement that ceded the Louisiana Territory to the United States for approximately $15 million. The French signed it two days later. Final approval of the agreement provided Americans with unimpeded use of the Mississippi River and territory equal in size to that already controlled by the United States. Any brief attempt to describe the enormity, importance, and success of the transaction would fail to do it justice.

Jefferson's second presidential term generated a related achievement. As early as 1783, Jefferson proposed an expedition to California. His grasp of the strategic importance of expansion into the Louisiana Territory was combined with his insatiable interest in scientific matters. For decades, he recorded the weather, tabulated plant growth, and registered animal life in Virginia. He sought a similar knowledge of the western territory. Jefferson chose Meriwether Lewis to lead an expedition to the Pacific Ocean. Lewis, his co-leader, William Clark, and a band of explorers left St. Louis on May 14, 1804. The party wintered with the Mandan Indians in what is now North Dakota. There they secured the services of a Shoshoni woman translator, Sacajawea. The expedition reached the Pacific Ocean in November 1805. Leaving the Pacific shore in March 1806, the explorers returned to St. Louis on September 23, 1806. During the 8,000-mile journey, Lewis and Clark wrote meticulous journals about the land they traversed. The expedition accumulated a wealth of knowledge about the Great Plains and the area that is now the American Northwest. The endeavor filled in a huge blank space on the map and encouraged the American people to claim the West.

THE DEATH OF A MATRIARCH, 1807

A triumph such as the Louisiana Purchase can mark a new era, just as death is the mark of closure. The death of Betty Hemings, who had lived for thirty-three years within a stone's throw of the Monticello mansion, certainly signified a new era for the plantation. She was the matriarch of a family of fifty or more persons who lived on Mulberry Row. Her family helped to build the Monticello mansion and the house on the Poplar Forest plantation. Her youngest son, John, most likely built the casket in which Thomas Jefferson rests. During portions of several years, Jefferson lived at Monticello without the company of other Jeffersons. From 1773 until his death fifty-three years later, whether he was at Monticello, in Paris, Philadelphia, Washington, or elsewhere, he was seldom out of contact with members of the Hemings family. Most of the time he had only to call and one would appear instantly. Jefferson biographers such as Dumas Malone left Betty Hemings out of her master's life, but her character loomed large on the Monticello plantation.

Betty Hemings died in 1807 at the age of seventy-two. Few slaves lived to that age. Her life reflected centuries of American history. It merged the past and the future in the rarest manner. Betty Hemings spawned and nurtured a clan that embodied massive societal change. Her mother was a full-blooded African, captured and brought to America in the eighteenth century. Betty Hemings saw two sons gain freedom in that same century. She must have known that at least a few of her grandchildren would somehow leave the vise of slavery and live as white persons, as they did. At least two of her children and several grandchildren became literate in a time when the education of blacks was illegal. Her children learned many skills that today are seldom associated with the enslavement of African Americans.

If the Thomas Jefferson/Sally Hemings liaison is viewed as an aberration, if Monticello is viewed as an aberration, then one might examine whether the cause for that aberration lies in another. Was the relationship between Martha Wayles Jefferson and Betty Hemings the phenomenon that created the distinctive circumstances of the Hemings family? Martha was thirteen years of age when her father's third and last wife died. She never knew the love of her biological mother, who died three weeks after she was born. It must have been difficult for a daughter to know that her mother died three weeks after her birth. Of course, the sensibility may have been different in an age when early death was more common. Who cared for Martha after her birth and until her first stepmother arrived? Her father's second wife presumably cared for Martha during her marriage to Wayles. This wife gave birth to four children of her own, one of whom died in infancy. How much love did Martha receive from a stepmother who raised three biological daughters of her own? Martha's father owned several plantations and actively traded slaves; as a self-made man, he lacked the family support network that most men of his ilk enjoyed. John Wayles attempted to care for his daughter through remarriage, but those attempts failed.

Whenever Betty Hemings entered Martha's life as a caregiver, the relationship continued until Martha's death in 1782. At the latest, the relationship began in 1760 with the death of John Wayles' last wife. At the earliest, it began at Martha's birth in 1748. Martha must have recognized that her father was also the father of Betty's new brood. Yet Martha's awareness of the social unacceptability of the arrangement may have been very limited. As the oldest child, she would not learn from siblings to scorn miscegenation. Her father had come to America as a single man; he was well liked and jovial. He suffered the deaths of three wives, and any sneering among neighbors must have been muted. Martha did not have a mother who was being hurt by her father's interest in a mulatto concubine. It is likely that Martha saw Betty Hemings only as capable, caring, and loving and as the fulfillment of a void in her life. Betty remained in Martha's life through difficult pregnancies, wartime displacement, and her final illness.

Martha's love for Betty and the acceptance of her children as family rose from circumstances cited. This is not to suggest that Martha regarded her half-sisters and half-brothers as siblings. Still, she accepted them as family in some fashion. Miscegenation was a common occurrence in Virginia; its presence at Monticello was not aberrant. Comprehensively, however, the life of the Hemings family at The Forest and Monticello was an aberration in that it was markedly affected by a history of compounded miscegenation and the repetitive loss of life among the Wayles and Jefferson families. The resulting lifestyle deviated considerably from the traditions of American slavery in the eighteenth century.

During the first twenty years following Monticello's creation, Jefferson did not free any slaves. Two of Betty Hemings' sons were freed in the 1790s. In the new century, emancipation of the Hemings clan accelerated; the first to gain freedom was Thomas, Sally's oldest son. Within two years of Thomas' 1802 departure, his cousin Jamie, the son of Critta Hemings, ran away.

Jamie Hemings was severely beaten by Gabriel Lilly while working in the nailery under his direction. James Oldham, a carpenter, described the event: "The Barbarity that he maid use of with little Jimmy was the moost crool. To my noledge Jimmy was sick for thre nights and the most part of the time

I rely thot he would not be of Livd he at this time slepd. In the room with me." Jamie Hemings was not able to work, according to Oldham, "and begd. Him to not punnish him." Lilly whipped the boy again, until he was not able to raise his head. Jamie escaped. A year later, in 1805, Oldham, who, was then living in Richmond, informed Jefferson that he had seen the boy. After contemplating whether Jamie should be placed in jail, Oldham took him in and looked to Jefferson for instruction. Oldham informed Jefferson that Jamie wished to return to Monticello if he were not placed under the supervision of Lilly again. Jefferson responded with accommodation, typical of his treatment of the Hemings clan. He indicated that Jamie would be placed in joinery work under the direction of John Hemings and Lewis. "I can readily excuse the follies of a boy," Jefferson explained. But Jamie did not return to Monticello as he had pledged to do; he slipped out of Oldham's grasp.[23]

Before Oldham found him, Jamie worked on boats on the lower James River; most likely he subsequently returned to work aboard coastal vessels and ferries in the Tidewater area. The story is crowned by a notation in Jefferson's Memorandum Book ten years later, signifying payment to James Hemings for finding an eyepiece, part of a surveying instrument. Jamie eventually returned to Monticello on good terms and apparently moved about freely, living in a twilight zone between freedom and slavery. One by one, the Hemings children maneuvered into this twilight zone in various ways and with varying degrees of success.

THE SAGE OF MONTICELLO

Jefferson returned to Monticello after completing his second term as president, satisfied with the westward expansion of the United States, the navy's successful campaign against the Barbary pirates, and the election of James Madison. At home, he witnessed the near completion of a forty-year labor of love. Jefferson had begun building Monticello in 1768. Martha Wayles Jefferson never saw or enjoyed a completed house. Jefferson himself described the house as never even half done.

When Jefferson returned from Washington on March 17, 1809, he found a grand home, nearly complete. Some work on the porticoes was yet undone, but the interior was at last finished. The house is elegant and enchanting. The interior is ornamented by decorations inspired by a host of classical buildings. The exterior is framed by extensive gardens and a breathtaking vista of the Virginia countryside. Influences of Andrea Palladio and Pierre Rousseau are strongly represented, as Jefferson studied and savored creations of both.[24]

Historian David McCullough reasons with unreasonableness as he describes Monticello:

On an inconvenient wilderness summit where no planter's establishment had any business being—up where there was no river to transport the product of his acreage, or even water enough to meet everyday needs—he put a house that itself made no sense, not by conventional standards. Compared to other "great houses" of Virginia, it was costly foolishness, eccentric in the extreme, such overt unreasonableness. To top it off, there was the dome, for its builders the most difficult and troublesome part of the entire scheme, which served no useful purpose. It was conceit piled on top of conceit. Unless . . .

Unless you were Jefferson, an artist, a visionary, a revolutionary, a romantic, a man not like others, who was himself, as the poet John Masefield said of Shakespeare, "the rare unreasonable" who comes along only once in a very great while.[25]

The grandeur of Monticello notwithstanding, Jefferson's attention and talent were also drawn to his other possessions. Jefferson inherited land from John Wayles in 1773, including Poplar Forest, a plantation located in Bedford County, which was continuously farmed and expanded. In 1781, when the British army drove the Jeffersons from Monticello, it was Poplar Forest which served as refuge. The plantation is located eighty miles southwest of Monticello, approximately fifteen miles from the Blue Ridge Mountains. The slaves who lived and worked at Poplar Forest were primarily descendants of slaves that Peter Jefferson, Thomas Jefferson, or John Wayles owned in decades past.

In 1806, Jefferson began to build a house at Poplar Forest, using a design he intended for construction at Pantops, the plantation he gave his daughter Maria and her husband. Pantops was located near Monticello, but no house had been built there. The couple decided to live at Eppington, a plantation near the old Eppes estate, Bermuda Hundred. The house that eventually was built at Poplar Forest is octagonal in shape, the first of its kind in America. John Hemings performed and supervised much of the construction of the octagonal structure.[26]

Jack McLaughlin ventured Jefferson's reason for building a second home at age sixty-three.

He was a man who revealed to others only what he chose to; he remained fixedly concealed behind what we would call his defenses—observing all but seldom revealing. Only with his close family, in the confines of the walls of Monticello, did he allow himself to be seen, to reveal his needs for, and his capacity to show, love and affection. These private feelings were not for public display; therefore, as Jefferson's fame grew during his presidency, and Monticello became increasingly an inn, his need to control his privacy intensified. His bedroom-library sanctuary, protected by locks and blinds, gave him a measure of control; when this was not enough, he built another house at Poplar Forest and periodically disappeared from Monticello, where he was on public exhibition, to the rural solitude of his Bedford plantation.[27]

During the years that the Sage of Monticello lived in retirement, John Hemings built furniture for Monticello and the various outbuildings. Martha Jefferson Randolph's children were particularly fond of the cabinets, tables, flower boxes, and such that he was requested to produce for them. While John was at Poplar Forest in 1825, Septima Randolph wrote to tell him of Jefferson's declining health. Hemings wrote back to the eleven-year-old as follows:

Dear miss Septima your letter came to me on the 23th and hapey was I to embreasit to see you take it upon you self to writ to me and let me know how your grand Paw was Glad am i to hear that he is no worst dear I hope you ar well and all the famely give my Love to all your brothers Gorg with Randolph speculy I shoul gite don the house on tusday that is tining it we have all the Tarrste [terrace] to do yet which is one hundred feet Long and 22 feet 8 inches wide yesterday we just hade one Lode of the stuff brought home fore the gutters and that is 25 mile off where it came from I am in hope I shal be able to com home by the 25 of Nomember Ef Life Last

I am your obediente seirvant
John Hemmings[28]

The source of John Hemings' education is unknown. He certainly did not attend school. Only one other written artifact survives from John Hemings' generation, a list of kitchen utensils, written by James Hemings. Neither is it known who taught James to read and write, but the possibilities in his case are much narrower. The most likely teacher was Martha Wayles Jefferson. It is probable that most of Betty Hemings' children were literate. Many of Betty Hemings' grandchildren were literate, though they violated Virginia law to become so. In contrast to Jefferson's often-quoted words from his *Notes on the State of Virginia*, which question the intellect of blacks, the sage knew of and likely fostered their education at Monticello and Poplar Forest.[29]

A Clan of Colored Woodsons Emerges in Greenbriar County

Lewis Woodson, the oldest of Sally Hemings' grandchildren, was a well-educated man, although how he became so is unknown. As an adult, Lewis

Woodson became an educator himself. Though he lived west of the Allegheny Mountains as a child, Virginia law prevailed there; the education of African Americans was prohibited. Woodsons repeatedly broke that law and other laws that degraded blacks.

Lewis Woodson's proficiency and confidence in writing and the early age at which he became an educator suggest that he received some formal education. When Lewis was born, there was no school of consequence in Greenbriar County. In 1808, Reverend John McElhenney, D.D., moved to the county, establishing the Lewisburg Academy. An excellent and energetic educator, he also preached frequently in small churches in Greenbriar County and adjacent counties. His preaching style was plain, but the man was very popular. He frequented the Rader Church, located a few hundred yards from the Woodson farm on Brushy Ridge. No document connects Reverend McElhenney to the Woodson family. It is not likely that Lewis Woodson attended the Lewisburg Academy, as it would have been illegal. Lewis Woodson's adult life had much in common with Reverend McElhenney's, who may have been a good role model for Lewis. And, if Lewis Woodson did receive some early structured education, Reverend McElhenney is a likely, albeit undocumented, source.[30]

The name Thomas Woodson was recorded in the 1820 U.S. Census as a free colored head of household along with five other African American residents of the county. Circumstances did not allow him to emulate his father's intellectualism or John Hemings' meticulous craftsmanship. But Thomas was interested in carpentry and gravitated toward fine horses, cattle, and a semi-nomadic lifestyle. Like his father, he added a dynastic quality to his family's sense of direction and expectation.

Among the other five free colored household heads were Fanny Leach and Hannah Grant, so Thomas Woodson's extended family represented half of the free colored population of the county. At the time, Thomas and Jemima had eight children. The younger six were Delila, Jemima, Frances, Thomas, James, and John P. Tom Woodson probably began to use the given name Thomas before 1820. Fanny Leach had named a son Thomas in 1807, so Tom may have formalized his name at that early date. Thomas Woodson was listed in the county tax records of 1820 as a white man. Inconsistency regarding the race of mulattos of light complexion was commonplace. No other Woodsons (black or white) lived in the county in 1820, in the prior decade, or in the decade to follow.

No record exists confirming that Thomas Woodson journeyed to visit his mother at Monticello while he lived in Greenbriar County. However, Thomas' younger brothers Madison and Eston (who were born after Thomas left Monticello) later moved to the very same Ohio town where Thomas moved after leaving Greenbriar County, so there must have been contact between Thomas Woodson and Sally Hemings after he left Monticello. Communication most likely flowed through Jefferson's Poplar Forest plantation, rather than through Monticello. Poplar Forest was seventy miles from Brushy Ridge and thus easily reachable on horseback. The ultimate question is, however, whether or not Thomas Jefferson visited his son. In 1818, during his only excursion west of the Allegheny Mountains, the seventy-five-year-old Jefferson visited the town of Ronceverte, located only five miles from Thomas Woodson's home on Brushy Ridge. Did father and son connect in Greenbriar County? Another of Betty Hemings' grandsons, Burwell, accompanied the ex-president on the mountainous journey. Did Burwell arrange a rendezvous?[31]

According to the 1820 U.S. Census, Thomas Woodson's mother-in-law Hannah Grant owned a slave named Sheldon Brock. Slave ownership by African Americans began soon after Africans were brought in chains to America in 1619. Initially, a slave code did not exist, and Africans were set free after seven years of servitude, just as white indentured servants were. In the seventeenth century a small percentage of free African Americans acquired land and slaves. Several free blacks owned plantations of substantial size in Northumberland County and in other counties in small numbers. In the decades prior to the Civil War a free black South Carolinian named William Ellison became a cotton gin manufacturer and used profits to buy land and slaves, becoming relatively wealthy. The number of African American slaveowners did not grow during the nineteenth century. None of the African Americans who obtained freedom by moving north, into the Midwest, or into Canada owned slaves, as it was illegal to purchase slaves in those regions. Although she had crossed the Allegheny Mountains, Hannah Grant remained within the boundaries of antebellum Virginia, where slavery was legal. Her ownership of Sheldon Brock, though as immoral as the ownership of blacks by whites, was similarly permitted under Virginia law.[32]

Thomas Woodson began to work for or partnered with the Renick family, driving cattle from Ohio to the east through Greenbriar County. Some Renicks moved to Chillicothe, Ohio, the first capital of the state. The younger generation of many Greenbriar County families moved into southern Ohio and Kentucky. The technology of the Industrial Revolution was beginning to create opportunity in the East and the Midwest, but was slow to arrive in the mountainous communities of western Virginia.

NOTES

1. Minnie S. Woodson, *Woodson Source Book* (Washington, D.C.: Privately printed, 1984), 1: quote by John S. Woodson (b. 1918).

2. Henry Morton Woodson, *Historical Genealogy of the Woodsons and Their Connections* (Columbia: E. W. Stephens, 1915), identification #88. This book documents the genealogy of the descendants of John Woodson, who came to Virginia in 1619. These Woodsons were white and were not the ancestors of Thomas Woodson and his descendants.

3. Julian Boyd, *The Papers of Thomas Jefferson*, vol. 2 (Princeton: Princeton University Press, 1950–), 458: location and ownership of James River ferries.

4. Drury Woodson's will, Cumberland County (VA) Will Book #2, 441.

5. Minnie S. Woodson, *The Sable Curtain* (Washington, D.C.: Privately printed, 1987), appendix 5: details on the western migration of the white Woodsons.

6. Obituary of the Reverend Lewis Woodson, *Christian Recorder*, vol. 16, no. 6 (Philadelphia: A.M.E. Church, February 7, 1878): citation of Rev. Lewis Woodson's place and year of birth.

7. Deed of property purchased by James Kincaid, Greenbriar County Deed Book #4, 110–11.

8. James Hugo Johnston, *Race Relations in Virginia and Miscegenation in the South, 1776–1860* (Amherst: University of Massachusetts Press, 1970), 213–14.

9. Ibid., 193: from William H. Hening, *Statutes at Large of Virginia* (Richmond, 1823).

10. Ibid., 194.

11. Ibid., 208–9: from *History of the City of Memphis* by James D. Davis.

12. Ibid., 167: from William H. Hening, *Statutes at Large of Virginia* (Richmond, 1823).

13. Fawn M. Brodie, *Thomas Jefferson, an Intimate History* (New York: W. W. Norton, 1974), 84.

14. John Chester Miller, *Wolf by the Ears: Thomas Jefferson and Slavery* (Charlottesville: University Press of Virginia, 1991), 241.

15. Andrew Lipscomb and Albert Bergh, eds., *The Writings of Thomas Jefferson*, vol. 14 (Washington, D.C.: Thomas Jefferson Memorial Association, 1903), 267–71.

16. Ibid.

17. John Stuart, "Memorandum," *Appalachian Springs* (Newsletter of the Greenbriar, West Virginia, Historical Society), November, 1998.

18. Hannah Grant's will, Greenbriar County Deed Book #3, 160–61.

19. Brodie, *Thomas Jefferson*, 377.

20. James A. Bear and Lucia C. Stanton, eds., *Jefferson's Memorandum Books*, vol. 2 (Princeton: Princeton University Press, 1997), 1126: departure from Monticello.

21. Ibid., vol. 2, 1208–12: Jefferson's return to and departure from Monticello.

22. Willard Sterne Randall, *Thomas Jefferson: A Life* (New York: Holt, 1993), 565: "marry . . . the British fleet."

23. Jack McLaughlin, *Jefferson and Monticello* (New York: Henry Holt, 1988), 113: "The Barbarity," and 114: "I can readily excuse."

24. Ibid., 331.

25. David McCullough, Introduction to *Thomas Jefferson's Monticello: A Photographic Portrait* (New York: Monacelli Press, 1997).

26. McLaughlin, *Jefferson and Monticello*, 257, 264.

27. Ibid., 327.

28. Ibid., 123.

29. Letter from Hannah to Thomas Jefferson, November 15, 1818, provided by Lucia Cinder Stanton of the Thomas Jefferson Memorial Foundation. Hannah (this was not Jemima's mother and not a Hemings) was enslaved at the Poplar Forest plantation.

30. Marcellus Zimmerman, "The Old Lewisburg Academy," *Journal of the Greenbriar Historical Society*, vol. 3, no. 1 (1975): 24.

31. William Laurance, "The Midland Trail," *The World and I*, May 2000, 143; Bear and Stanton, *Jefferson's Memorandum Books*, vol. 3, 1346–47.

32. Michael P. Johnson and James L. Roark, *Black Masters* (New York: W. W. Norton, 1984), xi–xiii: description of William Ellison.

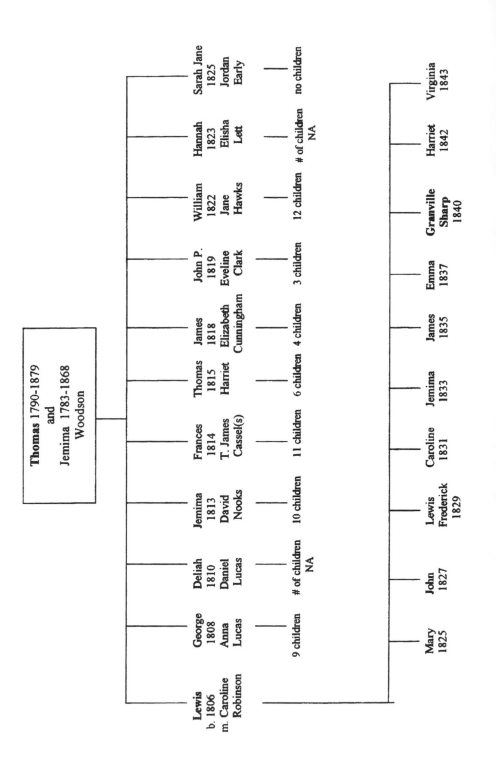

Thomas 1790-1879
and
Jemima 1783-1868
Woodson

Lewis
b. 1806
m. Caroline
Robinson
9 children

George
1808
Anna
Lucas

Deliah
1810
Daniel
Lucas
# of children
NA

Jemima
1813
David
Nooks
10 children

Frances
1814
T. James
Cassel(s)
11 children

Thomas
1815
Harriet
6 children

James
1818
Elizabeth
Cunningham
4 children

John P.
1819
Eveline
Clark
3 children

William
1822
Jane
Hawks
12 children

Hannah
1823
Elisha
Lett
# of children
NA

Sarah Jane
1825
Jordan
Early
no children

Mary
1825

John
1827

Lewis
Frederick
1829

Caroline
1831

Jemima
1833

James
1835

Emma
1837

Granville
Sharp
1840

Harriet
1842

Virginia
1843

CHAPTER FIVE

Freedom Secured

A gentle knock, a call of, "Come in," and I would enter, with a mixed feeling of love and reverence, and some pride in being the bearer of a communication to one whom I approached with all the affection of a child, and something of the loyalty of a subject.
> —Words of Ellen Randolph Coolidge (daughter of Martha Jefferson Randolph), which convey her feelings toward her illustrious grandfather[1]

Late in 1820 or early in 1821, Thomas and Jemima Woodson packed their children and household wares into Conestoga wagons and headed westward to Ohio on the Midland Trail, then a dependable, obstacle-free road. Their travel by water, in addition to the unavoidable ferry ride across the Ohio River, may have included a flatboat trip down the Kanawha River or even a steamboat trip down the Ohio River to Portsmouth, at the mouth of the Scioto River. The Woodsons settled in Chillicothe, located in south central Ohio on the Scioto River. Chillicothe had served as Ohio's first capital, but the state government had moved to Columbus in 1816.

Thomas Woodson rented a farm from Thomas James on a hill on the west side of Chillicothe. The hilltop view is stunning, rivaling the spectacular view from Mulberry Row at Monticello. Mulberry Row's southeastern view presents a plentiful array of rolling hills, which appear to willingly diminish their prominence to evade the horizon as it threatens to steal the existence of the very next hilltop. The view from the James farm location overlooks the town of Chillicothe as if the hill anointed the viewer as guardian angel of the town—a post most likely shared by another would-be angel standing upon a hill of equal prominence three miles away on the opposite side of the meandering Scioto River. The viewer on the other hill is merely too distant to discern. The view offered Thomas Woodson remembrances of Monticello and the family left behind. He was not alone, as the burgeoning population of the Midwest was made mostly of transplants who cut traditional ties and established new ones on the westward trek.[2]

Though the sensational view brought Monticello to mind, Thomas no doubt thought more of Brushy Ridge as he looked over the quaint town enlivening the Scioto River Valley. Fanny and Hannah were left behind in Greenbriar County. Ohio offered Thomas and Jemima the chance to raise their children in a place that offered greater economic opportunity and where slavery was outlawed.

In the Shawnee language, Chillicothe means "the place where people live" or village. Twenty-five years before Thomas Woodson settled in Chillicothe, the area contained several Shawnee villages. It was in this area that Shawnee raiding parties formed to attack white settlements in Greenbriar County, as noted in Chapter Four. When Mingoe, Miami, and Wyandot chiefs banded with the Shawnee to fight armies of the white settlers, they formed a confederation around the Shawnee chief Cornstalk, who lived in the Scioto River Valley. Two large armies of Virginians, one primarily from the Shenandoah Valley and the other from the Greenbriar and Clinch River areas, marched toward Ohio in 1774. Cornstalk raised an army of 1,000 to meet General Andrew Lewis' troops at Point Pleasant on the Ohio River. A fierce daylong battle failed to stop the frontiersmen from advancing. The two armies from Virginia crossed the Ohio, marching far into the heart of Shawnee and Mingo land, destroying villages and sending families scattering into the forest as winter approached.[3]

Fighting continued with only brief intermissions as the Native American confederation refused to relinquish their land without battle. White Americans pushed the tribes toward the northwest corner of Ohio but suffered two costly defeats, one led by General Hamar in 1790 and another led by Arthur St. Clair, who later became territorial governor of Ohio. In 1794, Native Americans, including the realigned Delaware tribe and the Ottawas, were broken at the Battle of Fallen Timbers. A treaty signed in Greenville, Ohio, in 1794 restricted the tribes to a reservation in the northern portion of the state, west of present-day Cleveland. Just six years later the Ohio government began to reduce the size of the reservation. Native Americans sided with British forces in the War of 1812 with predictable results. By 1820, the Wyandot tribe and remnants of other tribes, which once controlled large land masses, occupied small reservations and were forced to cultivate land in a similar fashion to whites to produce sufficient food from their restricted areas.[4]

ESTABLISHING AN A.M.E. FOOTHOLD IN THE MIDWEST

The Methodist church in Chillicothe, Ohio, retained a record of Thomas and Jemima's oldest son Lewis' presence there in 1818. His parents and siblings still lived in Greenbriar County at the time, though Thomas traveled between Greenbriar County and the Scioto River Valley several times on cattle drives. Lewis Woodson may have received a formal education or tutoring in Chillicothe, though specific documentation is lacking.

After settling in Chillicothe, the Woodsons attended the Methodist church. An account by the Reverend Dr. S. McAdow written decades later records the formation of a separate Methodist church for African Americans in 1821, soon after the Woodsons would have joined the congregation. McAdow's account appeared in a local newspaper in February 1874.

He recounted the motivation for leaving the Methodist church:

A feeling, however, obtained among them to worship separate and apart from the white Methodists. This feeling grew out of the fact that they had to occupy the gallery on the north side of the church and, on quarterly meeting occasions, although they communed at the same sacramental board, the white members communed first and the colored members last. This perhaps was the principal cause of the separation. They felt that they did not enjoy equal rights and privileges with their white brethren, notwithstanding they contributed their share in supporting the minister and defraying the contingent expenses of the church.[5]

The Reverend McAdow recalled:

The church was organized in the dwelling house of The Reverend Peter James, on the south side of Fourth Street between Mulberry and Paint streets. This was the first African Methodist Episcopal (A.M.E.) church organized west of the Allegheny Mountains by Reverend Paul Quinn, later Bishop Quinn. Their first place of worship was a one-story frame building on the south side of Main Street between Paint and Walnut, and one door east of the American House. After worshipping there for some time, they purchased a one-story frame building on the south side of Main street between Walnut and High.

Twenty-eight persons had been listed as colored in records of the Methodist church. It was that same group who formed the new church. Twelve couples were identified in those records, including "Thomas Woodson and his wife." Lewis Woodson is the only offspring listed by name on the entire list.[6]

The establishment of an A.M.E. church in Chillicothe paralleled the founding of the first A.M.E. church in Philadelphia in 1787. Richard Allen, who occasionally preached in St. George's Methodist Church in Philadelphia, led African American members of the congregation to form a church of their own in that year. The Bethel church was formed because black parishioners were not treated as equals at St. George's. On April 9, 1816, a group of at least sixteen men, including several men from Baltimore, two from Wilmington, Delaware, and one from New Jersey, assembled in Philadelphia. By resolution, a new denomination was established: "Resolved, that the people of Philadelphia and Baltimore and other places who may unite with them shall become one body under the name and style of the first African Methodist Church of the United States of America and that the book of Discipline of the Methodist Episcopal Church be adopted as our Discipline until further orders, except that portion relating to Presiding Elders." The resolution, offered by Stephen Hill and seconded by the Reverend Daniel Coker, both of Baltimore, not only united these men in worship, but committed them to spread their faith throughout America.[7]

Sixteen men joined the resolution, but expansion of the church was accomplished by a few who zealously traveled far and wide on horseback. The expansion of the A.M.E. Church allowed African Americans to worship without the humiliation they experienced among white congregations. By 1818, the denomination counted 6,784 members; nearly all were free African Americans. The church gained a strong foothold in Charleston, South Carolina, but when Denmark Vesey's plot for a slave insurrection was discovered, whites forced the closure of A.M.E. churches there. In 1822 the Reverend Morris Brown, the South Carolinian stalwart, escaped to the north with no more than his life.[8]

A.M.E. Church records indicate that Bishop Richard Allen sent Reverend George Boler to Chillicothe, Ohio, to organize the first A.M.E. Church west of the Allegheny Mountains. However, it was the Reverend William Paul Quinn's unrelenting resolve that actually fulfilled the mission, helping the Woodsons and other Chillicothe worshippers form Bethel A.M.E. Church there (now Quinn Chapel).

Reverend McAdow described the dress code of the "coloreds": "The colored Methodists of Chillicothe in olden times were unlike those of the present day. No jewelry or superfluity of apparel was worn by them. In this regard they dressed plain. You could tell them wherever you met them by their dress; the male members with their broad-brimmed hats and shad-bellied coats and the female members with their plain Quaker-looking bonnets and habits." The Woodsons made quite an impression on neighbors, as they were well remembered. Years later, a local man, John Waddle, recalled the community of African Americans who lived in Chillicothe in the 1820s and 1830s. He described the Woodson family as mulatto farmers. "They were very genteel and industrious people, the Old man and his sons always going well dressed and riding fine horses. They were rather exclusive and did not associate with the town darkies."[9]

Contrary to Waddle's anecdote, Lewis Woodson's activity seems to indicate that he had a very close association with the African American community. In 1827, at age twenty-one, Lewis formed the African Education and Benevolent Society in Chillicothe, the first organization of its kind in Ohio. Lewis had a fire in his belly for the elevation of his people; he consistently created new ways to accomplish his mission. Was his motivation an inherent gift, or was he motivated by the knowledge of his illustrious ancestry? The Sons of the African Society, formed in Boston in 1798, was among the first of the African American benevolent societies, which rapidly grew in number. Such organizations cared for the sick and arranged decent burials for those who died. By 1838 the number of African American benevolent societies in Philadelphia had grown to eighty.[10]

MIDWESTERN PROSPERITY

While Lewis Woodson focused on improving living conditions for African Americans, the Industrial Age was beginning to benefit all Americans. The change was more pervasive in Ohio than in the Greenbriar County highlands. Steamboats, by-products of James Watt's steam engine, began to ply the Ohio River in 1811. In 1807, Robert Fulton built the first commercially successful steamboat, the *Clermont*, for trade on the Hudson River. Two years later Robert Stevens sailed his boat, the *Phoenix*, from New York to Philadelphia, the first Atlantic voyage for a steamboat. Thereafter, the invention came into widespread use. It was the first form of transportation not dependent upon human strength, harnessed animal power, or the force of the wind. Burdens placed upon human bodies began to ease, and the need for universal education began to rise.[11]

Development of a canal system had an even greater effect than steamboats on Chillicothe and the Ohio interior. The canals actually reached beyond the rivers, opening interior land to production for markets far and wide. The state of New York built the Erie Canal between 1817 and 1825. It was hugely successful, paying for itself in ten years from tolls and spurring growth in New York City and the states of Michigan, Wisconsin, and Illinois. A migration pattern began wherein Europeans sailed to New York, then continued west instead of settling on the East Coast. Ohio's early governors, Thomas Worthington and Ethan Allen Brown, lobbied mightily for funds for a canal to connect the Ohio River with Lake Erie. In 1822, funds were appropriated for planning and engineering. On July 4, 1825, governors Jeremiah Morrow of Ohio and De Witt Clinton of New York raised great expectations as they delivered speeches and thrust the symbolic first shovels downward at Licking Summit, a point near the center of Ohio. The dig was on![12]

Construction of the canal was a massive undertaking. As no one contractor could complete the entire project, 110 sections were created for purposes of construction bidding. Over 6,000 bids were submitted. The canal was dug to a depth of four feet and a minimum width of twenty-six feet. In order to use natural waterways as much as possible, the Scioto, Licking, Muskingum, and Cuyahoga Rivers formed part of the canal system. Numerous locks were designed and built to raise or lower boats to the next level. The amazingly flat landscape of Ohio, where the maximum variation in elevation is approximately 1,000 feet, offered a perfect setting for canal building. Laborers received wages of twelve dollars a month when the project started, but later, as canal builders in Pennsylvania and Indiana competed for labor, fifteen dollars a month was offered. The Miami Canal from Cincinnati to Dayton was completed in 1828, but the Ohio and Erie Canal, reaching Chillicothe in 1831, was not completed until 1833.[13]

Like the Erie Canal, the project was a boon. The price of wheat in the interior tripled. Land prices rose, which helped the project directly, since the state paid for the canal in part through land sales. There was little through traffic between the Ohio River and Lake Erie, thus access to the interior was the critical benefit. Cities such as Akron and towns such as Newark sprang to life with canal construction. Canals washed away any remnants of the frontier atmosphere in Ohio. When northeastern Ohio was occupied by the Delaware tribe, their numbers, including women and children, totaled only 3,000. By comparison, 2,000 men labored on just one stretch of canal construction south of Cleveland in November 1825. Invention and engineering captured the imagination of those who sought to make their mark in this land of great promise.[14]

At least one canal boat plying the Ohio canal system was captained by an

African American, John Malvin. Malvin was born to a free woman in 1795 near Dumphries, Virginia, on the Potomac River, but his father was enslaved. As a teenager, Malvin was apprenticed to his father's owner. The owner, a Mr. Henderson, owned property in Wood County, Virginia, located on the Ohio River. Though Malvin was an indentured worker, not a chattel slave, he was severely whipped by Mr. Henderson's clerk while in Wood County. Malvin's skin color was a greater determinant of his treatment than any legal distinction. After Mr. Henderson died, Malvin returned to eastern Virginia to his parents' home. Having learned to read at the age of thirty-two from an old African American man, Malvin applied for and received papers proving his free status. This enabled him to leave the state without major difficulty. He traveled to Cincinnati and married while in the vicinity. He set out for Canada with his bride, traveling partly by canal; but when his wife hesitated to continue the journey, they made Cleveland their home in 1832. Malvin worked several jobs, including one as cook on a Lake Erie steamship, before he became a canal boat captain.[15]

At the age of eighty-four Malvin wrote his autobiography. It contains an interesting story about a white woman who paid fare for passage on his canal boat from the Akron area to Circleville, a town fifteen miles due north of Chillicothe, Malvin's destination. About nine o'clock in the evening, Malvin took the woman's hand to help her board. Upon her descent into the cabin, she was startled to see a female African American cook. Of the five male crewmen, three were white, two were African American. When one of the latter went below to fetch something, the sight of the crewmen caused the woman to become terribly unsettled, and to call for the captain. When Malvin appeared, she sprang to her feet, exclaiming with shortness of breath, "Well, I never! well I never! well I never!" Malvin ordered a fresh supply of bedding, but the woman sat up all night. In the morning she refused breakfast, as she was not feeling well. That evening, the woman refused dinner with the same report, but she did accept a piece of pie and later tea and biscuits. That night, the woman spent some time on deck, then retired to a good night's sleep. The next morning, she ate a hearty breakfast. Disembarking at Circleville, she thanked the captain. "Captain when I first came aboard your boat, not accustomed to traveling in this way, I supposed I must have acted quite awkward. Now, I must return my thanks to you and your crew for the fine treatment I have received. I never traveled so comfortably in all my life, and I expect to go north soon, and I shall defer my journey until you are going north, even if I am obliged to wait two or three days." Malvin never saw her again.[16]

THE RISE AND FALL OF BLACK LAWS IN THE NORTH

Despite the rising standard of living afforded by the early advances of the Industrial Revolution and improvement of the infrastructure, which permitted rapid development in Ohio, the blacks in antebellum Ohio faced special challenges. The state constitution barred African Americans from the ballot and prevented them from testifying against white men in court. Whites effectively could not be punished for violent crimes against blacks, even murder. The year after the state was founded, 1804, black laws were adopted, in part requiring black persons to submit certification of their free status before settling in the state. Blacks were required to register with the county clerk upon settling and were expected to post a $500 bond to insure good conduct. If an employer hired a black not in possession of a certificate, the employer was subject to fine. Blacks were excluded from state-funded poorhouses, insane asylums, and other institutions. They were, however, required to pay taxes.

Black laws were not typically enforced until 1827. In the years immediately thereafter, conditions for many black Ohioans regressed from horrible to untenable. Violence against blacks erupted on August 10, 1829, in Cincinnati, compounding the legal persecution. Nearly one-half of the black population was driven out; approximately one-fifth of the city's African American population of 2,250 moved to Canada. The town of Wilberforce, named after a British anti-slavery activist, was established a few miles north of London, Ontario, for displaced African Americans. Townspeople of Portsmouth, located at the confluence of the Scioto and Ohio Rivers, drove out eighty blacks who were unregistered or had failed to post bond. Political leaders in Cincinnati soon relented, but black Ohioans who remained were no doubt shaken.[17]

Only 337 blacks lived in Ohio at the turn of the century. The number grew to 1,890 by 1810 and to 4,723 by 1820. This rapid increase was matched by an astounding increase in the state's overall population, which grew from 42,000 in 1800 to 581,434 in 1820. The U.S. population, 4 million at the time of the Revolution, grew to 11.6 million in 1820, comprising 600,000 Native Americans, 9 million whites, and 2 million blacks, of whom 100,000 were mulattos. The large and rapidly growing slave population remained locked in the South; the number of manumissions and escapes was small in comparison to the natural increase of the enslaved population. Westward migration in America was an unparalleled event. By 1825 Ohio's population was the fourth largest among the states. The early black population of Ohio continued to increase, though it still hovered at 1 percent of the total population.

Two-thirds of Ohio's black population was mulatto, a very high proportion.[18]

When the state of Ohio began to fund education in 1829, black children were barred from such benefits. It was not until 1847 that the state began to fund black schools; in the meantime, blacks established private schools for their children. In 1827, Lewis Woodson organized education for blacks in Chillicothe; canal boat captain John Malvin started the first school for blacks in Cleveland in 1832. Cleveland began to fund education of blacks in 1843, a few years before state funding became available.[19]

Black laws effectively legalized a caste system based on skin color. Exclusion from publicly funded education and denial of the right to vote were further fundamental aspects of the institutionalization of caste. New England states never instituted comprehensive black laws. Mid-Atlantic and Midwestern states instituted black laws in the decades following the American Revolution, but dropped their enforcement before the Civil War. For free blacks, conditions in the North were never as harsh as in the South, though the difference often seemed slight. For instance, northern states never criminalized the education of blacks. Free blacks in the North fervently opposed slavery, helped enslaved blacks to escape, and unrelentingly petitioned for equal opportunity in their own communities. Gradually, their voices were heard and their ambitions realized. In so doing, the fight for liberty and inalienable rights for all men, as framed in the Declaration of Independence, continued.

THE SAGE OF MONTICELLO DIES

Life at Monticello always reflected the contradictions and intricacies of Jefferson's elusive inner self. The mixture of intellectualism, traditionalism, compulsion, and experimentation must have unnerved even the most loyal friends, relatives, and servants. Harriet and Beverly Hemings, Sally's oldest children living at Monticello, grew to maturity on Mulberry Row. Harriet was very beautiful, according to the former slave Isaac Jefferson, who chronicled his life at Monticello for a writer years after he left, and to Francis Bacon, a former overseer who gave an account after he had migrated to Kentucky. Harriet apparently worked at the weaver's cottage for a time. Like Sally's other boys, Beverly apprenticed with John Hemings as a carpenter/joiner.[20]

In 1822, both older children were set free and sent north. Decades later, Bacon would report that Harriet was "freed," as he was instructed to give her $50 and place her on a stagecoach to Philadelphia. Harriet's freedom apparently caused quite a stir in the neighborhood. Beverly left prior to Harriet, presumably to arrange or verify a place to live and work. Thomas Jefferson noted in his *Farm Book* that his offspring ran away, "ran 22." His description was misleading but, to his credit, the departures were noted. It is difficult to discern whether the departures were considered banishment or manumission by the residents of Mulberry Row, but they conformed with the promise Jefferson made to Sally Hemings years before; possibly a mixture of emotions marked the occasion. Harriet was the only female slave Jefferson ever freed.[21]

Jefferson had more control over the destiny of Harriet's and Beverly's lives than he did over Sally Hemings' other three children. It appears that Harriet and Beverly were sent away to join white society. It may have been Jefferson's desire that all of his children by Sally Hemings secured a similar fate. Yet, his desires competed with the traditions of the Hemings clan. Betty Hemings was alive during Thomas' early years on Mulberry Row. Eston, the youngest of Sally's children, never knew his grandmother. The correlation between the fates of these two brothers and the influence Betty Hemings may have had on Thomas provides fascinating food for thought.

During retirement Thomas Jefferson's fame endured; for idealists, Jefferson became an icon for the American Revolution. He took on new challenges. A letter dated September 7, 1814, to his nephew Peter Carr mentions one of his prime endeavors: "On the subject of the academy or college proposed to be established in our neighborhood, I promised the trustees that I would prepare for them a plan, adapted, in the first instance, to our slender funds, but susceptible of being enlarged." Jefferson founded the University of Virginia, personally surveying and staking the site. Along with architects William Thornton and Benjamin Latrobe, he designed most of the buildings, which reflect the Palladian influence, his preference, setting a standard for southern architecture. He helped to plan the curriculum, helped to select the faculty, many of them Europeans, and lobbied for appropriations.[22]

The War of 1812 again brought British troops to American soil. Congress' reference library was burned by the British, who entered the nation's capital. In 1815, Jefferson sold his entire book collection, 6,000 volumes, to the U.S. government for $23,950, formally establishing the Library of Congress. Most of the money went to pay Jefferson's debts, though the transaction did not provide lasting relief. When he died, his debts totaled $100,000.

In 1824, a notable reunion took place at Monticello when General Lafayette visited Jefferson. Both men had lived fulfilling, exciting, and demanding lives since the American and French Revolutions. Lafayette's time was more tumultuous, as France's destiny unfolded not in a smooth line toward aspirations of the Enlightenment but rather in an often violent stream of royalist seizures and new uprisings. Thousands of aristocrats were put to death by the guillotine. General Lafayette was thrown in jail for a time. Lafayette's wife, Adrienne, voluntarily joined her husband in prison and brought her daughters along with her. Napoleon, measuring the political advantages, freed the freedom fighter. Thus Lafayette retained his magnificent stature much as Jefferson did.

First landing in New York, Lafayette was met with heartfelt gratitude, and this spirit followed him throughout the land. Upon leaving Mount Vernon, where he paid his respects to the grave and memory of his dearest friend, George Washington, Lafayette was accompanied by James Madison to Monticello. The visit with Thomas Jefferson was warm and endearing, lasting four days. Lafayette, however, broke through the adulation to chide Jefferson for the continuation of slavery in the United States. Lafayette's travels ultimately lasted over a year, covering 5,000 miles. He spent considerable time with Andrew Jackson, who soon thereafter became president. Though Jackson was a slaveholder, both were military men; neither was accomplished in science, literature, arts, or the classics. Lafayette and Jackson struck a common chord; moreover, Jackson was simply younger than the eighty-two-year-old Jefferson. Jackson's memorable years were still ahead of him.[23]

The perpetual procession of building projects at Monticello ended when the west portico was finally finished. The adolescent triumphs, mishaps, and noisiness of Martha's children brought joy and love into Jefferson's life; he took an interest in their education, paying particular attention to their French lessons. Martha's daughter Ellen was Grandpa's most eager student. He also spent much time with his late daughter Maria's only child, Francis Eppes.

Disappointment, conflict, and anxiety also marked the period. Martha's oldest daughter, Anne, married a handsome but brutish man, Charles Bankhead, who drank heavily, was prone to brawls, and treated Anne poorly. Another granddaughter's father-in-law asked Jefferson to guarantee a loan, then defaulted, placing a heavy burden on the already precarious finances of Jefferson and his son-in-law Thomas Mann Randolph.

On July 4, 1826, Thomas Jefferson died quietly in his bed at Monticello. It was the fiftieth anniversary of the signing of the Declaration of Independence. Miles away, John Adams lay feeble in his Massachusetts bed, sighing, "Thomas Jefferson still survives." Adams would die later that day.

Jefferson was buried on July 5 in the graveyard at the foot of Mulberry Row. Wormley, a grandson of Betty Hemings, dug the grave, and John Hemings made the casket. The stone Jefferson designed was inscribed as he had directed: "Here was buried Thomas Jefferson, author of the Declaration of American Independence, of the Statute of Virginia for Religious Freedom, and Father of the University of Virginia."

In the end, Jefferson could not have freed his slaves even if he had been so inclined due to his indebtedness. During sixty-two years as a slaveholder, he had never prepared to free them. However, he did free five slaves in his will. In addition to Madison and Eston Hemings, Sally's only children then remaining at Monticello, he freed Burwell, who had served as his body servant, Joe Fossett, and John Hemings. These men were all sons and grandsons of Betty Hemings. Jefferson made a special appeal to the Virginia legislature to allow these men to remain in Virginia, as a state law enacted in 1806 called for newly manumitted blacks to leave the state.

Sally Hemings was "given her remainder" (the remainder of her life in undocumented freedom) shortly after Jefferson's death by Martha Jefferson Randolph. Subsequently, she moved to Charlottesville with her sons Madison and Eston. She chose to remain in Virginia; Jefferson's will allowed the choice by making Eston's and Madison's stay in the state possible. A few other Hemingses were also "given their remainder." Other Monticello slaves, 130 in all, including some members of the Hemings clan, were sold in 1827 at the auction block, as Martha's oldest son, Thomas Jefferson Randolph, sadly disposed of Monticello assets. Monticello, the lands, and the Shadwell mills were sold in 1828.

LEWIS WOODSON EXTENDS HIS STEADY HAND

Though circumstances of Lewis Woodson's adolescence were vastly different from those of his father's, at an early age Lewis Woodson married a woman older than himself, as Thomas had done. In 1823, at the age of seventeen, Lewis wed Caroline Robinson, who was born in Boutetort County, Virginia, in 1805. Caroline was of a darker complexion than Lewis, just as Jemima was darker than Thomas. Lewis was a leader in the African American community, and his life's ambitions were well formulated even at an early age. He knew that he would gain wider acceptance as an African American leader if his family, and particularly his children, resembled most African Americans. The lives of Lewis and Caroline unfolded in a different era, defined not only by time, but also by place; nonetheless, the bond they established obviously emulated the extraordinary bond between Thomas and Jemima. Their first two children, twins, died at twenty-two months of an unknown cause. Lewis and Caroline produced three more children, Mary, John, and Lewis Frederick, before 1830.[24]

In addition to helping establish the A.M.E. Church in Chillicothe and organizing the education of blacks there, Lewis Woodson asserted himself in another fashion, by writing a letter to *Freedom's Journal*, the first abolitionist newspaper in the United States. The weekly paper was printed in New York City. His letter, written December 22, 1828, from Chillicothe, appeared in the January 31, 1829 issue. In a previous issue of the paper, Lewis had read an offer by a Mr. Joseph Watson for the sale or lease of a section of land (less than 400 acres) in Guernsey County for the purposes of "colonization." Seemingly, Lewis wrote to *Freedom's Journal* to secure an address for Mr. Watson, not to have his letter published. The weekly printed the letter nevertheless, along with a notation explaining that it appeared "almost literally, and verbally, and in punctuation, as we received it," and questioning why segregation was the goal of so many Americans, when Lewis Woodson and others like him were capable of such fine writing.

Lewis' imagination was stirred:

Watson's offer . . . receives my most cordial approbation. Although the lot of land is too small to form a settlement of colored people up on, yet I feel a due degree of respect; and sincerely honor the gentleman who proposed the plan, though entirely unknown to me. My principle object in troubling you with these lines is to let you know that this mode of colonization is the mode which meets the cordial approbation of all the enlightened colored men in this and many of the other free states. If there could, by any means, be a lot from five to ten thousand acres obtained for us, or even three thousand acres of good land in one place, I am sure that the whole would be settled in one year.[25]

Lewis Woodson's vision far exceeded Watson's offer. The tenor of the offer was, however, generous in the sense that it was contrary to the strong movement that was afoot to expatriate African Americans to Africa. The American Colonization Society was formed in December 1816 to promote and support that effort. Reverend Daniel Coker, one of the Baltimorians who helped to create the A.M.E. denomination in 1816, sailed with ninety others to West Africa in 1820. In 1821, Richard Stockton, a U.S. naval officer, helped the American Colonization Society negotiate a treaty in West Africa which afforded stability to the settlement of African Americans.[26]

The Society was in essence a coalition of disparate ideas. At the time, the population of African Americans was 2 million. Their removal seemed farfetched. Society members realized that expatriation had to commence in earnest at once to be successful. Some members of the Society focused on the removal of free blacks only. Most whites viewed free blacks as a threat to peace, likely agitators for insurrection. Through the Society, white missionaries recruited black Christians to spread the faith in Africa. Removal of free blacks to Africa was seen as a real threat by some African Americans and as a Godsend by others.

Lewis Woodson favored separate settlement of blacks in Ohio. The greatest obstacle facing him was how to pay for the land, as most blacks were poor. Whites would not patronize black businesses, further limiting black income. The other concern was security, but implicit in Watson's offer was an acceptance of black settlement in Ohio. Lewis' stance may have been affected by the prospect of enforcement of black laws in Ohio and the agitation that preceded the Cincinnati "riot" of 1829. His letter continued, "Although we but normally enjoy it in this country but such a settlement would entirely alter our condition, there we should be all on perfect equality—we should be free from the looks of scorn and contempt—free from fraud—and, in time, free from all the evils attendant on partial and unequal laws."[27]

Woodson felt the pressure of the American Colonization Society. He addressed Watson without reservation: "Be assured sir, that this mode of colonization meets the decided approbation of the people of colour throughout the free states & perhaps, as much so in the slave states, though I know but little about this part of the country: what are their views and feelings. Africa, is with us, entirely out of the question. We never asked for it—we never wanted it: neither will we ever go to it."[28]

Such clear denunciations of the American Colonization Society's work were rare. Soon after the Society was formed, a large contingent of African American Philadelphians met in the Bethel Church. The vote against expatriation was unanimous; a committee of twelve was elected to monitor the menace. The Presbyterian minister, the Reverend Robert Finley, a founder of the American Colonization Society, soon thereafter arranged to meet with the committee. Finley's meeting with fellow Presbyterian the Reverend John Gloucester, the Reverend Richard Allen, and others was cordial. The committee entertained the question of the best location for colonization. The Reverend Finley left with the mistaken belief that the meeting had produced agreement. Such was the manner in which African American leaders chose to handle conflict in those times. Rather than challenge whites directly, locking into conflict, blacks often let whites think they were taking control or gaining complicity when they were not. Lewis Woodson adopted a more direct approach, occasionally standing apart from the mainstream of African American leadership.

At its heart, Lewis Woodson's loathing of the expatriation movement was more than a distasteful assessment of an errant political dictum or the rejection of the African continent. The source of Lewis Woodson's excited denunciation of the American Colonization Society and its mission was primal, extremely personal. In essence Lewis' outcry "neither will we ever go to it" was a rejection of expatriation and banishment, born in his own father's abrupt separation from the home of his own parents. Lewis vehemently rejected the forced separation and/or banishment of people from their root of origin. The African American press became a well-used outlet for Lewis Woodson's ideas.

Freedom's Journal began publication on March 6, 1827, with this opening prospectus: "As education is what renders civilized man superior to the savage: as the dissemination of knowledge is continually progressing among all other classes in the community: we deem it expedient to establish a paper, and bring into operation all the means with which our benevolent CREATOR has endowed us, for the moral, civil, religious and literary improvement of our injured race." The prospectus was signed by Samuel E. Cornish and John B. Russwurm, editors and proprietors. Cornish reemerged as a newsman of long standing after *Freedom's Journal* folded. The weekly publication flourished for only two years but made an enormous impact. Coeditor John B. Russwurm, an 1826 graduate of Bowdoin College, was enticed by the American Colonization Society to emigrate to Africa.[29]

HOME

Thomas Woodson and his family lived for nine years in Chillicothe, Ohio. They prospered there, and the family continued to grow. Thomas was pleased with the move to Ohio and sought to anchor the family's future there. In 1829, he bought 160 acres of land from Nathan and Margaret Brown in Jackson County, Ohio, located thirty-five miles southeast of Chillicothe. There must have been an earlier association with the farm, as Lewis' twins, who died in 1825 before reaching their second year of life, were buried on the grounds. The land cost $425. The Land Act of 1820 established a cost of $1.25 per acre for an 80-acre section of federal land. The Act of 1804 had previously established a price of $2.00 per acre for a minimum 160-acre plot.[30]

The Panic of 1819, brought on by contraction in the money supply, caused land values to fall. In the 1820s, Ohio land values rose again due to general economic health, population growth, canal building, and road improvement. The $2.60 per acre Thomas Woodson paid for the land was higher than the going rate for land used for cattle grazing. The price reflected valuation of good farmland. Tax records from 1828 indicate that Woodson owned five horses and a few head of livestock while he was in Chillicothe. Horses were most likely sold to pay for building material to construct a house on the Jackson County farm.

The parcel was located in a place that later carried the name Berlin Cross-roads. Southeastern Ohio was not as densely populated as the Miami River Valley, which stretched from Cincinnati to Dayton or the Cleveland area. If the move was made as an escape from urban-oriented violence and the persecution of blacks, then Jackson County was a good choice and remained so. The area offered decent farmland. Coal was later mined nearby, and the Buckeye furnace, also close by, provided nonagricultural employment.

A year later, in 1830, Thomas Woodson bought 50 acres from John and Emma Brown for $200, paying $4.00 per acre. The second deed of purchase, like the first, did not mention Jemima. Though manumission papers were filed in Greenbriar County for Hannah Grant and Fanny Leach, Jemima's mother and sister, none were filed for Jemima. None of the Greenbriar County or Cumberland County records gives the correct spelling of Jemima's name. In fact, the correct spelling appeared only in Ohio church records and on her gravestone. Her earlier identity is known because the name, whether it was Mima or Mummery Woodson, appeared along with those of relatives. The lack of manumission documents may have prompted the family to avoid using her name or for her to obscure it on county records. This explanation seems reasonable, but it leaves the question open as to how her older sister was able to become legally free while Jemima's condition remained in a precarious state.[31]

Fanny Leach, Jemima's sister, sold her land in Greenbriar County in 1824 to the Renick family, enabling her family to move to Ohio. The Leach family first appears in the census of 1840 for Jackson County, but they may have moved there much earlier. Fanny's husband, Lewis, who, it seems, remained a slave as long as he stayed in Greenbriar County, also moved to Ohio, as his presence in Chillicothe is chronicled in records preserved there. Census records do not reveal Lewis Leach's presence. He may have walked away from Greenbriar County when his owner died. Lewis Leach was described as "a light mulatto and a remarkably fine-looking man." Generations later, some Leach descendents lived as part of white society. Mulattos like Lewis Leach generally had an easier time escaping slavery.[32]

Hannah Grant, Jemima Woodson's mother, never moved to Jackson County, choosing to remain in the Greenbriar County highlands. Jemima gave birth to her tenth and last child, Sarah Jane, before the family moved to Jackson County; Fanny Leach brought eight children with her. The sense of kinship was strong among the cousins. Five names (Lewis, John, Thomas,

Hannah, and James) were common to both the Woodson and Leach families. There were no intermarriages, as the tradition of family intermarriage had faded throughout society. Nearly all of Jemima's sixty-two grandchildren were born in Jackson County, though all but a few left the county in adulthood. Family names such as Jemima, Fanny, and Sarah Jane spread through the third generation of the Leach and Woodson families. Fanny Leach's daughter Fanny married Benjamin Wilson. Their descendents stayed in Jackson County longer than the Woodsons and the Leaches.[33]

STEPPING INTO A BROADER STRUGGLE

Thomas Woodson's family did not leave Greenbriar County to join the struggle for African American freedom. Their goal was a better life. Ohio offered prosperity, and it was free of slavery. Equality remained a distant dream, but freedom, defined in an early nineteenth-century context, was secured. While the Woodsons and others formed the Bethel A.M.E. Church in Chillicothe, faith in God was taken close to heart and faith in the future became the bread of life. This fellowship began with a purely religious purpose in mind. Still, the Woodsons became inextricably engaged in the communal struggle of African Americans. Slaveholders feared that free blacks would incite a mass insurrection, and they also knew that free blacks would attempt to free family members and friends who remained in slavery. The Woodsons became entangled in the latter effort. As the Underground Railroad began to take shape, the Woodsons were among the early instigators.

In 1830 a national conference of the A.M.E. denomination was held in Hillsboro, Ohio, located halfway between Chillicothe and Cincinnati. African American refugees from the Cincinnati violence of 1829 who remained in or returned to the Cincinnati area must have found great comfort in knowing A.M.E. leaders convened in their midst. The founder of the denomination, Bishop Richard Allen, was seventy years of age in 1830 and died the following year. Leadership of the A.M.E. denomination had passed to the Reverend Morris Brown in 1828. Bishop Brown presided in Hillsboro; the Reverend Lewis Woodson served as secretary of the conference. Thus two men of great courage and vision joined to set a course for their church, if not for their people. The Reverend Lewis Woodson never met Bishop Richard Allen, but Woodson maintained a close association for decades with three other men who took on Allen's mantle, building the A.M.E. Church from the Atlantic to the Pacific. These men were Bishops Morris Brown, William Paul Quinn, and Daniel Payne, all of whom were present at Hillsboro. Their names now grace two universities and a seminary founded by the A.M.E. Church.[34]

For the next twenty years, the A.M.E. Church consolidated and strengthened its organization and significantly expanded the number of churches in the North. Reverend Paul Quinn moved his ministry to Chicago, then to St. Louis, fostering further expansion of the church. In many communities, the church was the only place where African Americans could publicly speak against slavery. However, congregations did more than talk. The A.M.E. Church clandestinely bolstered operations of the Underground Railroad; free blacks joined with white abolitionists in establishing routes for escaped slaves to gain freedom. Another common practice was raising money to buy the freedom of escaped slaves who were caught in the North. A.M.E. Churches also encouraged the purchase of "goods free from slave labor." Churches facilitated the distribution and purchase of African American newspapers and other abolitionist newspapers, sometimes voting on which paper would receive support from a particular congregation.

Two of Lewis' younger brothers, John and Thomas, became A.M.E. ministers as well. The church provided an outlet for the family's concern for the common good. No doubt Lewis' activism articulated values passed from Thomas and Jemima. In 1837, a few years after the Hillsboro conference Lewis would memorialize his ambitions: "Every youth should be educated; every minister should be a fountain of light; a copy of the 'Colored American' [newspaper] should be put in the hands of every family. To accomplish these or either of them, requires organization and the concentration of our whole moral and pecuniary power. And as to our possessing the requisite power and means, I have not the shadow of a doubt. All that is requisite to effect it, is the will."[35]

NOTES

1. Sarah N. Randolph, *The Domestic Life of Thomas Jefferson* (New York: Harper, 1871), 342.

2. Renick-Waddle Papers, in the archives of the Ross County Historical Society, Chillicothe, Ohio. This source indicated that the Woodsons rented the Thomas James farm. Beverly Gray of Chillicothe was able to determine the location of the farm and guided the author to the site and to several Chillicothe landmarks.

3. D. E. Crouse, *The Ohio Gateway* (New York: Scribner and Sons, 1938), 91: Shawnee meaning of "Chillicothe," and 57: unification of tribes. Also R. Douglass Hurt, *The Ohio Frontier* (Bloomington: Indiana University Press, 1996), 57: Battle of Point Pleasant.

4. Hurt, *Ohio Frontier*, 59.

5. Minnie S. Woodson, *Woodson Source Book* (Washington, D.C.: Privately printed, 1984), 45: from "History of Ross County," Ross County register, 1/3/1874.

6. Ibid., 46.

7. Charles H. Wesley, *Richard Allen, Apostle of Freedom* (Washington, D.C.: Associated Publishers, 1935), 152.

8. Ibid., 173: A.M.E. membership count, and 187: Brown's escape.

9. Renick-Waddle Papers.

10. Benjamin Quarles, *Black Abolitionists* (Oxford: Oxford University Press, 1969), 101.

11. Crouse, *Ohio Gateway*, 122: first use of steamboats on Ohio River.

12. Hurt, *Ohio Frontier*, 391.

13. Ibid., 393.

14. Hurt, *Ohio Frontier*, 392.

15. John Malvin, *North to Freedom: The Autobiography of John Malvin, Free Negro, 1795–1880*, edited by Alan Peskin (Cleveland: Press of Western Reserve University, 1966), 50.

16. Ibid., 62.

17. Ibid., 41; Hurt, *Ohio Frontier*, 387.

18. Hurt, *Ohio Frontier*, 375, 387.

19. Malvin, *North to Freedom*, 62–63 notes.

20. James A. Bear, ed., *Jefferson at Monticello* (Charolttesville: University Press of Virginia, 1967), 102: Harriet worked at the weaver's cottage.

21. Ibid., Robert C. Baron, ed., *The Garden and Farm Books of Thomas Jefferson* (Golden: Fulcrum, 1987), 386–87.

22. Adrienne Koch and William Peden, *The Life and Selected Writings of Thomas Jefferson* (New York: Modern Library, 1944), 642–43.

23. Fawn M. Brodie, *Thomas Jefferson, an Intimate History* (New York: W. W. Norton, 1974), 461–62: Lafayette chides Jefferson.

24. Woodson, *Woodson Source Book*, 161: 1830 U.S. Census (Ohio).

25. *Freedom's Journal*, January 31, 1829 (Schomberg Library, New York City).

26. Wesley, *Richard Allen*, 170: Reverend Coker sails to West Africa.

27. *Freedom's Journal*, 1/31/1829.

28. Ibid.

29. Ibid., March 6, 1827.

30. Hurt, *Ohio Frontier*, 345; Woodson, *Woodson Source Book*, 28: property deed, Jackson County (Ohio).

31. Deed of manumission for Fanny Leach, Deed Book 2, Greenbriar County, West Virginia, 712; deed of manumission for Hannah Grant, Deed Book 3, Greenbriar County, 160–61.

32. Renick-Waddle Papers: description of Lewis Leach.

33. U.S. Census, 1840, for Jackson County, Ohio.

34. Woodson, *Woodson Source Book*, 67: from *Year Book of Negro Churches*, comp. Bishop Beverly C. Ransom (Wilberforce, Ohio: Wilberforce University, 1935–36).

35. Lewis Woodson, letter in *Colored American*, December 2, 1837 (from *Woodson Source Book*, 95). This excerpt appears in the first of ten letters written to the *Colored American* by Lewis Woodson under the pen name Augustine.

CHAPTER SIX

The Rights of All

There is a natural aristocracy among men. The grounds are virtue and talents.
                    —Thomas Jefferson, letter to John Adams, October 28, 1813[1]

Thomas Woodson acquired more acreage in Jackson County than he could possibly cultivate himself. A smattering of evidence suggests that a number of people resided on portions of the Woodson property for a few years at a time. Though it seems Thomas secured a favorable financial standing, the purpose behind the transitional use of the property probably had less to do with the prospect of rental income than with the needs of the transients, some of whom might have been blacks who escaped enslavement. He was glad to be of help. Thomas and Jemima drew even greater satisfaction from the achievements of their large, ambitious brood.

Since Jemima was seven years older than Thomas, the union began when she filled the role of both wife and surrogate mother. During their residence in Ohio the age difference began to effectively disappear. As Lewis emerged as a prodigy and continued to assume more responsibility, another oddity loomed. Only sixteen years older than Lewis, it seemed as though Thomas had spawned a brother, not a son. No doubt this quirk of fate was obvious to family and friends. Thomas rejoiced in his blessings, supporting his prodigious son and encouraged his other sons and his daughters to follow Lewis' lead.

SALLY HEMINGS DIES

In 1835 Sally Hemings died in Charlottesville, Virginia, where she had moved after Jefferson's death to join her sons Madison and Eston. Her place of burial has not been preserved. The Hemingses purchased a house and additional lots on Main Street near Davy Isaacs and Nancy West. Davy Isaacs, a Jew whose father had emigrated from Frankfurt, Germany, to Virginia in 1747, operated a store on Main Street and counted Thomas Jefferson as a regular customer. Nancy West was a free colored woman who cohabited with Davy Isaacs but maintained her own identity as a property owner and a business operator. She published a local newspaper, the *Charlottesville Chronicle*. Between 1789 and 1817, Davy Isaacs and Nancy West produced seven children. Sally Hemings' son Eston married their sixth child, Julia Ann.[2]

Eston was listed as head of the Main Street household in the 1830 U.S. Census, which listed Eston, Madison, and their mother, Sally Hemings, as white. One "colored female adult" and five children were also listed. Madison married a mulatto named Mary McCoy in 1831. Eston and Madison worked as musicians and carpenters.[3]

After Sally Hemings' death in 1835, Madison and Eston moved to Chillicothe, Ohio, where their brother Tom (Thomas Woodson) had lived for nine years. Madison soon left Chillicothe for Pike County, located immediately south of Ross County and Chillicothe. A carpenter/builder, Madison Hemings built a warehouse for Great Lakes ship captain Joseph Sewell adjacent to the Erie and Ohio canal in Waverly, Ohio, along with several other area buildings. Madison lived as an African American. He made no secret of his relationship to Thomas Jefferson, nor did he flaunt it. He occasionally proclaimed connection to President Jefferson, but knew that whites would make every effort to discredit him. Most of Madison's children passed into white society; the family lines that did so lost cognizance of any connection with Monticello. The family lines living as African Americans passed along their connection to Sally Hemings and Thomas Jefferson.[4]

One account indicates that Chillicothe locals accepted the idea that Eston was the son of Thomas Jefferson. He was thought to resemble Jefferson, but Eston apparently attempted to play down the idea. It is possible that Madison Hemings was the one who implanted the family genealogy into the lore of Chillicothe. Eston bought property in Chillicothe and later sold part ownership to his mother-in-law, Nancy West, when he moved to Wisconsin in 1850. Eston changed his surname to Jefferson in Wisconsin, where he and all of his children lived as whites. He worked as a cabinetmaker there but died not long after his arrival. Several of his descendants were childless, but a small family line continued. Eston's descendents did not pass on a clear knowledge of his connection to Sally Hemings and Thomas Jefferson.[5]

Martha Jefferson Randolph moved to Boston for a time after her husband died and Monticello was sold, to live with her daughter Ellen Randolph Coolidge. Her youngest children, George and Septima, traveled there with her. Martha later lived in Washington for a short time with another daughter, then returned to Virginia, living at Edgehill with her son Thomas Jefferson Randolph. When her indigence thereafter became public knowledge, the state legislatures of South Carolina and Louisiana each voted a gift of $10,000. Martha Jefferson Randolph died in 1836, a year after Sally Hemings, and was buried in the family plot at Monticello.[6]

Martha instructed her sons, Thomas Jefferson Randolph and George Wythe Randolph, to always uphold the honor of their grandfather. She told them that one of Sally Hemings' children was born during a period when her father had been away from Monticello for fifteen months. While this account was not true, it would influence the thinking of historians for over a hundred years. Thus the southern miscegenation taboo, which coerced intelligent people to pretend not to know or understand what was blatantly apparent, prevailed.[7]

Martha's account passed from Thomas Jefferson Randolph to historian Henry Randall (who did not mention the Hemings controversy in his biography of Jefferson), then to historian James Parton. Parton reported several of Randolph's assertions, including that "he had never seen a motion or a look or a circumstance which led him to suspect, for an instant, that there was a particle more of familiarity between Thomas Jefferson and Sally Henings [sic], than between him [Jefferson] and the most repulsive servant." The Parton biography, which presented the most vigorous defense of Jefferson's "sexual misconduct" of that century, was published in 1874, a year after Madison Hemings gave a statement to an Ohio newsman. Parton presented the Randolph denial with more style and vigor than the Randolphs could have ever dreamed.[8]

Jemima Woodson's mother, Hannah Grant, died the year before Sally Hemings. Thomas and Jemima shared the same loss. Hannah filed a will in the Greenbriar County courthouse on June 10, 1834. The exact date of her death is not known. She used the will to free her slave, Sheldon Brock, whom she referred to as a "bound," a term sometimes used in reference to a slave but used more frequently in the prior century to describe an indentured servant. Hannah's use of the word was intended to soften the reality. Appointing Thomas Woodson as Brock's guardian, she designated money for purchase of "one half quarter section of land" for Brock. She willed ten dollars to "Louis [Lewis] Woodson of Ohio," who was actually then immersed in various missions in Pittsburgh. Hannah had many grandchildren, but Lewis is the only one mentioned by name in the will, a special remembrance.[9]

Like Betty Hemings' death, Hannah's marked the end of one era and the beginning of another for those intimately connected to her. It was a profound event for them. Prior to her death, some of her children gained freedom. Less is known about Hannah's origin than about Betty's; but each managed to push parts of their family out of slavery, triumphantly, maybe miraculously. Unlike Betty, Hannah secured freedom for herself as well. Like Sally Hemings she spurned the opportunity to move to the Midwest. During her last years in the Greenbriar County highlands, she recalled the memories of her enslavement on the Virginia Piedmont and lived another part of her life through reports of the prosperity that her children and grandchildren enjoyed in the heartland called Ohio.

YET THE TRUTH SURVIVED

Those who lived at Monticello passed into another life, but their legacies lived on, helped by a writer named Frances Wright. Wright, a wealthy young woman of Scottish decent, had begged Lafayette to allow her to join him on his trip to Monticello in 1824. She had been touched by the literature of Lord Byron, who spread potent notions of personal freedom and new sexual mores. Lafayette consented, and she did in fact meet Thomas Jefferson, reportedly engaging in lengthy discussions with the elderly sage.[10]

After the failure of Wright's ill-conceived "experiment," a racially integrated settlement in Tennessee where she planned to educate former slaves, she moved to on Cincinnati, Ohio. There she lectured, becoming the first woman in America to speak publicly about political matters. Her lectures stirred the town, and it must have been her references to Thomas Jefferson that drew the most concern. She claimed firsthand knowledge: "Mr. Jefferson is said to have been the father of children by almost all of his numerous gang of female slaves . . . when, as it sometimes happened, his children by Quadroon slaves were white enough to escape suspicion of their origin he did not pursue them if they attempted to escape, saying laughingly, 'Let the rogues get off, if they can; I will not hinder them.' "[11]

Wright's poignant but exaggerated account was recorded in Cincinnati by another writer from the British Isles, Frances Trollope, whose *Domestic Manners of the Americans* was published in 1832. The account did not mention Sally Hemings, the children, or others by name. The story gently echoed through time. It was raised above a whisper by abolitionists and later, after the Civil War, by Reconstructionists, but it was proffered more as innuendo than as fact.

When biographer Alice Perkins covered Frances Wright's life in 1939, Trollope's tale of the lecture heard in Cincinnati was recounted, except for the passage relating to miscegenation at Monticello. Apparently Perkins either did not feel the tale would stand without corroboration or thought that the passage of time and the deification of Jefferson rendered the tale irrelevant. In 1829 Frances Wright moved from Cincinnati on to New York City, living the balance of her life in America, witnessing Emancipation and the emergence of the women's suffrage movement. The Wright/Trollope account would not begin to have meaningful impact until the 1940s, a hundred years later, when it fell into the hands of another persistent researcher, Pearl Graham.[12]

VASHON, WOODSON, AND DELANEY

At the 1830 A.M.E. National Conference in Hillsborough, Ohio, the Reverend Lewis Woodson, Bishop Morris Brown, and the Reverend Paul Quinn collectively decided that Woodson would minister to a church in Pittsburgh and guide the expansion of the Ohio Conference from there. His wife Caroline, of course, supported the decision. Women of that time did not have equal say in matters of importance. The Pittsburgh community had clearly and repeatedly expressed a desire for an A.M.E. church; Lewis Woodson found that his talents were fervently appreciated.[13]

In 1808, the African Church had been organized in a home on Front Street in Pittsburgh and was chartered in 1818. The same year Sunday school began in a separate location, between Third and Fourth Streets. Members of the African Church petitioned the Baltimore Conference of the A.M.E. Church for admission into the denomination. In 1822, the Reverend Paul Quinn was sent to Pittsburgh to minister there, fulfilling the request. The church was able to purchase a building on Strawberry Way in 1827. The congregation must have grown, because in 1830 another purchase was made, this time on Front Street.[14]

Moving from Columbus, Ohio, in 1831, Lewis assumed the ministry in Pittsburgh. The following January, Lewis formed the African Education So-

Historical Table of the Organizations, Annual Conferences and Place of Meetings.   277

Conference.	Month	D.	Year	Place of Meeting	B'iip Pr'zg.	Secretary.
Philadelphia	April	9	1816	Philadelphia..	Allen	Richard Allen, Jr.
Baltimore ...	April	1	1817	Baltimore	Allen	Richard Allen, Jr.
New York...	May		1820	N. York City	Allen	Jos. M. Corr
Pit'b'g or West'n	Aug		1830	Hillsboro, O..	Brown	Lewis Woodson
Indiana......	Oct	2	1840	BlueRiv., Ind	Brown	M. J. Wilkerson
N. England	June	10	1852	New Bedford	Payne	T. M. D. Ward
Missouri	Sept	13	1855	Louisville Ky	Payne	J. M. Brown
California ...	April	6	1865	Sacramento...	Campbell	J. B. Sanderson
S. Carolina..	May	15	1865	Charleston ...	Payne	T. G. Steward
Louisiana...	Nov	1	1865	New Orleans	Campbell	John Turner
N. Carolina	Mch		1867	Wilmington...	Wayman	G. W. Brodie
Virginia	May	10	1867	Richmond....	Wayman	J R V Thomas
Georgia......	May	30	1867	Macon	Wayman	T. G. Steward
Florida	June	8	1867	Tallahassee...	Wayman	B. W. Quinn
Pittsburg.....	April	3	1868	Pittsburg	Wayman	D. E. Asbury
Kentucky ...	Sept	8	1868	Louisville	Payne	T. H. Jackson
Tennessee...	Sept	10	1868	Nashville	Shorter	B. L. Brooks
Texas	Oct	22	1868	Galveston.....	Shorter	Johnson Reed
Arkansas ...	Nov	16	1868	Little Rock...	Campbell	W. A. Rector
Mississippi ..	Oct	8	1868	Vicksburg	Shorter	Hiram R. Revell
Alabama.....	July	25	1868	Selma	Brown	Lewis Hillery
Illinois	Aug	1	1872	Bloomington	Wayman	E. A. McIntosh
New Jersey..	June	20	1872	Trenton.......	Shorter	F. J. Cooper
N. Georgia..	Jan'y	9	1874	Augusta	Ward	W. D. Johnson
West Texas..	Dec	2	1875	San Antonio..	Brown	W. R. Carson
Kansas.......	Oct	4	1876	Fort Scott.....	Shorter	T. W. Henderson
West Tenn..	Oct	4	1876	Clarkesville...	Wayman	D. E. Asbury
S. Arkansas	Oct	26	1876	Arkadelphia .	Ward	J. T. Jenifer
North. Miss	Nov	15	1877	Coldwater ...	Campbell	A. R. Green
E. Florida...	Oct	27	1878	Polatka, Fla..	Campbell	J. R. Scott, Sr.
ColumbiaSC	Dec		1878	New Berry...	Brown	S. S. Goosely
N. Alabama	Dec	11	1878	Florence......	Campbell	C. L. Harris
N.E. Texas..	Nov	27	1879	Corsicana	Ward	T. B. V. Davis
Indian... . {	Oct	25	1879	Yellow Spr'gs Ch'ctawNat'n	Ward	J. F. A. Sisson
W Kentucky	Oct		1880	Paducah Ky..	Campbell	O. P. Ross
North. Ohio	Sept	7	1882	Lima..........	Shorter	T. H. Jackson
N. Missouri..	Sept	19	1882	Hannibal, Mo	Ward	G. W. Gaines
N. Louisiana	Dec	29	1882	Shreveport ...	Caine	E. E. Makiell
Iowa	Aug	15	1883	Des Moines ..	Ward	G. H. Shaffer
S. Kansas...	Sept	20	1883	Lawrence.....	Ward	J. H. Hubbard
Macon, Ga..	Jan'y	31	1883	Sandersville ..	Dick'rs'n	W. C. Fanton
Cent'l. Texas	Dec		1883	San Antonio..	Caine	A. Grant
W. Arkansas	Nov	25	1885	Arkadelphia..	Ward	J. M. Collins
Michigan....	Aug		1886	Terre Haute I	Campbell	J. Bass
Colorado	Sept		1886	Lincoln, Neb	Brown	J. H. Hubbard

Year Book of Negro Churches, compiled by Bishop Beverly C. Ransom (Wilberforce, Ohio: Wilberforce University, 1935–36).

ciety with businessman John B. Vashon, a successful bathhouse operator, as its president. Woodson served as secretary. The school, staffed solely by blacks, attracted many of the "respectable citizens" of Pittsburgh. The society bought a building from the Methodist Church on Front Street and paid Lewis a teacher's salary of $150 per year.[15]

Having stabilized Bethel Church and established the school, Woodson turned to the mission of expanding the Ohio Conference. In 1833, a nine-day conference was held in Pittsburgh. Bishop Morris Brown presided; the Reverend Lewis Woodson assumed a familiar role as secretary. The Reverend Paul Quinn was among those present. Fifteen ministers and seven interns attended. The Conference reportedly had grown to include twenty-four churches, divided among five circuits. Total church membership of 1,194 was reported. In later years, the Ohio Conference boundaries would include Indiana, Michigan, and parts of Kentucky. Thereafter, the North Ohio Conference was created along with other conferences; the Ohio Conference consequently contracted.[16]

Pennsylvania instituted gradual abolition of slavery in 1780. Any person born after March 1, 1780, could not be a slave for life in the state. Abolition of the indenture of whites was immediate. By 1800, there were only 500 enslaved persons in Pennsylvania, 64 of whom lived in Allegheny County, where Pittsburgh is located. When Lewis Woodson arrived in Pittsburgh, there was very little, if any, slavery in the city.[17]

In the late summer of 1831, John B. Vashon and Reverend Woodson befriended a young man of nineteen who had recently arrived in Pittsburgh. Most African Americans came in contact with Vashon, the owner of a bathhouse and barbershop, soon after arriving in Pittsburgh. The young man, Martin Delany, became a student in Lewis Woodson's school.

Martin Delany came from Charlestown, which is now located in West Virginia, but at the time was in the Old Dominion, Virginia. His mother was free; his father was enslaved. Born May 6, 1812, Martin was the youngest of three children. He thirsted for knowledge but was not well educated. After an itinerant peddler sold him a primer in exchange for some bent spoons and blunt knives, Martin began to teach himself to read. When townspeople discovered this and threatened to lock Martin's mother in jail, she fled to Pennsylvania, settling in Chambersburg with her children in 1820. Martin Delany's father followed, finding a job in a paper mill. Martin attended primary school there, but the high school was expensive; no tuition aid was offered. Consequently, Martin sought work and eventually found himself helping to construct the Pennsylvania Canal. He wished to attend Dickinson

College in Carlisle but was unable to do so. At that point Delany set out on the 150-mile journey to Pittsburgh.[18]

In Pittsburgh, Delany lived with the Vashon family for a time, sharing a bed with Vashon's son George. He found work on the Pittsburgh waterfront and attended Reverend Woodson's nearby school at night. Delany began to read a new abolitionist newspaper, *The Liberator*, published by William Lloyd Garrison in Boston. Soon Delany decided that he wanted to practice medicine and approached a local doctor, Andrew McDonald, seeking an apprenticeship. The doctor agreed, and through him Delany learned the practice of bloodletting and applying leeches. The 1837 *Pittsburgh Business Directory* lists Delany, Martin R., as a cupper, bleeder, and galvanizer. The practice of medicine at the time was appallingly archaic by today's standards.

William Lloyd Garrison began publication of *The Liberator* on January 1, 1831. Garrison traveled to several cities, meeting with black activists. Abolitionist Lewis Tappan wrote, "It was their united and strenuous opposition to the expatriation scheme that first induced Garrison and others to oppose it." Garrison became a staunch and powerful advocate of abolition. Unlike most white abolitionists, he opposed expatriation of African Americans and formed meaningful relationships with African American leaders. Reflecting upon twenty-five years of observation, the African American abolitionist Dr. J. McCune Smith noted that it was hard to tell "who loved the other the most, Mr. Garrison the colored people or the colored people Mr. Garrison?" By early 1832, Garrison had enlisted blacks in several cities as newspaper agents, including John B. Vashon. African Americans carried *The Liberator* through its infancy. In December 1832, Vashon advanced Garrison $50 and later $60. By 1834, the newspaper had built its subscriber list to 2,300; whites comprised one-fourth of the number.[19]

On October 21, 1835, Vashon lunched at Garrison's house in Boston. Later that day, Garrison was attacked by a mob. When he was placed in jail for safekeeping, Vashon visited him, bringing a new hat to the frazzled abolitionist. Vashon traveled a great deal for a man of his time. His 1835 trip predated extensive railroad construction. Vashon most likely used horse-drawn coach from Pittsburgh to Philadelphia or to New York City, then traveled by steamship to Boston, a total journey of nine or ten unpleasant days. He attended antislavery and "Negro" conventions and joined the boards of several organizations. When the American Anti-Slavery Society formed in December 1833 in Philadelphia, Vashon was named to the board of managers, along with five other blacks, including Robert Purvis of Philadelphia and the Reverend Peter Williams of New York.[20]

In the early 1830s, African American leaders held conventions in East

Coast cities, where most free blacks lived. The free black population of Baltimore was the largest by far. At the last of these conventions in 1835, the American Moral Reform Society, spearheaded by Philadelphian William Whipper, was formed. Lewis Woodson became the secretary of the Pittsburgh auxiliary, placing himself in a dilemma. The Society's basic tenets fostered moral reform, industry, integrity, and temperance—all convictions agreeable to Lewis. However, the Society opposed racial separation and tied initiatives for black advancement to the collaboration of sympathetic whites. Lewis Woodson rejected the entanglement of black progress with the sympathy or patronizing expressions of whites. Lewis stressed self-determination and strengthening institutions within the black community.[21]

AUGUSTINE

Wanting to avoid contention with Whipper, yet needing to express convictions he deemed critical, Lewis Woodson assumed the pseudonym "Augustine" in a series of essays published in the abolitionist newspaper the *Colored American*, which was printed in New York by African American publisher Samuel Cornish. A deft tone was set in the first of Lewis' Augustine letters: "Since the commencement of the great abolition movement in our country, many highly respectable and intelligent colored men have fallen into the opinion, that we have less to do in our moral elevation, and that it will require less to raise us to respectability and usefulness now, than formerly." Lewis considered toil and sacrifice the most fundamental aspect of African American uplift, and he largely rejected the assistance of white abolitionists. "Consequently, unless we within and among ourselves become elevated and worthy, we should still be cut off from polite and elevated society, though all the world around us were in our favor."[22]

Candor was the strength of Lewis' message. His writings fully recognized the depth of the deprivation that African Americans experienced and outlined the principal resources needed to improve conditions for his people:

There are also others, who think it impolite and improper for us to acknowledge and speak of ourselves as a distinct class, in the community in which we live. . . . They have been the holders and we the held. Every power and privilege have been invested with them, while we have been divested of every right. . . . If the school, the pulpit, and the press be the natural and legitimate means of our moral elevation . . . that elevation, to be effectual must . . . be brought to bear . . . by ORGANIZED and systematic effort.[23]

115

He compared the circumstances of African Americans to those of other nationalities:

A few individuals of any class of men, being civilized, enlightened and refined, does not procure for their class such a character. This is the case with Ireland, Spain, Turkey, and Russia. Not but there may be found in all these countries, many who excel in whatever is elegant, polite, and refined; but because a majority of their population is low, ignorant, and degraded, it establishes for them a corresponding national character. So, on the contrary, France is characterized for her politeness; Scotland for her morality and profound learning. . . . Not but there may be found in all these nations, many individuals differing essentially from these national characteristics, but because a majority of the individuals who compose them, are such, it establishes for the whole, such a national character.[24]

Contrary to William Whipper's contention, Woodson argued that the black church should not work toward integration among white congregations. He argued for independence: "Prejudice, the offspring of slavery, shuts us out alike from the pulpit and the house of God, with our fairer brethren;— it shuts their eyes, stops their ears, steels their hearts against us, and cuts [us] off from all friendly intercourse with them—and leaves it with ourselves alone to sink to perdition, or rise to immortality. It is to the pulpits of our own congregations that I wish to direct the attention of the reader, as being the only source from which shall cause the moral regeneration of our race."[25]

The letter printed by the *Colored American* on July 28, 1838, marked a crescendo, not of a literary or a political nature, but in the realm of emotion. Referring to the Declaration of Independence as a rational act, justified by prevailing "antipathies," Lewis Woodson urged African Americans toward separate settlement on land tracts large enough to support black schools and churches, as opposed to the scattering or mixing of blacks into rural communities. Just this once he brought his father into the debate, though not by name: "My father now resides, and has been for the last eight years residing in such a settlement, in Jackson County, Ohio. The settlement is highly prosperous and happy. They have a church, day and Sabbath school of their own."[26]

The ten letters Lewis Woodson wrote to the *Colored American* under the pen name Augustine comprise the earliest manifesto for African American self-determination. The central themes were self-reliance, moral elevation, institution-building, and unity. Unlike other leading black abolitionists, Lewis never advocated expatriation to Africa or a slave uprising. For a time he did accept immigration to Canada or the West Indies as an option, since those places were near enough to prevent abandonment of the African American slave population trapped in the South. It is probably an overstatement to claim that black America set its course by rallying to the message of the Augustine letters, but it is clear that the letters articulated with uncanny and unequalled accuracy the course that was in fact taken.

Lewis anticipated the success of the abolition movement. He recognized a need to prepare for the end of slavery, and it seems in retrospect that those preparations must have hastened emancipation itself. "Slavery must soon be abolished; and, if so, where are the men to supply the wants that will then be created? Brethren, we are far behind the spirit of the age. God is holding out his blessings to us, will we be ready? When HE demands our action, will we be prepared?" "The elevation of three millions of immortal beings from the lowest depths of moral degradation, to the proper level of humanity, is a work to which the head and pen of the mightiest sage is barely adequate."[27]

Lewis Woodson and Martin Delany were elected as Pittsburgh delegates to the "Annual Convention of Colored Men of New York City." The convention, however, was never held. The pair no doubt made the best possible use of the trip, greeting abolitionists in New York and Philadelphia. Later Delany became disenchanted with his bleeding and cupping practice and decided to travel to the South and Southwest to learn about those parts of the country and living conditions of blacks there. He boarded a steamship headed down the Ohio and Mississippi Rivers, touring Mississippi, Louisiana, and Texas. Greatly disturbed by what he encountered, Delany returned to Pittsburgh in 1840. In 1843, he established the *Mystery*, the first African American newspaper printed in Pennsylvania, and he married Catherine Richards, a member of an old African American Pittsburgh family whose patriarch had bought land from John Penn, a son of William Penn. Delany's newspaper office was only a few doors away from Lewis Woodson's residence. The location is now occupied by PPG Place, an office tower complex that houses headquarters of the successor of the Pittsburgh Plate Glass Company.[28]

Delany's *Mystery* was not a profitable enterprise, as the number of abolitionist and African American newspapers continued to grow. In 1847, Frederick Douglass, the famed African American orator, traveled to Pittsburgh to address antislavery meetings. Douglass enlisted Delany to help start a newspaper in Rochester, New York. The *North Star* was named for the star Douglass followed through the forests to freedom. Delany served as its first editor and toured with John Mercer Langston, a graduate of Oberlin College, delivering antislavery speeches and selling newspaper subscriptions.

Realizing that the practice of medicine was becoming more advanced, and seeking an education that would elevate him above the customary procedures of bleeding and cupping, Delany applied to Harvard Medical School. He was accepted with the stipulation that he immigrate to Liberia under the aegis of the American Colonization Society upon completion of his training. Other black applicants accepted this scheme but finished the medical program at Dartmouth before leaving for Africa, as Harvard students objected to the admission of blacks. Delany rejected the plan and did not enter medical school, but he did sail to Africa with his family in 1859 to explore the prospect of settlement there. His stand against immigration to Africa softened; however, he continued to strongly reject forced emigration and the role of the American Colonization Society.

Fire!

At two minutes past noon on a sunny, windy day in April 1845, the bell of the Third Presbyterian Church in Pittsburgh rang with an unusual and alarming rhythm. Fire! A wooden shed near the corner of Second Street and Ferry Avenue (now Boulevard of the Allies and Stanwinx) caught fire. The first fire company to respond was the Vigilant. The wind sent embers toward other clapboard buildings, spreading danger to adjacent structures. The water system, installed in 1828 and enlarged in 1844, was used to fight the blaze, but water soon ran low, as it had not rained for two weeks. The fire spread across to Front and Third Streets, as wind whipped into the fire from changing directions. At Second Street, the Globe Cotton Factory was destroyed within minutes, creating an inferno. Workers and residents ran for their lives. Brave efforts to save the Third Presbyterian Church were unsuccessful. The 160-foot steeple, aflame, warned those across Fifth Avenue of unspeakable disaster. Bethel A.M.E., Lewis Woodson's church, located on Front Street (later First Avenue), quickly succumbed to the inferno.[29]

Fire terrorized Pittsburgh for hours. Near 6 P.M., the devilish wind ceased its mischief. The fire destroyed 1,100 buildings in all, nearly double the number burned in the New York Fire of 1835. Ten to twelve thousand people were left homeless. In seven hours, sixty acres of the city burned to the ground—representing three-quarters of the improved real estate value in Pittsburgh.[30]

Locals responded with bravery and resolve. Insurance companies were of little assistance. In 1829, the Commonwealth of Pennsylvania forbade companies to sell fire insurance unless they had an office and a charter in the Commonwealth. Consequently, one-quarter of the insurance policies in force in 1845 had been provided by companies situated in Pittsburgh. The offices of these companies and the value of many of their investments had been lost in the fire. Some of the companies operating from Philadelphia went bankrupt. The Bethel A.M.E. Church gave $61.28 to the Allegheny Relief Association, a figure that compared well to the donations of other churches. Generous contributions were received from all over the United States. Contributions from New York State totaled $23,265. This generosity significantly eased hardships caused by the fire.[31]

The A.M.E. Church relocated, but not until 1873 did it acquire a structure which fit its standing in the community. In that year, the church moved to Wylie Avenue in the Hill District. Lewis Woodson's home was not damaged by fire; but, when rebuilding commenced, he moved both his residence and his barber business close to the site where the Great Fire had started.

THOMAS WOODSON, FARMER

When Lewis Woodson, using the pen name Augustine, identified the Ohio community where his father lived he did not give his father's name. Anonymity was a family practice. In no way does this suggest that Lewis was not proud of his father. He was exceedingly proud. Exposure of the family's unusual history and its leadership role, especially in the Underground Railroad, would invite prying questions and possibly acrimony. It is easier to win a battle if the enemy does not know which soldiers are the officers.

The June 29, 1842 issue of the *Philanthropist*, the organ of the Ohio Anti-Slavery Society, printed an article on the success of black farmers in Jackson County. It reported on a settlement located six miles from the town of Jackson that contained 161 persons, "most of whom were former slaves in Virginia. . . . They own 2,055 acres of fine land." One Thomas Hoodron was said to own 150 hogs and 400 head of cattle and to have grown 1,500 to 3,000 bushels of corn as well as a large quantity of hay. "Four of his sons are school teachers. The people are putting up a good house for a permanent school." A white neighbor is quoted as saying, "The Negroes are all that care anything about education around here. . . . still they are treated with great injustice by whites; but not withstanding every obstacle they are making steady progress in moral and intellectual improvement."[32]

There was in fact no Thomas "Hoodron" in the county. Thomas Woodson, who remained anonymous to most readers of the article, paid a total of $2,425 for his land in Jackson County. According to the *Philanthropist* the land was worth $12–15,000. In 1850 Thomas Woodson placed a value of $6,750 on the land when reporting to the U.S. Census. Whatever the precise figure, the land value was rising, and the abolitionist newspaper clearly embellished the success of farmer "Thomas Hoodron." Although the *Philan-*

thropist used Thomas Woodson to exemplify the success of blacks (albeit with an intentionally misspelled name), he was listed as a white man in the U.S. Census near this time, the only time the federal census would label him as such. Though the *Philanthropist* made its point successfully, it did so because readers did not know all of the details. If readers had known the subject farmer was listed in the census as being white the point would have been lost. It was difficult to accurately use the Woodsons to exemplify anything other than their boundless tenacity.[33]

Other evidence of Thomas Woodson's bent for anonymity indicates that while in Jackson County he sometimes used the name Tom Corbin for disguise. Tom Corbin Road is the name of a local road that runs across the land Woodson once owned. Yet there is no record of a Tom Corbin in the U.S. Census. Corbin also appears as the middle name of one of Thomas Woodson's youngest granddaughters, Lucy Corbin Woodson. Oral history has survived which indicates use of the name by Thomas Woodson in some manner. It's likely that he used the name because of his connection to the Underground Railroad or to further disguise his connection to Thomas Jefferson. All church records, deeds, and wills reflect unabridged use of one name, Thomas Woodson.

In the 1850 census, Harriet, George, and William Woodson, children of Thomas and Jemima, were listed as adult heads of households in Jackson County. This Harriet was the widow of Thomas Woodson (Jr.), third son of Thomas and Jemima. Thomas Woodson (Jr.) died at the age of thirty-one in 1846, leaving Harriet with six children. John P. also died at an early age, thirty-four, in 1853. Berlin Crossroads, as the community was then known, was a fixture on the Underground Railroad. Members of the Woodson family now embrace the premise that one or both of the brothers were killed by slave catchers who discovered that they were helping escaped slaves. This history is probably accurate, although its origin is untraceable.[34]

In addition to providing editorial content for the *Colored American* as Augustine, Lewis Woodson was also the newspaper's Pittsburgh agent. His brother Thomas followed suit by becoming an agent for the *Palladium of Liberty*, a black newspaper printed in Columbus, Ohio. Historian Floyd Miller presumed that this particular Thomas Woodson was Lewis's father, but he was probably Thomas Woodson (Jr.), born in 1815. The family continued to grow and prosper despite the racial hostility that surrounded their enclave. During the height of the Civil War, Morgan's Raiders, a Confederate cavalry battalion, invaded southern Ohio, reaching Berlin Crossroads. A local man's horse was shot from under him at the road crossing. It is not known if the target of the attack was Buckeye Furnace or Underground Railroad stations, but the attack did not have long-term consequences for the county or for the Woodson family.[35]

LEWIS WOODSON, VOTING RIGHTS ACTIVIST

When the first Africans were brought to Virginia in 1619, no law sanctioned, defined, or regulated slavery there. At first, Africans were treated like white indentured servants and freed after seven years. A comprehensive slave code was not enacted until 1670. In parallel fashion, when northern states passed acts of abolition after the American Revolution, blacks assumed the rights of free men. Gradually, the states surrounding Pennsylvania restricted those rights. States denied the voting right to blacks as follows: New Jersey, 1820; Delaware, 1792; Maryland, 1809; Ohio, 1817; and New York (invoked a property test), 1821. By 1837, a movement was afoot to deny voting rights to blacks in Pennsylvania.

Small numbers of blacks voted in Allegheny (Pittsburgh), Bucks, Dauphin, and other Pennsylvania counties after the Gradual Abolition Act of 1780 became law. Blacks in Philadelphia were not able to vote, however, and the prospect for progress there was dim. Philadelphia blacks were attacked in 1834 and 1835 (reported as a riot) and forced to concern themselves with self-preservation rather than civil rights. In 1835, a black man from Luzerne County, William Fogg, was turned away from the poll by a man named Hobbs. Fogg sued and won the favor of the county court, but Hobbs, backed by politicians, appealed. The ruling set in motion politicians who opposed sharing the right to vote with blacks. The Pennsylvania Supreme Court eventually ruled in Fogg's favor but not until after a state constitutional convention eliminated the voting right of blacks.[36]

A state constitutional convention was in session on June 19, 1837, when John Sterigere, a former state representative and former U.S. congressman, offered a motion to insert the word "white" before "freemen" in the section of the constitution that addressed suffrage. Sterigere believed that "the Negro is only fit for slavery" and attempted to make political hay of Governor Joseph Ritner's abolitionist leanings.[37]

Even before Sterigere made the motion, blacks in Pittsburgh were aware of the prospects for trouble. On June 13, a mass meeting of African Americans was held in Pittsburgh to discuss the threat to their voting privilege. They decided to compose "The Memorial of the Free Citizens of Color in Pittsburgh and Its Vicinity Relative to the Right of Suffrage." Today the document is known as the "Pittsburgh Memorial." It contains several sections: a petition, which includes an elegant extract from the 1790 Pennsylvania Constitution; a survey of the black community in Pittsburgh; and a statement from the Pittsburgh tax collector. A list of petitioners provides an excellent picture of the early stalwarts of the African American community in western Pennsylvania. The highest taxpayers cited were John B. Vashson and Charles Richards. Five signers are depicted as Committee members responsible for the Memorial. John B. Vashson is listed first; Lewis Woodson, Secretary of the Committee, is listed last. The Memorial reflects traces of Lewis Woodson's writing style, but it was not written entirely by his hand.[38]

On January 20, 1838, the Pennsylvania constitutional convention voted to restrict suffrage to white males only. Later in the year, Robert Purvis of Philadelphia composed a protest document, "Appeal of Forty Thousand Citizens Threatened with Disenfranchisement, to the People of Pennsylvania." The elegant appeal was not enough, however. In October 1838, white male voters ratified a new constitution that restricted suffrage to their ranks.

Chronicles of several Europeans who traveled through the United States between 1815 and 1845 to study its political system and culture provide rich and relatively impartial pictures of the nation. Alexis de Tocqueville's *Democracy in America* chronicled the predicament of African Americans. His synopsis is blunt and revealing:

In the North the white no longer distinctly perceives the barrier that separates him from the degraded race, and he shuns the Negro with the more pertinacity since he fears lest they should some day be confounded together.... Among Americans in the South, Nature sometimes reasserts her rights and restores a transient equality between blacks and the whites.... But if the relative position of the two races that inhabit the United States is such as I have described, why have the Americans abolished slavery in the North of the Union, why do they maintain it in the South, and why do they aggravate its hardships?[39]

In reality, conditions were clearly more precarious for blacks who lived in the South, whether enslaved or free. The black code was more rigid in the South; the code was regularly enforced there, and slavery as an institution permeated everyone's everyday life. This account documents that blacks in the North lived in an atmosphere of animosity just as intense as that in the South but somewhat different in character.

LEWIS WOODSON, BUSINESSMAN AND FATHER

Lewis Woodson was certainly disappointed by the new Pennsylvania Constitution. The right to vote conveys both tangible and symbolic powers. Its denial established disenfranchisement in more than one way. Paradoxically, public funding of a black school began in Pittsburgh in 1837. The African Education Society was thereafter disbanded. This was an enormous step forward for African Americans. The education of blacks was illegal in the South, and taxes collected from blacks in the North had not been used to educate their children in prior years. Blacks for the most part were poor; many used part of their meager income to buy the freedom of relatives from southern slaveholders. The financial relief brought by public funding of black schools was momentous, even though the funding itself fell short of standard appropriation. Publicly funded education for blacks in the North became a reality only a few years after public education for whites. The benefits were immediate and long-range, symbolic and fundamental.[40]

As early as 1837, Lewis Woodson operated a barbershop at Liberty and Seventh Streets in Pittsburgh, which today is the heart of the downtown business district. In 1847 John B. Vashon operated his bathhouse, barbershop, and saloon at Market and Ferry Streets, closer to the wharfs along the Monongahela River. Charles Richards, a steamboat steward at the time, was one of the first stalwarts of the African American community in Pittsburgh to live in the neighborhood then known as Haiti and later known as the Hill District. The Hill District became the focal point of the African American community.

By 1857 three Woodsons were listed in a Pittsburgh business directory, Lewis and two of his sons, John and Lewis. John Woodson, born in 1827 in Ohio, practiced his barber trade in the Perry Hotel. Lewis Frederick Woodson (b. 1829) shared a location with his father. The evidence indicates that the careers, marriages, and ambitions of the new generation of Woodsons were closely associated with the patriarch, Lewis.[41]

As he aged Lewis Woodson became less driven by political and social issues and turned to building a network of family enterprises. Around the same time, James G. Birney, a former American Colonization Society agent, transcended the idea of expatriating blacks and used his wealth to forge into presidential politics through the Liberty Party, founded in 1840 with the singular goal of emancipation. His transition symbolizes the institutionalization and politicalization of abolitionism. With the Liberty Party, and then the Free-Soil Party, in motion, the role of clergy in the abolition movement, even that of black clergy, was simply overshadowed.

Pittsburgh was booming! Steamboats not only plied the Ohio River, making the city a gateway to the west, but they led to the creation another crucial industry, shipbuilding. From the start of steamship travel, many boats that plied western rivers were built in Pittsburgh. The firm of Robinson and Minis won the distinction of building the first large iron-hulled steamboat, the *Valley Forge*, in 1839. Locals were bewildered that it stayed afloat as well as wooden boats. Pittsburgh boatyards produced 100 boats in 1840 alone, most for use on canals. The construction of steam-powered boats increased demand for steel. Pittsburgh was already a smoke-filled assemblage of hills and rivers; new industry only made conditions worse. By 1816 one traveler complained, "Pittsburgh is gloomy, because dark dense smoke rises from every part, and a hovering cloud of vapor obscures the view." In spite of condescending remarks from passers-by, hard-working locals of many nationalities rather enjoyed having bread on their tables and savored freedoms their parents were unable to imagine.[42]

REVEREND LEWIS WOODSON, FOUNDER OF WILBERFORCE UNIVERSITY

The black population in Ohio rose from 9,568 in 1830 to 36,673 in 1860, a fourfold increase. The needs of this population grew rapidly. By comparison, the African American population of the state of New York grew from 44,870 to 49,005 in the same period, a gain of less than 5,000. Lewis Woodson focused on the needs of the growing population of free blacks, especially in the west. *The Encyclopedia of African Methodism* reveals, "The Ohio Conference was the first Conference to take a definite stand for education and temperance." The following resolution, introduced by Lewis Woodson in 1833, memorializes the beginnings of his effort: "Resolved, As the sense of this conference, that common schools, Sunday Schools, and temperance societies are of the highest importance to all people; but more specifically to us as a people, that it shall be the duty of every member of this conference to do all in his power to promote and establish these useful institutions among our people." Thankfully politicians also recognized this need. With the establishment of public primary and secondary education for blacks in Pennsylvania, the African Education Society, which Lewis Woodson had founded, was disbanded. Since he had already begun to push the church toward satisfying the educational needs of African Americans, he began to push it toward the domain of higher education.[43]

In 1844, the Ohio Conference, meeting in Columbus, selected and purchased a tract of land "for the purpose of erecting a seminary of learning, on the manual labor plan, for the instruction of the youths among us in the various branches of literature, science, agriculture, and mechanical arts, and also for those who may desire to prepare for the ministry." A tract containing 172 acres was purchased for $1,720, paid in installments. It was located twelve miles west of Columbus, two miles north of the National Road. The school was established as the Union Seminary.[44]

Separately, a few years later, leaders of the Cincinnati Conference of the Methodist Episcopal Church decided to establish a school of higher education for blacks and selected a site near Xenia, Ohio, known as Tawana Springs. The site was previously used as a resort and was known as a station on the Underground Railroad. It was also known as a place where white fathers relocated with their African American mates and their children. The school opened in 1856 as the Ohio African University.

Commitment was deep, resources small. The first principal of the Ohio African University was assisted by one person, his wife. In 1858 the Reverend Richard S. Rust, D.D., a graduate of Wesleyan University, became president, and the faculty was bolstered by three graduates of Oberlin College, including Sarah Jane Woodson, who taught in the English Department. (Having finished Oberlin in 1856, she was among the first six black women to graduate from college.) She was the youngest daughter of Thomas and Jemima Woodson and thus the youngest sister of Lewis Woodson. She was the first African American faculty member at the school, and as such was the first African American to teach college. Sarah Jane was also one of the first women of any race to teach college in the United States (if not the first). The board of trustees, at the new university was composed of twenty-four members, included four African Americans. Among these four were Bishop Daniel A. Payne and the Reverend Lewis Woodson. Bishop Payne, a member of the board's executive committee, lived on the campus.[45]

During the Civil War, the Ohio African University found it difficult to sustain operations. Reverend Rust informed Bishop Payne that the Methodist Episcopal Church would sell the campus to the A.M.E. Church if the latter could raise the funds to pay off the university's indebtedness of $10,000. In June 1862, the campus closed. Bishop Payne contacted several men, including Dr. Willis R. Revels, Philadelphian Stephen Smith, and Reverend Lewis Woodson. Smith did not respond, but others encouraged Payne to raise the money and buy the campus. Woodson wrote Payne, promising he "would be one of one hundred men to give one hundred dollars." The board of trustees pressed Payne for a timely answer, declaring that the state of Ohio wished to purchase the site for an asylum. When the trustees set a deadline of noon on March 11, 1863, Payne responded affirmatively.[46]

Union Seminary, the A.M.E. school established in 1844, was moved to the newly acquired campus, which was renamed Wilberforce University after the renowned British abolitionist. Bishop Daniel A. Payne, a graduate of Gettysburg Theological Seminary, became president. Sarah Jane Woodson, who left the school in 1860 after two years, returned in 1865 for two more years as preceptress of English and Latin and as lady principal and matron. Only one other college had been founded to educate African Americans before the Civil War. Ashmun Institute, later named Lincoln University, was founded in 1854 by Presbyterians in southeastern Pennsylvania.

Upon returning to America from their exploratory trip to Africa, Martin Delany's wife and children moved to the Wilberforce University campus in Ohio. On February 8, 1865, Delany met with President Lincoln to argue for the appointment of black officers in the Union Army. During the war, 188,000 African Americans were enlisted. President Lincoln assigned Delany the rank of major in the U.S. Army. He was the highest-ranking African American officer, but he was never assigned a troop command. After the Civil War, he moved to South Carolina, working for the Freedmen's Bureau. He asked his family join him there, but to no avail; they stayed in Ohio. Delany continued to work for the state of South Carolina. After serving a term as lieutenant governor before the Reconstruction era ended, he later joined his family in Wilberforce. His restless soul had finally found a home.[47]

GOING UP TO YONDER

Jemima Woodson passed into the hereafter in 1868 at age eighty-five. It is not known whether Lewis Woodson was able to travel to Ohio in time for his mother's burial. He did travel to Jackson County at some point during that year, remaining in the vicinity for some time.

Jemima Woodson lived even longer than her mother, Hannah Grant, and Betty Hemings. She witnessed extraordinary change, as they had, but during a very different time and ultimately in a new place, one that would typify the new age. Betty Hemings saw Africans unloaded from ships, shackled, and chained. She and Hannah Grant lived through the Revolutionary War. They often subordinated their needs and self-interest to those of their masters in hope that the next day would bring reward and a better life in return. Jemima Woodson spent a lifetime with one husband, raising a huge and industrious family. She was amazed at the steamboats that came to master the rivers, then amazed at the railroads that raced across the land. She saw her youngest daughter, Sarah Jane, graduate from Oberlin College and become the first African American to teach at a college; she witnessed the Civil War and Emancipation. Chattel slavery was abolished. If her children faced obstacles, Jemima knew they would overcome them, as the challenges the family had already hurdled had been the hardest.

In 1869, Rachel Hill Cassel, mother-in-law of Frances Woodson Cassel (the fifth child of Thomas and Jemima), donated nearly two acres of land for the construction of a school for the African American community of Berlin Crossroads, Ohio. Although not the first school in the settlement, it was built to last. The original trustees were James Woodson (the seventh child of Thomas and Jemima), James W. Stewart, and Major Shepherd, the latter two being Rachel's sons-in-law. The Rachel Cassel Educational Center, as it was known, served its original purpose until about 1930. It was demolished in 1970 when the Appalachian Highway was widened.

The third generation of Woodsons followed the legacy of Thomas and Jemima Woodson and their gifted son, Lewis. Thomas Wesley Woodson, the only son of James Woodson, was born in 1853 in Berlin Crossroads and went on to become a distinguished A.M.E. minister. He was ordained by Bishop Daniel A. Payne in Dayton, Ohio, in 1891 and obtained a doctor of divinity degree from Morris Brown College in 1913. He ministered to many churches during his life, including Quinn Chapel in Chillicothe, Ohio. Thomas Frank Cassel became a lawyer and moved to Memphis, Tennessee, along with his first cousin Benjamin Frank Woodson, who was a carpenter-builder. T. Frank Cassel was elected as the first African American member of the Tennessee legislature, during the Reconstruction era. Sarah Jane Woodson Early spent her last years in Nashville, the state capital, after a long life devoted first to education and later to the temperance movement.

At least two Woodson descendants enlisted in the U.S. Army during the Civil War, Cyrus Creighton Cassel and James White, both grandsons of Frances Woodson Cassel. Lawrence Woodson, one of William and Jane Woodson's twelve children, became an educator, teaching at the Randall Academy in Jackson County before moving elsewhere.

Most of the Woodson grandchildren were raised in Ohio, but Lewis and his wife Caroline had of course taken their three young children with them from Ohio to Pittsburgh, where seven more children were born to them. Like Thomas and Jemima's children, some moved away and others stayed close to their parents when they matured. Before the Civil War, the older children began to marry and start families of their own.

Lewis' oldest daughter, Mary, married Jethro McGuire and stayed in Pittsburgh. Lewis Frederick Woodson married Nancy Tanner, remaining in Pittsburgh for some time but later moving away like most of his own eleven children. Nancy Tanner's father, Hugh Tanner, was one of the signers of the Pittsburgh Memorial. Her brother Benjamin was a graduate of Avery College in Pittsburgh and of the Western Theological Seminary. Benjamin Tanner became an A.M.E. minister and in 1868 was appointed editor of the *Christian Recorder*, the denomination's newspaper. The assignment placed him in Philadelphia, where he became an A.M.E. bishop and on occasion preached at the Mother Bethel Church there. His son Henry Ossawa Tanner would become a world-renowned painter. One of Nancy Tanner Woodson's daughters, also named Nancy Woodson, married a Philadelphia minister who was part of Bishop Tanner's circle of friends; she moved to Philadelphia.[48]

Many of the grandchildren carried threads of the Hemings/Woodson legacy forward. Many family members became educators; some entered the ministry; others retained some connection to the construction trade as contractors or landlords. Most carried on strong oral traditions generation after generation, though such a large family was bound to grow apart.

Thomas Woodson bought and sold land throughout the 1840s and 1850s, including eighty acres in 1853 for seven times the per acre price he paid in 1829. He also sold land to the Jackson County Coal & Iron Company. Apparently not all of the transactions have been uncovered, because in 1870 it seems he retained as much land as he owned in 1840 despite land sales. The Woodson patriarch made a will in 1855. In 1875, at the age of eight-five, he sold fifty acres of land to daughter-in-law Jane Woodson, William's widow, in exchange for her promise to care for him for the remainder of his life. By then he had outlived four of his sons. Only Lewis and James still lived. Daughters Delila and Jemima had long before left Jackson County, and contact with Jemima was lost.[49]

Earlier, Thomas Woodson had told his children they were the grandchildren of Sally Hemings and Thomas Jefferson. In his last years, he told grandchildren who remained in Jackson County of his biological origin and his departure from Monticello. Young Woodsons such as Thomas Wesley Woodson and Minerva Woodson, Jane's daughter, who as a child lived on the same farm as her grandfather, heard the oral history directly from him. Thomas Woodson passed on knowledge of his extraordinary origin and life, handing down a legacy of self-reliance, strong family traditions, and a defiance of injustice.[50]

Sections of Thomas Woodson's deed of fifty acres to Jane E. Woodson, October 14, 1875.

NOTES

1. Quoted in Robert Andrews, *Famous Lines* (New York: Columbia University Press, 1997), 29.

2. Judith Justus, *Down from the Mountain* (Perrysburg: Privately printed, 1990), 77, 78, 105, 106.

3. Ibid., 77: 1830 census record.

4. Ibid., 78: account of Madison's work in Ohio.

5. Ibid., 89: sale of Chillicothe house.

6. Jack Mc Laughlin, *Jefferson and Monticello* (New York: Henry Holt, 1988), 380: financial help for Mrs. Randolph.

7. Fawn M. Brodie, *Thomas Jefferson, an Intimate Life* (New York: W. W. Norton, 1974), 296.

8. James Parton, *Life of Thomas Jefferson* (Boston: James R. Osgood & Co., 1874), 569: citation of Randolph family denials.

9. Minnie S. Woodson, *Woodson Source Book* (Washington, D.C.: Privately printed, 1984), iii: Will of Hannah Grant, Greenbriar County (W. Va.), Deed Book #2.

10. A. J. G. Perkins, *Frances Wright, Free Enquirer* (New York: Harper & Brothers, 1939), 3–10: description of Frances Wright; Brodie, *Thomas Jefferson*, 461: Wright's appeal to Lafayette.

11. Frances Trollope, *Domestic Manners of the Americans* (London: Whittaker, Treacher and Co., 1832), 97–98.

12. Perkins, *Frances Wright*, 213–14: Perkins' omission.

13. Woodson, *Woodson Source Book*, 67: from Rev. Beverly C. Ransom, *Year Book of Negro Churches*, 276: record of 1830 A.M.E. Conference.

14. "Bethel A.M.E. Honored with Historical Marker," *Pittsburgh Courier*, September 30, 1995.

15. Woodson, *Woodson Source Book*, 68: from the Constitution of the Pittsburgh African Education Society, printed in the *Liberator*, 2/25/1832.

16. Bishop R. R. Wright, *Encyclopedia of African Methodism* (Philadelphia: A.M.E. Church, 1947), 456.

17. S. Trevor Hadley, *Only in Pittsburgh* (Cincinnati: Educational Publishing Resources, 1994), 182.

18. Ibid., 145: early life of Martin Delany.

19. Benjamin Quarles, *Black Abolitionists* (Oxford: Oxford University Press, 1969), 19: quote by Lewis Tappan, and 18: quote by J. McCune Smith from *Frederick Douglass' Paper*.

20. Ibid., 21: Vashon-Garrison encounters.

21. Floyd Miller, *The Search for a Black Nationality* (Urbana: University of Illinois Press, 1975), 95.

22. Woodson, *Woodson Source Book*, 95–96: from the *Colored American*, 12/9/1837.

23. Ibid., 95: from the *Colored American*, 12/2/1837.

24. Ibid., 96: from the *Colored American*, 12/9/1837.

25. Ibid., 101–2: from the *Colored American*, 1/13/1838.

26. Ibid., 109–10: from the *Colored American*, 7/28/1838.

27. Ibid., 105: from the *Colored American*, 1/27/1838 and 2/10/1838.

28. Ibid., 88: Floyd Miller, "The Father of Black Nationalism," *Civil War History*, vol. 17, no. 4 (December 1971).

29. Tom Kondis, "The Inferno," *Pittsburgh*, November 1976.

30. Marcellin C. Adams, "Great Fire of 1845," *Western Pennsylvania History Magazine*, May–June 1942; Dorothy Kantner, "Old Diary Reveals Spark by Spark Account of Blaze," *Sun Telegraph*, March 26, 1955.

31. J. Heron Foster, *A Full Account of Great Fire at Pittsburgh* (Pittsburgh: J. W. Cook, 1845).

32. Woodson, *Woodson Source Book*, 32: from the *Philanthropist*, 6/29/1842.

33. Ibid.

34. Ibid., 132, 138: deaths of Woodson men from gravestones in Woodson Cemetery, Jackson County, Ohio.

35. Ibid., 54: mention of raid by Confederate calvary from "The Decline of Roads," *Columbus Dispatch Magazine*, 4/3/1960.

36. Eric Ledell Smith, "The Pittsburgh Memorial," *Pittsburgh History*, vol. 80, no. 3 (Fall 1997): 106–7.

37. Ibid.

38. Ibid., 106–11.

39. Alexis de Tocqueville, *Democracy in America* (New York: Knopf, 1945), 381.

40. Woodson, *Woodson Source Book*, 66: from James P. Wickersham, *A History of Education in Pennsylvania*, (Lancaster: Inquirer Publishing Co., 1886), 254.

41. Isaac Harris, *Harris Directory* (Pittsburgh: Privately printed, 1857).

42. Leland D. Baldwin, *Pittsburgh: The Story of a City, 1750–1865* (Pittsburgh: University of Pittsburgh Press, 1937), 190: boat production; and Hadley, *Only in Pittsburgh*, 226: "Pittsburgh is gloomy."

43. Wright, *Encyclopedia of African Methodism*, 455; Nancy C. Curtis, *Black Heritage Sites: The North* (Chicago: American Library Association, 1996), 179: establishment of school at Wilberforce; E. Franklin Frazier, *The Free Negro Family: A Study of Family Origins Before the Civil War* (New York: Arno Press, 1968), 8: population growth.

44. Wright, *Encyclopedia of African Methodism*, 455.

45. Woodson, *Woodson Source Book*, 147: biographical information on Sarah Jane Woodson.

46. Ibid., 86: from Bishop Daniel A. Payne, *Recollections of Seventy Years* (New York: Arno Press, 1888), 150.

47. Hadley, *Only in Pittsburgh*, 152.

48. Rae Alexander-Minter, "The Tanner Family: A Grand Niece's Chronicle," in *Henry Ossawa Tanner* (Philadelphia: Philadelphia Art Museum, 1991), 23–26.

49. Woodson, *Woodson Source Book*, 141–42: deed of sale, Thomas Woodson to Jane E. Woodson, 10/14/1875.

50. Conversation between Thomas Woodson and Minerva Woodson as per interview with General John King, March 15, 1999.

Granville Sharp Woodson

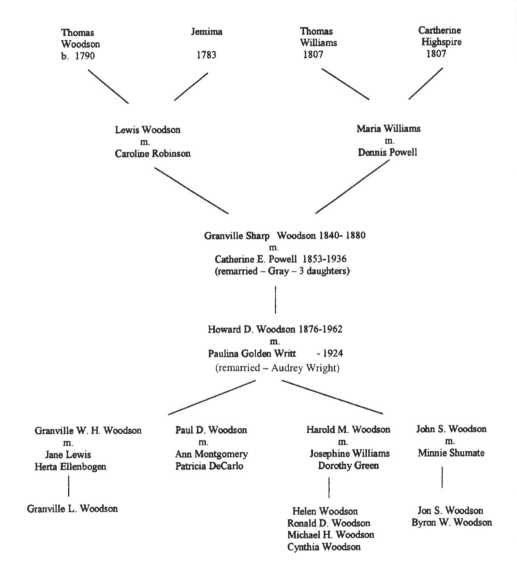

Thomas Woodson b. 1790 — Jemima 1783 — Thomas Williams 1807 — Cartherine Highspire 1807

Lewis Woodson m. Caroline Robinson — Maria Williams m. Dennis Powell

Granville Sharp Woodson 1840-1880
m.
Catherine E. Powell 1853-1936
(remarried – Gray – 3 daughters)

Howard D. Woodson 1876-1962
m.
Paulina Golden Writt – 1924
(remarried – Audrey Wright)

Granville W. H. Woodson
m.
Jane Lewis
Herta Ellenbogen

Granville L. Woodson

Paul D. Woodson
m.
Ann Montgomery
Patricia DeCarlo

Harold M. Woodson
m.
Josephine Williams
Dorothy Green

Helen Woodson
Ronald D. Woodson
Michael H. Woodson
Cynthia Woodson

John S. Woodson
m.
Minnie Shumate

Jon S. Woodson
Byron W. Woodson

CHAPTER SEVEN

The Color Line

We shall never have a science of history until we have in our colleges men who regard the truth as more important than the defense of the white race.

—W.E.B. Du Bois[1]

When the United States Congress chose a route for the National Road that passed through the river town of Wheeling, the development of western Pennsylvania and Pittsburgh's claim to be "The Gateway to the West" were threatened. Pittsburgh's position, however, was reinforced by completion of the Pennsylvania Canal system in 1934, a project largely financed by the Commonwealth of Pennsylvania, which attempted to mimic the very successful Erie Canal in New York State. The system utilized railway lines from Philadelphia to the Susquehanna River, river and canal to Hollidaysburg, the "Old" Portage Railroad over the Allegheny Mountains, and, starting in the town of Johnstown, a combination of the Comemaugh River and canals onward to Pittsburgh.[2]

Railroad construction along the nearly flat Erie Canal route posed few challenges, but the Allegheny Mountains presented a formidable obstacle to Pennsylvanians. The "Old" Portage Railroad was not a real railroad, but an engineering marvel that employed steam engines to pull cars by cable up inclines that were too steep for a steam locomotive. Cargo and passengers had to be transshipped. A telegraph line was strung across the mountains in 1846, another precursor to the real challenge.

In 1847 Philadelphia and other towns within Philadelphia County subscribed to stock in the Pennsylvania Railroad in the amount of $4 million, enabling a daring venture. The California Gold Rush of 1849 turned enthusiasm for westward migration into an absolute frenzy. Over the next few years the previously uninhabited mountains between Hollidaysburg and Johnstown would test the mettle of financiers, civil engineers, laborers, and politicians. The Commonwealth of Pennsylvania funded the construction of the "New" Portage Railroad, which was a real railroad, and the Pennsylvania Railroad used it to begin all-rail service from Philadelphia to Pittsburgh on December 10, 1852.[3]

The Pennsylvania Railroad sought a faster route, control of the entire line, and enormous profits, and thus built a rail line parallel to the Portage line, tunneling through the mountain range at a cost of $450,000. The Summit Tunnel, 3,612 feet in length and situated 202 feet below the top of the mountain, was an unparalleled achievement in terms of organization, engineering, technology, and finance. The Portage line was abandoned. Beginning in February 1854, the Pennsylvania Railroad served the entire distance from Philadelphia to Pittsburgh with its own trains in as little as thirteen hours, a trip that took three or four weeks only forty years before then. This link in part underpinned the industrial explosion that occurred in Pittsburgh in the late nineteenth century. Pittsburgh became the center of the steel industry, and its glassmakers continued to innovate and dominate. Workers were attracted from the East Coast and from Europe. In time the union movement developed, as well as other opportunities for social and political change.[4]

As mentioned in Chapter Six, Martin Delany was one of the workers drawn to the Pennsylvania Canal system in search of employment. The makeup of the population of Hollidaysburg, as recorded in the U.S. Census, reflects the enlistment of African Americans in local construction efforts:

Year	White population	Black population
1820	78	—0—
1830	136	—0—
1840	1,804	89
1850	2,290	130
1860	2,331	120

Growth in Hollidaysburg stagnated when the Pennsylvania Railroad bypassed the town. Some blacks moved westward, as only whites could secure the stable employment offered in nearby Altoona by the Pennsylvania Railroad Company. Daniel Hale Williams, the pioneer of open-heart surgery, was born in Hollidaysburg in its heyday. His father, also named Daniel Williams, who worked on the Pennsylvania Canal system for over twenty-five years, met Martin Delany when both worked in Mifflin County, Pennsylvania, in 1830. After Daniel Hale Williams moved on to Chicago, he achieved Martin Delany's long-held dream, that of becoming a doctor.

The Civil War had little effect on the daily lives of the Woodsons of Pittsburgh. The Reverend Lewis Woodson helped to reopen the college at Wilberforce; other family members concentrated on expanding the family's financial base in and beyond the barber business. In 1864, Caroline's name appeared in a business context for the first time. She was listed as a bonnet cleaner located at 15 Fourth Street in downtown Pittsburgh. Five Woodson businesses were listed in the city directory that year; business was good. The customer base expanded as African Americans who had fled to Canada as a result of the Fugitive Slave Act of 1850 returned, and as emancipated southerners began to trickle north.[5]

In 1868, the city directory mentioned six Woodson businesses. Three of the names were new to the roster: James, Granville, and Jemima Woodson, all children of Lewis and Caroline. James was a handsome young man with a beautiful wife, the former Anna Bird Moles of Baltimore. Granville Sharp Woodson, the youngest son, was possibly the most ambitious; when his name first appeared in the business directory, two barbershop locations were attributed to him. Granville had been named for a British abolitionist, Granville Sharp. Granville married Catherine Elizabeth Powell, whose father had taken his family to Haiti in 1863 to await the outcome of the Civil War and returned to Pittsburgh in 1869. Jemima, whose position was near the middle of the brood, operated a millinery shop; she never married.[6]

CELEBRATION

With the crash of drumsticks onto the tight skin of snare drums, the blare of trumpets, and the slow rhythmic oompah of the tuba, it was hard for the celebrants to stand still. Music of the Great Western Band instilled the urge to march, dance, or just move through the crowd to greet friends and neighbors. The procession gathered at Water Street in downtown Pittsburgh on Tuesday, April 26, 1870, to celebrate the Fifteenth Amendment to the Constitution of the United States. Chief Marshall of the Parade George D. Ware welcomed participants. He acknowledged the secretaries who volunteered to help publicize the event, including Lewis Frederick Woodson. After a dozen speakers praised the amendment, the parade began. Aides, including Granville S. Woodson, T. R. Roach, and five others, directed the procession. The parade traveled around the downtown area, then ventured across the Seventh Street Bridge to the North Side, then still called Allegheny City. It returned downtown via a suspension bridge and ended at Wood and Liberty Streets, near one of the Woodson barbershops. The parade typified the times; Americans were thankful for a great many things and frequently indulged in celebration.[7]

The Fifteenth Amendment reads in part, "The right of citizens of the United States to vote shall not be denied or abridged by the United States or by any State on account of race, color, or previous condition of servitude." With this and the Thirteenth and Fourteenth Amendments, the party of Lincoln, the Republican party, made equal rights of African Americans part of the law. The Thirteenth Amendment abolished slavery, and the Fifteenth granted the right to vote to all males (it did not mention women). During Ulysses S. Grant's administration, the law was actually enforced by federal troops garrisoned in the South. In 1877 Grant's successor, President Rutherford B. Hayes, stepped back from enforcing the Constitution by restricting troops to military camps and allowing southern politicians to deny the right to vote and other rights to blacks. Blacks looked to the rule of law as their salvation, thereby celebrating laws the federal government would soon ignore.[8]

Granville Woodson held onto the large intricately designed poster that was hung in his barbershop to advertise the parade. When another celebration was organized in 1873, he hung its announcement in the barbershop too. A great deal of social contact took place in barbershops; they were excellent places to advertise local events. The poster read, "Fellow citizens of Western Pennsylvania we invite you as brothers and companions in the long bitter years of servitude, which you and our ancestors have passed, to gather once more around your watchfires of Liberty." On July 24, a Jubilee of Freedom was held in Friendship Grove in Pittsburgh. Chief marshall of the day Harrison Taylor spoke. Others, including Granville Woodson, also addressed the crowd but were limited to fifteen minutes each.[9]

The celebration in 1873 was more solemn in tone than the 1870 commemoration, as it was becoming clear that not all of the expectations spawned by Emancipation and the three new constitutional amendments would be realized. Lives of African Americans in the South were still tied to the economies of cotton and tobacco. Lynching and intimidation underpinned a caste system that still limited economic opportunity. While Jim Crow practices in northern cities were not as perniciously enforced, northern blacks were nevertheless degraded. Despite these obstacles, and as their only alternative, blacks in the North and South established businesses, schools, churches, and social organizations. Frederick Douglass, Booker T. Washington, and others led the emerging "nation within a nation," realizing the vision Lewis Woodson had projected in his Augustine letters forty years earlier.

Lewis Woodson's religious sensibility and his penchant for educational achievement were passed on to younger generations. George Frederick Woodson, a son of Lewis Frederick and Nancy Tanner Woodson and a grandson of Lewis and Caroline, attended Pittsburgh's Central High School, Wilberforce University, and later Drew University in Iowa. Emma Woodson, one of the younger daughters of Lewis and Caroline, became an administrator at Avery College in Pittsburgh, a position she assumed when George B. Vashon, a graduate of Oberlin College, became principal at Avery.[10]

Avery College, located in Pittsburgh, was founded in 1849 as the Allegheny Institute and Mission Church. Its benefactor was Charles Avery, a wealthy white businessman. He had made his fortune by successfully pursuing a number of ventures and reinvesting his profits. He sold patent drugs and potions and later cotton. Avery also invested fortuitously in copper mining in Minnesota. A devout Methodist, he began a pattern of philanthropy. Charles Avery died childless in 1858, leaving a fortune of $800,000 (at a time when the average house cost about $1,000). After providing generously for his wife, the bulk of his fortune was designated to assist disenfranchised African Americans. The largest sum was targeted for resettlement of African Americans on the West Coast of Africa. A nearly equal sum was used to further the education of African Americans in the United States and Canada. Specific grants were made to Avery and Oberlin Colleges. The Avery Trust funded school operations, school expansion, and new school construction both before and after the Civil War. Wilberforce University was another Avery recipient. Avery College educated members of the Woodson family and their neighbors, but it ultimately failed to grow in stature, as no other great benefactors were attracted. Its leadership lacked inspiration and vision. At the turn of the century, Avery College acquired a hospital and nursing school component; but again failing to attract strong leadership, it closed in 1911.[11]

Despite the lack of specific documentation, it is certain that Charles Avery and Lewis Woodson crossed paths. Though Avery supported African American immigration to Africa, he also generously supported Oberlin College, a predominantly white school that admitted blacks. Avery was not a patronizing segregationist, but rather a true humanitarian, interested in tangible solutions to the pervasive dilemmas of his time. Had he and Lewis Woodson been able to communicate as brothers of the same mission, each would have been astounded at the harmony of their ideas.

VANISHING CONNECTIONS TO THE PAST

Lewis Woodson died in January 1878 at his home at 15 Fourth Avenue. His death was noted in all the Pittsburgh newspapers then in print. The Pittsburgh *Commercial Gazette*'s obituary made clear reference to Lewis Woodson's ties to the Underground Railroad, which would have gone unrecorded had he died before the Civil War ended. Granville was the executor of his father's estate.[12]

Nearly one hundred years later, historian Floyd Miller called Lewis Woodson "the first [African American] to articulate a genuine nationalist-emigrationist creed and place it in a coherent ideological framework" and labeled him a contender for the title of "Father of Black Nationalism," a title to which Martin Delany also had some claim. Miller discovered that Woodson was Delany's teacher and mentor, identified Woodson as the real "Augustine," and surveyed the magnitude of his achievements. Certainly recognition should be assigned to both of these great men. The contributions of those who led the free black community in the United States in the 1820s, 1830s, and 1840s have been largely overlooked by historians. Men like the Reverend Morris Brown and the Reverend Lewis Woodson took enormous risks and sometimes had to act in secret or assume aliases (and sometimes, as in Brown's case, had to run for their lives). Black leaders like Martin Delany and Frederick Douglass emerged only a few years later, but in a quite different era. When they met with U.S. presidents, the first blacks to do so, their stature was recognized. Yet Delany and Douglass certainly knew whose footsteps they followed.[13]

Lewis Woodson made an impact far beyond his writings. His talent and drive were evident early in life. He did not owe his accomplishments in the field of education to white paternalism. In that respect he presented African Americans with a model for self-reliance, never despairing or accepting mediocrity as an alternative. Yet the events surrounding the writing of the Pittsburgh Memorial and the founding of Wilberforce University strongly suggest that Woodson maintained constructive relationships with some whites. Those relationships were nurtured with some measure of secrecy, and the identities of Lewis Woodson's white collaborators have certainly been lost. He actualized a tremendous passion for justice and equality. He was, assuredly, a wonderful father. He firmly believed in the rights of all, at a time when politicians regularly compromised them. Separatism was for Lewis Woodson not a preferred path but a necessity for survival.

In 1879, only a year after the death of his accomplished son, Thomas Woodson died in Jackson County, Ohio, at the grand old age of eighty-nine. His grandson the Reverend Thomas Wesley Woodson was executor of the estate. Thomas had previously disposed of his land, and remaining assets were divided among the family.[14]

Thomas Woodson's life is largely unimaginable. In a word, it was triumphant, but any single word ignores its complexities, its contradictions, and its entanglement in America's greatest dilemma. As a boy, Tom could not have appreciated his special circumstances. Did his banishment initially cause great despair? Did he place banishment behind him by force of inner strength, or did the prospect of freedom and the appeal of westward movement leave little time for contemplation of his loss? Was his attraction to Jemima, a woman much darker than he in complexion, an act of defiance? Was the seamless bond between Thomas and Jemima Woodson a carnal attraction or a mutual commitment to the elevation of an imperiled race? Or was it both? Did Thomas and Jemima largely escape the harshness racial prejudice, or did they lose two sons because of their work on the Underground Railroad? How did a life marred by family separation at a tender age become filled with the love of so many wonderful children, in-laws, and neighbors? What allowed this legacy of achievement and fulfillment to prevail?

With the deaths of Thomas and Lewis Woodson, connection to earlier times was broken. The break was dramatically and unexpectedly compounded in at least one family line when in 1880, Granville Woodson died at the age of forty. His father, grandfather, and great-grandfather had lived long lives, but his was cut short. Granville left a wife, Catherine, and one son, Howard Dilworth Woodson, who was then four years old. Granville's brother-in-law, Lemuel Googins, was the executor of his estate. Googins had married Granville's sister, Harriett. He managed property Granville Woodson owned, including five houses on Roberts Street in the Hill District. The rent collected supported Catherine and her son and paid for Howard's education.[15]

With Granville's death the wellspring of verbal links to the past was certainly lost. Only that which he and his father had impressed upon his wife could then be relayed to Granville's only child. Only if they had informed her of the ownership of various papers that the Reverend Lewis Woodson left to his children could she then tell her son where to look when he came to age to learn of his heritage.

Catherine soon remarried. Her husband, Jesse Grey, was the offspring of a wealthy white businessman and his African American mistress. This particular robber baron was born in the British Isles and was a friend of Andrew Carnegie. Howard Woodson grew to manhood in the Hill District home of Jesse Grey. Catherine and Jesse Grey produced three daughters.

Like his older Woodson cousins, Howard Woodson attended Pittsburgh's Central High School. The building in use when Howard attended was near his home in the Hill District and was the first to be built as a high school in Pittsburgh. Central High School started in 1855 in a rented space on Smithfield Street near the current location of Kauffman's Department Store. The first class consisted of thirty-four boys and girls. In 1868, the school moved with 170 students to larger accommodations. The new space quickly became insufficient, as enrollment more than doubled, to 370 students. Education became a prerequisite for meaningful employment during this time, when a growing number of middle class families began to frown upon child labor. In September 1869, construction of a new building commenced with considerable fanfare. The new school, built for 600 students, contained an auditorium with an ample stage, a library, special rooms for chemistry and physics, office space, and fourteen classrooms. Howard Woodson entered the school in 1892.[16]

Students of all ethnic backgrounds attended the school. Aside from the Anglo-Saxon and Irish majority, others were sons and daughters of Italian, Slavic, and Jewish immigrants who had recently arrived in America. Only a few African Americans were students there. Most teenagers in Pittsburgh continued to work in factories; high school was a mark of privilege. Howard Woodson maneuvered through the tensions and joys of adolescence, focusing on a good education. He "showed ability in mathematics, and won the respect of both students and faculty," according to *The Colored American Magazine* and graduated with high honors.[17]

A NEW CENTURY

In 1897, Howard entered the Western University of Pennsylvania, now known as the University of Pittsburgh. The school had been established in 1787 as the Pittsburgh Academy. Howard set his sights on a degree in civil engineering. America enjoyed a booming economy at the end of the nineteenth century. Absorbing the optimism of the era, he prepared for a successful and challenging career by obtaining skills that were in great demand. The industrial might of the nation was not evident in every corner of the American landscape, but it was very apparent in Pittsburgh. Steel mills belching gray clouds of smoke and the fancy horse-drawn carriages carrying industrialists to the mansions of Shadyside and Sewickley symbolized America's ingenuity, competitive spirit, and rapid growth.[18]

The university, then located in Allegheny City (now called the North Side), grew rapidly. It benefited from very able leadership in the person of Chancellor William Jacob Holland, Ph.D., Sc.D., D.D., LL.D. During Holland's ten-year tenure, a medical school, a school of dentistry, and a law school were added. Holland also greatly expanded graduate studies. The enrollment grew from 95 students to 691; this growth occurred before the school acquired the more attractive and convenient campus it now occupies.[19]

Chancellor Holland accepted and instituted coeducation. He admitted sisters Stella Mathilda Stein and Margaret Lydia Stein, who graduated in 1898. Their graduation reflected the emerging struggle for gender equality. At the end of the nineteenth century, women had not yet gained the right to vote, but they had managed to raise their status through the temperance movement by declaring superiority over a despised class, alcoholic men. They also proclaimed women's education as a necessity for a healthy society. Howard was the second African American to graduate from the university. Later in life he maintained a healthy affection not only for the city of his birth but for the university. There can be no doubt that he encountered some unpleasantness there, but on balance it served him well.[20]

After graduating, Howard Woodson traveled for a few months in the South and West. Upon his return in August 1900, he accepted a well-paid position at the Pittsburgh Plate Glass Company, one of Pittsburgh's premier enterprises. He then worked for the Pittsburgh Coal Company as an assistant engineer and transitman. Howard's ambitious restlessness and the fact that he worked only until each construction job was finished, meant that he changed jobs often. In 1904, he secured a larger paycheck at Orient Coal & Coke Company in Uniontown, Pennsylvania, and the next year he worked as a draftsman for Cambria Steel Company in Johnstown. In 1905, he began work as a structural draftsman for the American Bridge Company in Chicago.[21]

Howard Woodson changed jobs yet again in Chicago, taking a position with Daniel H. Burnham & Company, where he earned a yearly salary of $1,664 as a structural engineer. After the Great Chicago Fire in 1871, real estate developers looked to maximize the value of downtown property by building taller buildings. Within a few years, the sons of Elisha Otis created the hydraulic elevator, and Daniel Burnham and John Root designed the first all-steel skeleton, nine stories tall, for the second Rand McNally Building, which was completed in Chicago in 1890.

Howard Woodson went to work for Daniel H. Burnham & Company

after the firm won the contract to design the structural steel components for the railroad station planned for Washington, D.C. Howard designed the roof structure. Union Station is an engineering marvel and a beautiful expression of American verve and confidence. Woodson's residence in Chicago was propitious in several ways. He was able to work with the most talented men in his field and was challenged with one of the most difficult and conspicuous projects of his time.[22]

By then well established and well connected within his profession, Howard Woodson married Paulina Golden Writt of the Homewood section of Pittsburgh. Paulina, one of the five children of John and Susan Writt, was raised in a large house on Susquehanna Avenue. Her father was a caterer. The origins of the Writt family are not known, but they intermarried with families who had lived in Pittsburgh for generations.

REACHING THE GOAL

Howard moved to Washington, D.C., in 1907, securing a position with the Treasury Department to design government buildings. As the need for such services grew, Woodson's job evolved into that of procuring engineering and architectural services from private firms. His initial workplace was in the Treasury Building, immediately east of the White House. At the time very few African Americans held professional jobs in the federal government. Civil Service regulations gave Woodson a measure of protection unavailable in private industry. Though co-workers occasionally tried to dislodge him from his employment and on one occasion made a huge fuss over his use of the men's room, Howard Woodson, small in frame but large in resolve, stood his ground. Jesse Grey, his stepfather, maintained connections with powerful Pittsburgh scions who looked out for Woodson's interests when asked to do so.

Howard Dilworth Woodson's first child, Granville Writt Howard Woodson, was born in 1909. Howard and Paulina used all of the family names they could. (The use of more than four names was considered gauche.) The second son, Paul Dilworth Woodson, arrived two years later. Paul is, of course, the masculine form of Paulina. In naming the first two children, all of the parents' names were used except for Paulina's middle name. Howard's father's name, Granville, was added for good measure.

The proud father turned his attention to making Washington a permanent home. He bought land in a remote corner of the city, Far Northeast Washington. This land, near the top of a steep hill, afforded a modest view of a narrow valley formed by Watts Branch, a creek that empties into the Anacostia River. Howard bought the land cheap, as no city water service was available at the site. In 1914, he began building houses. Woodson placed his home on the crest of the steepest part of the hill. He built five other houses at the same time, selling them for a profit.

Howard faced the same dilemma Thomas Jefferson faced at the top of Monticello. He designed an oversized well and placed a large water tank in the attic of his house to supply water for the six houses he constructed. In 1923, city water service finally reached the site. A portion of the hilltop was leveled to install the service more easily. Howard designed and developed five additional houses farther down the hillside and elsewhere in the neighborhood between 1915 and 1918. At the same time he continued to work for the federal government.

Howard Woodson bought his first automobile, an Essex touring car, in 1922. The Essex had no permanent windows except the windshield. When rain threatened, the family fastened "windows" made of a semi-clear plastic-like material to the doors. They traveled to Pittsburgh in the Essex each year to visit relatives and to keep tabs on the Roberts Street rental houses Howard had inherited from his father.

Paulina eventually bore five more children, but three of them died as infants. Harold Merriman Woodson, born in 1916, and John Stanton Woodson, born in 1918, survived. Paulina was a housewife, attending to her children's needs and caring for her well-appointed home. The family raised chickens in the backyard, as did many of their neighbors. When not consumed by household tasks, Paulina played piano; she was a fine musician.

Paulina Golden Writt Woodson died in 1924. Her oldest son, Granville, was then fifteen, and the youngest, John, was six. Howard Woodson went on without his beloved wife. Granville soon went off to college; John helped out by regularly shopping for groceries.

A 1925 Studebaker served as the next family car. The Studebaker was an enormous piece of machinery and sported the newest feature in the automobile industry, a radiator, placed in the floor behind the front seat. In 1926 Granville entered the University of Pittsburgh, his father's alma mater. Harold and John spent parts of a couple of summers with their mother's sister, Emma Writt Richards. The Richardses had two boys, Writt, the oldest, and Robert, who was John's age. Harold and John also visited their grandmother's house on Camp Street in the Hill District.

Howard's mother, Catherine, was self-assured and resolute. She was an attractive woman with a serene appearance but was not easily humored. Her grandchildren remembered her frequent comments about white ethnics embodying a measure of resentment or hostility, most directed toward the Irish.

Ever since the Irish began to immigrate to America in large numbers in the 1840s, relations between the African Americans and the Irish were filled with stress. Jobs were the central point of contention. During the Potato Famine of the 1840s, the Irish came to America hungry, illiterate, and willing to work the most menial jobs. Over time Irish immigrants managed to push African Americans out of many fields of employment. Many of the nineteenth-century urban riots in Philadelphia, Pittsburgh, and other cities were the result of Irish and African American tensions. The most deadly riot in American history occurred in New York in 1863, when Irishmen resisted being drafted into the Union Army during the Civil War. The freedom of African American slaves was understandably not a high priority for them. Over 1,000 people were killed in the New York riots.

Catherine Grey knew that most immigrants wanted, more than anything, to discard their ethnicity to become Americans. She resented their ability to make the transition. When she shopped for groceries, she often asked the clerk for items, giving ethnic-oriented descriptions. "I'll have some Irish potatoes," she would say, knowing well that the potatoes had never crossed the Atlantic Ocean. Or "Is that Polish sausage?" The clerks were probably annoyed, but nevertheless Catherine seemed to feel she was evening the score.[23]

Catherine Powell Woodson Grey traveled to Washington in 1928 to visit her son and grandsons, staying a few weeks. During this time she told Harold and John the family oral history. Standing on the small wood-plank back porch, she told the boys that Lewis Woodson, their great-grandfather, was an industrious, serious, and successful man, highly respected in Pittsburgh in his time. She told them that Lewis' father, Thomas Woodson, was a prosperous Ohio farmer and the son of President Thomas Jefferson. Catherine said that she heard the history and legacy of Thomas Woodson from Lewis Woodson; her pride in association with him was evident. She must have been equally proud of her son.

Catherine Grey was able to trace her own maternal grandfather's family to Joseph Williams, who was born in 1760. She was a cousin of Dr. Daniel Hale Williams, who performed the first open-heart surgery. She was immensely proud of these histories and connections. She no doubt found strength in them and considered the oral histories she passed on to her grandchildren the most valuable gift she could impart.

Howard Woodson had invested some of his savings in the stock market, so the crash of October 1929 was not fondly remembered in the Woodson household. All of his money was not in the stock market, however, so he was able to take advantage when an attractive piece of real estate in his neighborhood, a corner lot at Deane Avenue (now Nannie Burroughs Avenue) and 49th Street, became available in 1930. Within a few years he built a gasoline station at the busy intersection. After a few years of nonfamily management, Paul, then twenty-six years old, began to operate the enterprise.

Howard bought another Studebaker in 1930. Paul and Harold drove the car to Pittsburgh in 1936 to vote in the presidential election, since residents of the nation's capital could not vote for president. The next year Harold wrecked the Studebaker, leaving his father without an automobile for a while.

A New Deal For Real

President Franklin Roosevelt's New Deal made the elimination of slums and the creation of decent, affordable housing federal government mandates. Much of the land housing authorities and redevelopment agencies bought, using powers of eminent domain, was occupied by African Americans. Whole communities were destroyed, and the fabric of African American urban life was unsettled by the process. Small businesses were closed and their clientele displaced. The Pittsburgh Housing Authority bought the five houses Howard Woodson owned on Roberts Avenue, and the Pittsburgh Redevelopment Authority bought the Bethel A.M.E. Church on Wylie Avenue. The buildings were certainly not slums, but the governmental agencies nevertheless demolished them.

Public housing was constructed on the Roberts Avenue site. The church relocated to nearby Webster Street. Despite promises to redevelop the Hill District, much of the vacant land created by government-funded demolition was not built on for forty years. During those years no taxes were collected on the land. Many of the high-rise housing projects built in the 1950s throughout the nation were torn down after being occupied for only three decades. After fifty years of government intervention in urban neighborhoods, the benefits were difficult to discern, and the experience of the Hill District is arguably the nation's worse example.

From the time Howard Woodson completed the houses on Fitch Place, he began a relentless advocacy for improved conditions in his Far Northeast Washington neighborhood. Early on, he became secretary of the Northeast Boundary Civic Association. Though Howard Woodson never knew his grandfather Lewis, his penchant for public service seemed to emulate his grandfather's drive. Howard even became the secretary of organizations he joined, much like his grandfather.

Washington was governed by three commissioners, appointed by politicians; residents did not enjoy democratic government. Washingtonians voiced their concerns through civic associations. Woodson was not only active in his local association but was a leader of the Federation of Civic Associations, as its first vice president and later as the chairman of its Public Works Committee. Howard knew all of the commissioners of the District of Columbia and all the House and Senate District Committee members as well. He maintained a special friendship with Senator Everett Dirksen, a powerful Republican from Illinois. On two occasions Howard Woodson traveled back to Chicago to vote.

Howard pushed for construction of schools to meet the needs of the rapidly growing population of his neighborhood. He demanded increased police protection, specifically requesting the assignment of African American police, while taking care not to denigrate white policemen. He requested street lighting and tree planting. As an engineer, he thoughtfully assessed the need for road construction and flood control. Howard and his associates in the Federation of Civic Associations knew the District of Columbia budget as well as or better than the commissioners.

Washingtonians did not have the voting right, and Howard Woodson felt disenfranchised; as a result he often wrote editorials for the local daily newspapers, usually under the name Howard Dilworth, using his middle name as his surname. As a federal employee he needed the sheild of an alias when criticizing either the federal or local government. His grandfather, the Reverend Lewis Woodson, had used the pen name Augustine between 1837 and 1841. Thomas Woodson used the alias Tom Corbin, possibly as an outgrowth of Underground Railroad work. Blacks had not secured the freedoms enjoyed by others; consequently generation upon generation of Woodsons were obliged to find in creative ways to keep the fire burning.

After retiring from the federal government, Howard continued his civic roles. He took on many private design contracts as a structural engineer. As patriarch of the burgeoning Woodson family in Washington, he spent time with his five grandsons and two granddaughters. He bought his last automobile, a sleek four-door Packard, when he was sixty-five years of age.

Jesse Grey died in 1932. Catherine lived with her children during the balance of her life. She lived in Washington with Howard from 1933 to 1935. With the onset of senility, residence with a daughter in Ohio became the better choice. She died in Ohio in 1936, fifty-six years after the death of her first husband, Granville Sharp Woodson.

Howard Woodson's sons attended segregated public high schools in Washington. Granville and John attended the venerable Dunbar High, an academic school. Paul and Harold attended Armstrong, which emphasized manual trades. Granville and John, the oldest and youngest, respectively, were the tallest, 5' 11" in height. Paul and Harold grew to 5' 9" like their father. The boys were dark in complexion, with the exception of John, who has a medium brown complexion. All of them were more muscular than their father; all were strikingly handsome.

Harold and John put their youthful energies to work creating a tennis court on the west side of the Fitch Place house. Friends joined the endeavor, including Odell and Wendell Shumate, the brothers of John's girlfriend, Minnie. When Howard saw that the boys were serious, he engaged a local man who sold vegetables from a horse-drawn cart. A scoop was attached to the horse by a harness to remove dirt, leveling part of the hill. The brothers worked on the project intermittently, so months passed before the tennis court was finished. It proved to be very popular and received much use.

After receiving a degree in civil engineering from the University of Pittsburgh, Granville worked for the Department of Interior, designing improvements and managing construction projects. President Roosevelt formed the Civilian Conservation Corps (CCC) in order to relieve unemployment created by the Great Depression. In 1935, 500,000 young unmarried men were placed in camps to build roads and make other improvements all over the nation. Often, Department of Interior personnel designed projects which were then built by the CCC. Granville designed new roadways and the placement of monuments and plaques for the Gettysburg battlefield to accommodate increased tourism. He worked at other Pennsylvania sites, including the Pymatuning Reservoir in the northern portion of the state. Granville married Jane Lewis of Pittsburgh, whose father was publisher of the the *Pittsburgh Courier*, at the time among the most notable of the nation's African American newspapers.

The Department of Interior moved Granville to Tuskegee, Alabama, in 1940 to prepare the site for construction of an airfield. African American pilots were trained there in preparation for action in World War II. He worked with the notable African American architect Hilliard Robinson on the airfield project. Granville entered the army but suffered from asthma and was relieved of military duty soon after joining. He worked for the Budd Company in Philadelphia during part of the war, then went to Liberia in 1943 to assist with the construction of an airport there called Roberts Field. Short-range fighter planes were ferried to the North African front via South America and Roberts Field. They lacked the range needed for a more northerly crossing of the Atlantic Ocean. Roberts Field was built to facilitate that traffic.

Howard Woodson married again in 1943. It was the second marriage for Audrey Wright also. Howard expanded the rose garden and the western end of his tiered lawn. Audrey convinced him to dispense with the tennis court, declaring that she had not been engaged to "run a country club." The posts that held the net were uprooted, and the area was seeded with grass. The "boys" were all grown by then and off to various spots around the world.

In 1947, Granville returned to Washington, D.C., where he planned school construction for the D.C. Public School System. He was enticed back to Liberia in the 1950s, taking his son Granville, as his marriage by then had fallen apart. Draining swamps to rid the nation of malaria was one of his primary duties. Unlike many African American college graduates of his generation, Granville actually practiced the profession for which he was trained. Thousands of college-educated blacks worked as letter carriers or bus drivers until segregationist practices eased further. Shortly after his final return from Liberia, Granville married a German woman, Herta Ellenbogen.

Paul Woodson briefly attended St. Augustine College, a historically black college in the South, then worked as a carpenter, building houses in Highland Beach, Maryland, a resort community. He operated his father's service station for a while, then entered the Army Air Force. Paul was based at Tuskegee in Alabama, but was trained to maintain engines at the Pratt and Whitney factory near Buffalo, New York.

After the war, Paul married a well-known nightclub owner, Ann Montgomery, who was fifteen years his senior. He became acquainted with many popular entertainers of the day, such as Lena Horne and Pearl Bailey, as well as prizefighter Joe Louis, whose manager settled in Buffalo with more than his rightful share of Joe's money. Paul co-managed the business, a combination of nightclub, lounge, and hotel, in central Buffalo. The joint was jumping; the Little Harlem Hotel was a center for entertainment, political deal-making, and illegal lottery operations. Paul and Ann, who remained childless, lived ostentatiously, but not beyond their means.

Harold Woodson, who married early in life and started a family, did not attend college. He joined the Marines in 1944. Though he worked as a mail clerk, he came closer to combat than his brothers. His African American unit was assigned to the South Pacific, first landing on Tinian, in the Mariana Islands, 1,000 miles east of the Philippines. The adjacent island, Saipan, was first taken after fierce combat claimed the lives of 27,000 Japanese and 3,000 Americans. Americans shelled Tinian heavily from Saipan before landing there. Harold's unit landed on Tinian in early August after the primary battle was over, but Japanese soldiers had hidden themselves. Three months of dangerous hide-and-seek maneuvers were necessary to ferret out Japanese who fought to the death and would not surrender.[24]

Harold landed on Iwo Jima, a small island much closer to Japan than Tinian, three days after the initial beach invasion there. The American high command again faced a daunting prospect. The Americans needed to dislodge two Japanese airfields on Iwo Jima. The Japanese fortified the island with 21,000 troops, strengthened by a network of trenches, tunnels, and pillboxes. The Japanese command had no intention of rescuing their troops and expected them to fight to the death. The Marines completed their famous assault to gain the high ground at the top of Mt. Suribachi after five days of fierce combat, but still the fight continued. During the next four weeks and some of the bloodiest fighting of World War II, Americans took 200 Japanese prisoners. Over 20,000 Japanese fought to the death. The Marines suffered 6,800 deaths and 18,000 men wounded. The island was only eight square miles in size; there was no escape from that hell on earth once it was entered. Harold subsequently went on to duty in China before returning to the United States.[25]

At home in Washington, D.C., Harold Woodson worked for the navy as a civilian. He was a printer. After his first wife died, he remarried and raised five children. Golf and jazz were his avocations. Uncle Harold never talked about what he saw on Iwo Jima when he returned home. It's a missing piece of family lore that I wish we had.

NOTES

1. Quoted in Annette Gordon-Reed, *Thomas Jefferson and Sally Hemings: An American Controversy* (Charlottesville: University Press of Virginia, 1997), 105.

2. Leland D. Baldwin, *Pittsburgh: The Story of a City, 1750–1865* (Pittsburgh: University of Pittsburgh Press, 1937), 192–93.

3. William Bender Wilson, *History of the Pennsylvania Railroad*, vol. 1 (Philadelphia: The Pennsylvania Railroad Co., 1895), 157.

4. Ibid., 159: the Summit Tunnel.

5. Isaac Harris, *Harris' Directory* (Pittsburgh: Privately printed, 1864).

6. Minnie S. Woodson, *Woodson Source Book* (Washington, D.C.: Privately printed, 1984), 163: biographical data on James Woodson.

7. Posters advertising the celebrations are in the collection of John S. Woodson, grandson of Granville S. Woodson.

8. Constitution of the United States.

9. Collection of John S. Woodson.

10. Woodson, *Woodson Source Book*, 214: from the *Encyclopedia of the African American Church*, comp. Richard R. Wright, Jr. (Philadelphia, 1947), 309–10.

11. Charles A. Rohleder, "Pittsburgh Prepares to Honor Avery, Pioneer Philanthropist," *North Side Ledger*, December 27, 1929; James Parton, *People's Book of Biography, or the Short Lives of the Most Interesting Persons* (Hartford: A. S. Hale & Co., 1868), 122–27.

12. Woodson, *Woodson Source Book*: obituary, *Pittsburgh Commercial Gazette*, 1/15/1878.

13. Floyd Miller, *The Search for a Black Nationality* (Urbana: University of Illinois Press, 1975), 94; Woodson, *Woodson Source Book*, 88; Floyd Miller, "The Father of Black Nationalism," *Civil War History*, vol. 17, no. 4 (December 1971).

14. Woodson, *Woodson Source Book*, 40: probate of Thomas Woodson's will.

15. Ibid., 163: death of Granville Woodson.

16. Ibid., 227: education of Howard D. Woodson, from *The Colored American Magazine*; S. Trevor Hadley, *Only in Pittsburgh* (Cincinnati: Educational Publishing Resources, 1994), 91: establishment of Central High School and construction of new building.

17. Woodson, *Woodson Source Book*, 227, education of Howard D. Woodson, from *The Colored American Magazine*.

18. Ibid., 228: Howard Woodson's college education.

19. Robert C. Alberts, *Pitt: The Story of the University of Pittsburgh* (Pittsburgh: University of Pittsburgh Press, 1986), 39: Chancellor Holland.

20. Ibid., 42: coeducation.

21. Woodson, *Woodson Source Book*, 231: H. D. Woodson's resumé.

22. Ibid., 231: Howard Woodson's early employment.

23. Interviews with John S. Woodson (b. 1918) during 1999 provided significant material for this chapter.

24. James L. Stokesbury, *A Short History of World War II* (New York: William Morrow & Co., 1980), 340: Marine landing on Tinian.

25. Ibid., 368: casualties on Iwo Jima.

Thomas and Jemima Woodson, c. 1840. Photo provided to the Thomas Woodson Family collection by Jane Faithful.

Thomas Woodson and two of his sons, probably James and Thomas, c. 1845.
Photo provided to the Thomas Woodson Family collection by Mary Kearney.

The Reverend Lewis Woodson, eldest son of Thomas and Jemima. Lewis was an
institution builder, educator, minister, and abolitionist who was called the father of
Black Nationalism by historian Floyd Miller.

George Woodson, second son of Thomas and Jemima. George married Anna Lucas and became a farmer in Jackson County, Ohio. Photo provided to the Thomas Woodson Family collection by Mary Kearney.

Frances Woodson Cassell, who raised a large family in Jackson County, Ohio. Most living descendants are Midwesterners.

The Reverend John P. Woodson, second son of Thomas and Jemima. John P. became a minister in the African Methodist Episcopal Church, and his death in 1853 may have been due to his involvement with the Underground Railroad.
Photo provided to the Thomas Woodson Family collection by Mary Kearney.

Sarah Jane Woodson, youngest child of Thomas and Jemima, was one of the first African American woman to graduate from college, and the first to teach at the college level. She married an A.M.E. minister and wrote his biography after his death.
Photo provided to the Thomas Woodson Family collection by Mary Kearney.

Granville Sharp Woodson, named for the famous British abolitionist Granville Sharp, eighth child of Lewis and Caroline Woodson. He was a barber and landlord.

Catherine Powell Woodson, wife of Granville Sharp Woodson. After Granville's early death, Catherine remarried. One of her daughters from her second marriage married Robert Smalls, son and namesake of a Reconstruction-era congressman.

Oliver Highgate, son of Caroline Woodson Highgate.

Ada Highgate, daughter of Caroline Woodson Highgate. Howard D. Woodson
settled Ada's estate in Midland, Michigan.

Howard D. Woodson (front row, fourth from right, with mustache). Howard nurtured many friendships and belonged to a number of organizations.

Howard D. Woodson (back row, fifth from right) working as an engineer with the Treasury Department.

Paulina Golden Writt Woodson with sons Granville W. H. and Paul D., c. 1912.
Photo taken at the Scurlock Studio—Washington, D.C.

John S. Woodson, youngest son of Howard and Paulina Woodson. John was gregarious and became one of the finest athletes at Dunbar High School in Washington, D.C.

Cautious by nature, Minnie studied the Woodson clan before accepting membership. She found the Woodson verve and passions exciting and rewarding.

Fawn M. Brodie. Used by permission, Utah State Historical Society, all rights reserved. Photo no. 921 #11764.

Byron W. Woodson, Hanau, Germany. Byron learned to count in German, but forgot his second language when he returned to the United States.

Minnie and John Woodson on the *Queen Elizabeth 2*.

Byron and Trena Woodson with sons Byron and John at the first Woodson family reunion in Pittsburgh in 1978. Photo provided by Trena Woodson.

Kellie, John and Byron Woodson at the Jersey shore.
Photo provided by Trena Woodson.

Byron and Trena Woodson with Mary Jefferson, flanked by her sons Justin and
Colby, on the West Lawn at Monticello. Mary is an Eston Hemings Jefferson descendant. Photo provided by Trena Woodson.

Trena Woodson presents a copy of the *Woodson Source Book* to Shay Banks-Young, a Madison Hemings descendant. Photo provided by Trena Woodson.

Byron Woodson with Connye Richardson. Minnie Woodson was quite excited when she met Connye's mother, Norma Woodson McDaniel, in the hallway of an elementary school, discovering an unanticipated family link.
Photo provided by Trena Woodson.

Byron Woodson and Colonel James Truscott, president of the Monticello Association, standing below Monticello's East Portico, May 2000. Photo provided by Trena Woodson.

Jean Jefferson, Mary Jefferson, Michele Cooley-Quille, Nina Boettcher, screenwriter Tina Andrews, Shay Banks-Young, Shannon Lanier, and the next generation sitting on the tombstone of Thomas Jefferson. Photo provided by Trena Woodson.

Michele Cooley-Quille, daughter Alex, and husband Alan, May 2000. Photo provided by Trena Woodson.

Trena with grandchildren—Kellie's daughters Breeana and Daniesha, 1999.

Trena, Byron, and John Woodson attend younger son Byron's graduation from the
University of Pittsburgh, 1999. (John graduated from Pitt in 1998.)
Photo taken by Rod Parker.

Jefferson's descendants: Woodsons, Eppeses, Jeffersons, Hemingses, and Randolphs, May 1999. Photo provided by Trena Woodson.

CHAPTER EIGHT

Harvesting Strands
of the Past

When I first married into the family this was the oral history I heard. So
I said, I'm going to prove this right or wrong.
— Minnie S. Woodson, *Washington Post*, December 1, 1977

On the surface John Woodson did not seem to have an intellectual bent. He
joined the football, baseball, and swimming teams and seemed to know
everyone at Dunbar High School. Often bragging about racing the trolley
home—and winning, of course—he was boisterous and gregarious. Above
average height at 5' 11" and powerfully built, John moved with assuredness
and purpose.

When he met Minnie Shumate near the end of their high school days, he
was surprised at having overlooked her. When he first took serious notice,
he asked, "Where have you been?" They lived in the same section of Washington, D.C., though not in the same neighborhood. When he learned of the
budding friendship, Minnie's older brother, Odell, warned her that John was
a ruffian, a reputation gained from swinging on vines in the woods of Far
Notheast Washington. However, Minnie was ahead of her brother by then.
She quickly discovered that John always seemed to know more than she
expected him to and invariably saw things from intriguing points of view.
Odell revised his judgment when he was enlisted to help construct the tennis
court at John's house.

John Woodson began to visit Minnie at her modest wood-frame home in the dusty bedroom community of Deanwood, just east of the Baltimore and Ohio railroad tracks, which ran along the east bank of the Anacostia River. Often they played chess. Minnie did not really love the game, but it allowed them to spend time together without causing much trouble. John was two years older, but both were in the class of 1937. He had fallen behind, and she was ahead of students her age. Like John's father, Howard Woodson, Minnie's parents had always placed a high value on education; her father had trained in veterinary medicine. Her older brother, Lincoln Wendell Shumate, would over time acquire an M.D., LL.D., and M.B.A. After a wide-ranging career, he finally settled on psychiatry. Odell became a dentist. Minnie was impressed by Howard Woodson's civil engineering degree, since higher education among older residents of their neighborhoods was uncommon.

Advancing the budding courtship, Minnie accepted an invitation to cook a Sunday meal for the Woodsons. The meal was fine, but the rolls came out almost too hard to eat. Dad advised his family not to fret; the rolls could be put to good use knocking out a burglar should one appear. Minnie, who was about to reenter the dinning room, heard the comment, turned, and bolted onto the porch, crying her heart out. Time would never quiet John's mischief.

Upon marrying into the family in 1940, Minnie heard the oral history; the Woodson men were descended from Thomas Jefferson. Fascinated by what she heard and by their lack of interest in uncovering the full story, she promised herself to prove the history either wrong or right, but there was no time then to do so. Minnie and John's marriage was more like a reservation, as they did not immediately live together. They were still college students. John attended Howard University. Minnie left Howard, where she had begun as an art major, finishing her degree at Minor Teachers College. The wartime population of Washington had swelled by an additional 500,000 people, and apartments had become scarce.

At the outset of World War II, John decided to avoid the war, which intellectuals at Howard University bemoaned as "a white man's war."

The existence of Nazi concentration camps was not known at the time. He sought a job with a deferment, receiving one helping to build the Pan American Highway through Central America. John took trains through Missouri, Texas, and Mexico to Honduras. Determined to make his time in the mountains of Honduras a rewarding adventure, he took in the language and culture.

After nearly a year, he was transferred to Haiti. He knew a few Haitians, as some upper class Haitian families sent their children to Dunbar High School. He loved being in Haiti, not in small part because Minnie was able to join him there. Soon, however, Minnie found herself nursing a malaria patient who was near death. John had contracted the disease in Honduras, after which it remained dormant for a few months. It now posed a serious threat to his life. Minnie's close watch, pampering, and intense faith helped to pry John's life from malaria's deadly grip.

A son, Jon, was born in December 1944. Two of John's brothers and three of Minnie's brothers had sons by then; so Minnie and John, the younger pair, were falling right into place. John did join the army near the end of the war, signing on for Officers Candidate School in the Engineer Corps. He shipped off to Austria as a second lieutenant with an African American unit. The army was strictly segregated. Blacks were organized into battalions; the black battalions were part of regiments composed mostly of white battalions. As the traditions of segregation loosened, more of the commanding officers of black battalions were black.

The effects of segregationist rationalization went beyond official protocol. When John started sending profits from liquor sales in the dance hall to the United Negro College Fund, army brass ruled it out, announcing, "No money to the Nigger College Fund." Some of the officers John met in Austria became lifelong companions. Many of them stayed in for the twenty-year hitch, but John left active duty in 1948 and joined the reserves.

John Woodson learned German while in Austria, so by the time he returned to the United States he was conversant in Spanish, French, and German. His versions of these languages all carried dialects, Honduran, Haitian, and Austrian, but at that point he was able to converse with most of the people on three continents. Yet there was never any need for foreign languages in his predominantly African American community of Far Northeast Washington.

RECONNECTING BEGINS

Woodsons migrated to every region of the nation. During World War II some Woodsons met each other by chance. Without a complete family tree they could not understand the connections. Sometimes disconnected events brought family members together.

On May 14, 1945, Ada Highgate, a pianist who had never married, died in Midland, Michigan, at age seventy-eight. Her older brothers, Frederick and Oliver, had died a few years before. The three Highgates were offspring of Aaron Highgate and Caroline Woodson Highgate, both graduates of Avery College in Pittsburgh. Aaron and Caroline, both teachers, had moved from Pittsburgh to Canada. The family lived in a few Canadian towns before moving first to Saginaw, then to Midland, Michigan. Oliver, the oldest son, was a successful barber. Imagining the lives of the Highgates is difficult. No other African Americans lived in Midland at the time.

Surviving photo portraits reflect a degree of sophistication in their lifestyles. Handsome photographs of Oliver and Ada show the same elegant surroundings for each and were most likely taken in a studio, but Oliver's spiffy attire and Ada's elaborate ruffled dress were probably their own. None of the three siblings had any children; consequently, they left no closely related heirs.

Howard Woodson learned of Ada Highgate's death through relatives. By this time he was retired and had time on his hands. Howard assumed the task of representing a group of cousins in the settlement of the Highgate estate. He held a keen aversion to wastefulness. Although Howard had never met the Highgates, he was determined that their assets were to be distributed properly. Though Howard had three half-sisters, he was his father's only child.

The settlement process brought him into contact with several Woodson cousins. He discovered that Lewis F. Woodson (b. 1829) married Nancy Tanner of Pittsburgh and that Nancy was the sister of the A.M.E. bishop Benjamin Tanner. This connection brought Howard in contact with the prominent Philadelphia lawyer Sadie Tanner Mossell Alexander. Howard was able to uncover only a few of his many cousins. Like him, many relatives had left the Pittsburgh area, and their whereabouts were unknown. With the approval of his cousins, Howard traveled to Midland to probate the estate.

In the early 1950s the Woodsons of Washington had two sets of information comprising the family history, the information Howard gathered while probating the Highgate estate, and the oral history tying the Woodsons to Thomas Jefferson. The oral history John Woodson (b. 1918) first heard from his grandmother, Catherine Grey, only included the names of Thomas Jefferson, Thomas Woodson, John Woodson (of Goochland County, Virginia—no blood relation), and Lewis Woodson. The Washington Woodsons knew nothing at the time of an ongoing albeit fragmented controversy regarding Sally Hemings and Thomas Jefferson. Nor did the family know that a scandal had raged during Jefferson's first term as president. Sally Hemings' name did not flow through the generations along this line of the Woodson family. The family would later learn of its role as a part of the longest-running paternity controversy in American history.

BYRON WRITT WOODSON

New forces were stirring the aspirations of young blacks; at the time many of those forces were rooted in the nation's capital. Eleanor Roosevelt's acknowledgement of black leaders and their desires was certainly one impetus for change. Ralph Bunche, an African American who taught at Howard University over a twenty-year period but who achieved fame for his work with the State Department and the United Nations, won the Nobel Peace Prize in 1950. President "Give 'em Hell" Harry Truman was another force for change.

Minnie and John settled into a newly built apartment complex close to where they were raised. Son Jon was then three years old, and another child was on the way. Many of their friends from Dunbar High School who were raised "uptown" moved there also. Many of the men had recently returned from duty in the armed services. This was the baby boom. The nation's attention turned from foreign wars to formulas, diapers, and trips to the zoo. Every baby-boomer had an array of real aunts and uncles, a godmother and godfather, "play" aunts and uncles, cousins, godsisters, and a slew of inseparable friends, born as well to this close-knit community.

I was born on December 31, 1947. My name, Byron Writt Woodson, includes my grandmother's maiden name, Writt, as well as the Woodson surname. Names do not define a personality or character. Yet, for the last few centuries, names have given an indication of the sex of the newborn, along with social standing, ethnicity, and family lineage. Many of the male children in the generations following American independence were named for presidents. Tens of thousands of boys were given Thomas Jefferson, Benjamin Franklin, or George Washington as first and middle names. After the turn of the twentieth century, this practice became less common, as parents used the names of famous military men and other names of distinction.

In choosing "Byron" my parents displayed a cosmopolitan and literary interest. George Gordon Noel, sixth Baron Byron of Rochdale, was known beyond his romantic poetry for his chaotic love affairs, carnal exploits, travels throughout Europe, and inspiration for a cult which emphasized personal freedom. Names of title were not a British invention. The well-informed could use lengthy names to decipher all sorts of connections and to determine inheritance rights and the destiny of a child. The number of names increased, generally, with accrued status of the parents. Marie Joseph Paul Yves Roch Gilbert du Motier, Marquis de Lafayette, though a revolutionary, could never throw off his nobility without discarding such a name. Of course, on the other end of the social scale, slaves, serfs, villeins—those who lacked "natural rights"—held onto just one name.

While the Roman Empire controlled most of Europe, most Europeans were enslaved. The emancipation of the European masses started in A.D. 700. The use of surnames paralleled growth in individual rights and freedom. By the thirteenth century, European serfs (villeins in England) began to cast away the most persistent vestiges of slavery. During the transition from slavery to serfdom the nobility lost the privilege of unlimited sexual favor upon the manor, and marriage among serfs became a protected right.[1]

A study of one abbey in thirteenth-century England traced a one hundred-year period wherein surnames were uncommon at the outset, common after sixty years, and firmly established after one hundred years. Many surnames were derived from occupations, such as Carter (as in pushcart), Miller, Baker, Smyth, Carpenter, and Taylor. Other surnames were acquired from places (i.e., Woods, Hill, Rivers, etc.).[2]

When Africans were brought to America, Virginians reverted to the practice of giving slaves only a single name. It was an important method of weakening family ties. Typically, African Americans took on a surname as soon as they left slavery. Many took the name of their masters, but anthropologists have not fully studied the pattern.

With the Enlightenment, flaunting of extended names became gauche. In France, the guillotine pushed lengthy names into a danger zone. An egalitarian middle ground was reached with three names. In the mid-nineteenth century, all three names were often used as, with John Quincy Adams and John Wilkes Booth. The names of those in the lower classes grew in length as names of aristocrats shortened. Byron Writt Woodson has always suited me just fine.

JIM CROW GROWS TOO OLD TO CROW

Dad was recalled into active army duty during the Korean conflict. He was stationed in Fort Lewis in the state of Washington, but instead of being assigned to Korea, he was shipped off to Germany on the U.S.S. *Darby* with the entire 1279th Combat Battalion, an African American National Guard unit based in Detroit. Mother, Jon, and I flew in a DC3 to England, then on to Germany to join him.[3]

Though President Truman had issued an executive order to desegregate the armed forces in 1947, little was done by field commanders. Early in 1952, Truman, fed up with the delay in desegregation, sent an ultimatum through the Pentagon to Supreme Headquarters—Allied Forces Europe (SHAFE) in

Heidelberg, threatening to relieve commanders if desegregation was not implemented immediately. Truman had relieved the famous World War II corps commander General Douglas MacArthur from command in Japan a year earlier because of what Truman considered to be insubordination and over-aggressiveness involving China. Thus Truman's threat could not be taken lightly. Starting in March 1952, troops in the American zone of occupation in West Germany desegregated. The 1279th was disbanded.

Dad was then assigned to the 4th Engineer Battalion, an all-white unit from Georgia, Mississippi, and Florida, first with a desk job as a supply officer. After six months, he was in command of a platoon again, the only African American commissioned officer in the newly integrated battalion. The battalion commander made it clear that army regulations dictated that every soldier treat others with respect and that the chain of command would prevail. Our family moved from Hoecst to Hanau as a result of the reassignment. Though schools, restaurants, and other establishments were segregated in much of the United States, segregation was no longer a part of the U.S. Army life in Germany.

Mother taught kindergarten at the Hanau Kaserne school for dependents. I was in her class during the second year of our stay. African American soldiers no longer suffered the humiliation of Jim Crow practices. Families of African American officers living on foreign army bases enjoyed freedoms not available in "the land of the free and the home of the brave." Cold War tensions did not affect base life much. The time was idyllic in many ways. The German economy was still shattered; so was the value of the Deutschmark. Army pay did not allow for a lavish lifestyle, but the U.S. dollar went pretty far in postwar Germany.

At the time we did not know of Thomas Jefferson's 1788 tour of Hanau and Frankfurt, the very place where we then lived. Jefferson was there to visit a friend who was a Hessian military officer. The American 7th Army was in Hanau to occupy former Nazi facilities. It seems that a military presence there dated at least to the twelfth-century reign of the Holy Roman Emperor know as Barbarossa. Sightseeing along the Rhine, visiting the Romer, a centuries-old local government building in the old center of Frankfurt, watching hull races on the banks of the Main River, having a glass (or sip for a little tike) of Riesling with dinner, we enjoyed the Rhineland as our forefather had well over a hundred years before us.

When Dad's tour of duty ended, we boarded the S.S. *United States* in Bremerhaven. It was the fastest steamship ever built, with a bow shaped like an axe blade and smokestacks raked steeply toward the stern. It looked the part, built for speed! The ship stopped at Southampton and Le Havre before entering the Atlantic. Though Mother and Dad were seasick during much of the trip, it left a deep and fond impression upon them. The trip was a symbol of success; residence in Germany had been a good time. We enjoyed Thanksgiving dinner on board and after a five-day ocean passage entered New York Harbor, passing the Statue of Liberty. Ironically, as we returned home, certain freedoms and a measure of dignity were lost.

Mother's father, Thomas Jefferson Shumate, died soon after we returned from Germany. I knew him only through pictures and family stories. An unseemly sexual violation caused my grandfather's birth and engendered Mother's visceral rejection of racial divisiveness. Even now my understanding of this history grows. Family conversation, remembrances in particular, usually focused on the Woodsons, not the Shumates. Mother seldom spoke of her father's past. I learned some of grandfather Shumate's story from my father after my mother's death.

Mother's written research of her own family's genealogy came to me through a cousin after Mother's death. Mother did not give a copy to me. I didn't learn much about my maternal grandmother's family either, though she lived with us for five years. She was a sweet, religious, and pious person, forgiving and not at all introspective. Minnie Mae Mosely Shumate was an African American of dark brown pigmentation. Her father was a minister; the family was musically inclined. My grandmother was grandfather Shumate's second wife. Three children by his first wife looked white enough to pass but lived among African Americans and married African Americans of light complexion.

Mother was an African American of light complexion. Her parents were born in eastern Mississippi near the end of the nineteenth century. My maternal grandfather's maternal grandmother was a full-blooded Choctaw from Alabama who was abducted into slavery. A few years before her abduction, the United States Army had ravaged the Choctaw Nation, which eventually signed the Treaty of Dancing Rabbit Creek, agreeing to move west of the Mississippi River. This Choctaw woman's life reflected all of the horrors of pre–Civil War Mississippi. Her mistress, who abused her, sent her to her brother, who was a widower with children. When the young Choctaw became old enough, she gave birth to four children by the widower. The youngest child was named Martha. When an escape failed, the four mixed-race children were sold.

Martha was bought by Joseph Lowry, a lawyer of Scottish descent, born in South Carolina, who then lived in Lauderdale County, Mississippi. Shortly after the Civil War and Emancipation, Martha married an African American sharecropper, Solomon Shumate. The last of Martha's seven children, Thomas Jefferson Shumate, was not Solomon's son, but a product of a rape perpetrated by Joseph Lowry's son Waldover (alias Waldo). At this time sharecroppers could only protest such crimes by leaving the area. Justice was simply not available to nonwhites; protest in Mississippi invited death by lynching. Sadly, the virtually unavoidable debt owed to landowners or the general store kept many African Americans tied to places from which they wished to escape.

Joseph Lowry did ensure that Thomas Jefferson Shumate received a good education. On July 5, 1891, Thomas married Anna Wotten who produced the three of Thomas' children who looked nearly white, before she died young. Thomas Jefferson Shumate's second wife was my grandmother. After minor disagreements with neighbors, a note was pinned on his house, threatening harm to his wife and daughter if he did not leave Mississippi. My grandfather Shumate moved his family to Washington, D.C. He attended veterinary school with scholarship aid from the Bureau of Indian Affairs and became a meat inspector for the government.

Race was always a painful issue for Mother. Dad and his brothers viewed racism as a product of ignorance. They considered racists to be underachieving whites who were trying to gain a modicum of dignity by disparaging African Americans. Racism in their view was a sickness that could and should be fought and cured with education, truth, and the pursuit of justice. To them, inequality was a political and competitive issue. In contrast, the racial conditions in America troubled Mother both emotionally and intellectually. She seemed to ask, "How can people think that they are different from people that are their blood relations? Why is there so much hatred? How and when can we stop this ridiculous and savage behavior?" Gradually, well into adulthood, I came to understand that the violation of my great-grandmother's marriage and, more particularly, the rift between my grandfather and his dark-skinned Shumate half-brothers was a source of great consternation for my mother. She inherited a great deal of her father's pain, an identity rift, and a distinct inability to reconcile America's racial divide.

Mother was troubled by her experiences in church as a child, which exemplified her dilemma. Grandmother attended an all-black evangelical church. Children in Sunday school taunted Mother by calling her "the little white girl." Grandfather attended a white church. It apparently did not have Sunday school or, if it did, she did not ever attend it or mention it. She did speak of sitting in the rear of the church. She did not say whether she sat apart from her father, but the treatment she received there clearly troubled her. In adulthood, Mother did not attend church. She generally rejected anything that separated people by race. Even today few congregations are racially integrated.

The pernicious Jim Crow traditions seemed to make a habit of intruding on our family's peace and happiness, most often when we were trying to enjoy ourselves. I remember being denied service at a restaurant in Louisiana while we were returning from vacation in Mexico. We were a thousand miles from home, and we wished to eat. It was that simple. Whites expected blacks to yield to the incomprehensible pointlessness of these traditions without comment. Dad tended to resist any effort to deny to him equal access on the basis of his skin color. Mother would virtually stop breathing during such confrontations. She was pained by the treatment her family received, horrified by the hatred that white Americans expressed toward African Americans, and indignant toward the justifications that American politicians gave for segregation.

Mother was an attractive person with a quick smile, but she laughed only in the company of family and a few close friends. A certain wit never left her. She did not make acquaintances easily. "Why" was a common word in her vocabulary, but not spoken singularly like a two-year-old. Mother's "why" was followed by long reaching inquiries, often unanswerable.

Pictures of Mother as a young lady reveal glowing beauty. Some of it was lost as she bore children. The births were difficult. She was not a doting mother, but was watchful and wise. Jon and I always knew that a standard had been set for us to emulate. We knew mediocrity should not enter or leave our home. Both our parents were strict enforcers of that rule.

LEWIS WOODSON, LIVE AND IN LIVING COLOR

After living with my maternal grandmother for two years in the house in which Mother was raised, we moved into a house Dad built on land given to him by his father. Howard Woodson, or "Pop," as the adults in the family called him, lived a short distance away, farther up a steep hillside. Pop was a very quiet, reserved, and dignified man. Of course, he was already eighty years old when I came to know him. I was always amazed at the reverence bestowed upon him by all, though he did not seem to be a demanding person at all. I admired him immensely but was not awed by him. I knew my grandfather was a very disciplined man but also full of kindness. Sometimes I looked at his face, trying not to stare; to me he seemed to carry a faint but evasive smile, like Mona Lisa.

The first Lewis Woodson was born in 1806 in Virginia. Since then, there have been several Lewis Woodsons. In the late 1950s Lewis Frederick Woodson enrolled in Howard University in Washington, D.C. This one was born in 1933 near St. Louis, Missouri. He was a warm, friendly, and spiritual man who learned early on that wherever he went, a relative was only a few miles away. He boarded with Pop Woodson, who was then a widower while he attended Howard University in the late 1950s. Lewis was a large man with an engaging chiseled face that somehow exuded both masculinity and a boyish quality. His complexion was very pale. He rejoiced in the Christian fellowship of the A.M.E. Church. Lewis studied architecture, which, I am sure, delighted my grandfather.

Lewis brought more family history to the Washington Woodsons. He told of the connection between the Woodsons and the Payne Seminary at Wilberforce University in Ohio. His grandfather, George Frederick Woodson (b. 1861), served as dean of the seminary for many years in the early 1900s. His Uncle George (b. circa 1902), a mathematics professor at nearby Central State University, continued to live in Wilberforce, where Lewis had spent childhood summers with his grandparents.

Lewis (b. 1933) recited the same oral history regarding the family connection to Thomas Jefferson. This was the first time I was aware of corroboration of the oral history, which had come to us from Dad's grandmother, Catherine. I began to comprehend and relish the oral history handed down from one generation to another for 145 years. Lewis' grandfather left Pittsburgh in the late 1870s to attend Wilberforce University and Drew University. From this we knew that the oral history went back as far as the late 1870s. The further the oral history was pushed back in time, the more credence it possessed as far as we were concerned.

Lewis was fourteen years older than I. Despite the age difference, we formed a strong mutual affection, not based on common interests, but on bonding of a decidedly primal nature. Like me, Lewis worshipped the ground upon which his grandfather walked. Lewis' grandfather was dead (mine was still alive), but when I learned of his various offspring, I wanted to meet them.

Lewis' half-brother, Blair, lived in New Jersey. Blair's oldest child was also named Blair and was my age. During the summer of 1959, Lewis took "little" Blair and me for a three-week visit to St. Louis, where Lewis' mother lived. Barreling through the small towns and past the tall cornfields of Ohio in Lewis' bright yellow 1958 Impala coupe, we first stopped in Wilberforce. There I met Uncle George and his family. We also met a cousin whose butcher made the hottest breakfast sausage in Indiana. St. Louis was a barrel of fun because Lewis, who always had a warm, friendly demeanor, bounced with joy at seeing old friends and, of course, relatives. It was infectious. Blair and I were taught to give a strong handshake by a cheerful old man who frequented Grand Boulevard. To even things out for Blair, we drove to the blissfully remote river town of Murphysboro, Illinois, to visit Lewis' mother's relatives. Folks there were blessed with all the catfish one could ever care to see or eat.

On the return trip we met Uncle George's sister, Grace, who retired in Ohio after a teaching career at West Virginia State University. It was clear there was no shortage of Woodson relatives, just a shortage of time to find and meet them. I had a great time on that trip and still maintain friendships with some people I met then. Our roll through the Midwest took place when interstate highways were a few lines scratched on blueprint; my vivid memories of that trip not only take me to a different place but to a decidedly different era.

Lewis soon married and began a family, but sadly the marriage did not last. Lewis' mother, who was light in complexion, never accepted his wife, whom Lewis nicknamed Sandy. Sandy was slim, tall, and attractive, and her personality was warm and genuine, but her mother-in-law could not accept her brown complexion.

Lewis also had employment problems. Although he received a degree in architecture, he failed to pass the licensing examination. Once he received a job with an architectural firm as a draftsman. Soon after he was hired, the firm gave a picnic; Lewis attended, taking Sandy and the two children born by that time. The following Monday Lewis was fired. The firm apparently thought Lewis was white. Lewis never tried to be anything he was not. Like most people, he just wanted to be accepted for the content of his character. He did not wear a sign around his neck saying that his father's father, whom he loved dearly, had a dark complexion. Lewis was no match for this hostility. He did not have within him whatever he needed to fight back.

Pop Woodson died in 1962, the year I entered high school. The instant I heard of his death, I could not imagine life without my eighty-six-year-old grandfather. The pall that overcame me seemed to say, "Whose lead will we follow?" I soon accepted his death and my imminent maturity.

THE NEW FRONTIER

During those years, my family took two epic vacations. In 1960, after Dad fulfilled his two-week army camp duty at Fort Knox, Kentucky, we drove to Acapulco, Mexico. Mexico had not entered the world market economy then. It was exotic and romantic. Life unfolded at a surreally slow pace, which allowed one to savor the warm colors and warm, dry climate, as if a painter were creating each scene on a traveling canvas.

In the summer of 1963 Dad went to Ft. Leavenworth, Kansas, for army duty. Mother, Jon, and I flew to Denver to meet him. We drove southwest in a 1962 Pontiac station wagon to Mesa Verde National Park and a Native American reservation nearby. Native Americans there were cave dwellers, living as they had for hundreds of years. It was even more of a throwback in time than the trip through north-central Mexico. We also stopped at the Grand Canyon. Jon and I walked down Bright Angel Trail to Indian Springs, about a four-mile trek. It took two hours to walk down and five exciting, challenging hours to climb back to the South Rim. We visited Mother's multitalented brother and his fifth wife in Los Angeles and one of Dad's army buddies at Fort Ord.

After we left Yellowstone National Park on the return leg, the trip seemed interminable. Rather than becoming a point of fascination, the howl of coyotes at night became a real bother. Three of Dad's army buddies had planted themselves in Detroit upon leaving active duty, so the city was a mandatory stop. Ironically, Jon and I watched Martin Luther King's stunning March on Washington on television from a Detroit living room.

The Kennedy years were a good time. Dad's best friend from high school, Elmer Terry, took some courses in computer technology. He left his letter carrier job at the U.S. Post Office, landing a job with the National Aeronautics and Space Administration (NASA). Job opportunities for African Americans opened in the federal government. No longer were African Americans required to have a connection to the mulatto offspring of a robber baron to get a job above the level of janitor. Competency was becoming the criterion for employment. African Americans filled new jobs at the Department of Transportation and at other new and old federal agencies.

Mother and Dad were full of life, as were their brothers. With tuition payment assistance from the Veterans Administration, Dad completed a degree at George Washington University and became an oceanographer with the Naval Oceanographic Office. The job required that he travel all over the world, a demand Dad was all too happy to satisfy. He traveled to Korea and to Iceland and many places in between. He came home from each trip a different color, his skin announcing each change in sunlight. His eyes turned hazel as he grew older; his thick crop of hair turned shocking white. Always handsome, Dad took on a more exotic appearance as he grew older. Mother obtained a master's degree and left the classroom, becoming a reading specialist. She vowed not to earn a doctorate unless Dad obtained a master's degree.

During my senior year of high school, Dad doubled the size of our house. Built on the same steep hillside in Far Northeast Washington, the living room was on the upper floor and two bedrooms were below. Dad put me to work mixing mortar and carrying bricks on Saturdays, while he played golf. The same carpenter who helped build the original house was hired to build a huge new living room with a conversation pit. A carport and a room for a pool table were below. Neighborhood cronies helped me stake claim to the pool table through constant use.

Though I performed well amid the all-black student body in my junior high school and was salutatorian of my class, I was not allowed to choose where I would go to high school. I went to Western High School, at the opposite end of the city from our neighborhood, where Dad thought I would receive the best education. The student body was predominantly white. I rebelled by making poor grades, thinking I would be sent back to my neighborhood school according to school policy. However, because Uncle Granville was an assistant superintendent in the school system, that's not what happened. One day I received a message to report to Mr. Horn, the assistant principal, whom I had never met or spoken with before. I knew the issue was my grades and gleefully prepared to look disappointed to hear about my expulsion. When I entered Mr. Horn's office, I was quickly greeted with a surprising fate: "Young man, I know your uncle and he is a fine man. I want you to report to my office four days a week at 3:00 and we'll see what we can do about your grades." When he said the word "uncle" I knew I had been trapped by the Woodson clan.

Realizing that I was destined to stay at Western High, I began to earn decent grades; yet, when I reached my senior year, my cumulative average remained far below par.

Following Mother's direction, I requested that the school send my transcript to colleges. The counselor refused because of my poor grades. My College Board scores were high, but she was adamant about my inability to gain admission to college. I was wasting her time, she said. Mother made phone calls for six weeks to numerous school administration officials, becoming very agitated in the process. Finally, the counselor relented.

She agreed to send the transcripts out and called me into her office to discuss my applications. I wished to apply to three schools including the University of Pittsburgh and Duquesne University. The woman, who was middle-aged and who had worked most of her career in a legally segregated school system, shook her head in protest. "Duquesne, no you can't go there. You can't even say the word." Pittsburgh was Fort Pitt before it became a city, and it was called Fort Duquesne before the French lost it to the English.

I was as familiar with Duquesne as I was with Forbes Field or the Squirrel Hill Tunnel, or the Monongahela River for that matter; but my counselor could not imagine as much. "The word is Duquesne," she said in a searing voice, pronouncing it precisely as I had. She could not fathom that I could pronounce the word correctly. Blacks, she presumed, came from the South and knew nothing of other parts of the country, thus she could only imagine hearing the wrong pronunciation from me and in her agitated state heard what she wanted to hear. As she vented, I wondered why she was assigned the smallest room in the entire school. The ceiling was extremely high; the problem, however, was not cubic volume but the floor area of the room. It did not allow me to put much distance between the two of us. She had already been forced to send out my transcript. I was not about to argue about how to pronounce "Duquesne" and risk further delay. During the confrontation over the release of the transcript, I had become more determined to attend college.

In 1969, I graduated from Lincoln University, the oldest historically black college, located in southeastern Pennsylvania about fifty miles outside of Philadelphia. Lincoln was a wonderful experience for me. Its location in the rolling hills of Pennsylvania isolated the small student body from big city distractions. Since most students were from either the big northeastern cities or small towns in the South, there was little connection with the surrounding farm community. Students who sought a faster pace traveled to Philadelphia or Washington, D.C., for weekend parties or political activism. Bonds formed at the school were particularly strong.

I witnessed the social turmoil of the late 1960s firsthand, but was not measurably affected by it. I was in Washington, D.C., when Martin Luther King was murdered. When I saw sofas being thrown out of downtown department store windows, I understood the anger but didn't see solutions in those actions. "Burn baby burn" and "I may be unemployed but I am somebody," popular slogans of the time, never grabbed me. If there was one phrase that captured my appreciation of the period, it was uttered a few years earlier. The great civil rights activist Fannie Lou Hamer told the 1964 Democratic National Convention in Atlantic City, New Jersey, which had seated an all-white Mississippi delegation, that her racially integrated Mississippi Freedom Democratic Party delegation would not accept tokenism in place of full participation. She explained, "We ain't come all this way fo[r] no two votes, and I is tired." Those words were etched in my memory and in my heart.

FIRST FAMILY TREE

Dad brought home a family tree, found among some of Pop's papers. Uncle Harold had inherited Pop's house, so the process of going through Pop's papers proceeded slowly and intermittently. There was no hurry. Mother and Dad created a new family tree, adding new information. The newest Woodson, my niece, Marnee, born that year, was added along with other names. The amount of fresh information was small, but the tree symbolized our growing interest in the past. Every piece of information we gathered was more fascinating than we had anticipated.

Mother had suffered an accident as a child as a consequence of which, one of her kidneys was removed. She lived a fairly normal life as far as her health went, but I think she felt somehow she would not live a long life. She and Dad planned early retirement.

Just before her 1972 retirement from the District of Columbia Public Schools, Mother met Norma Woodson McDaniel, a second-grade teacher in the Aiton Elementary School. In a hallway Norma told Mother that her paternal grandfather had lived in Findlay, Ohio, and that her parents had attended Wilberforce University. Yet Norma was not descended from anyone named Lewis Woodson (b. 1806).

As the two realized common threads of family history, Mother was puzzled by the lack of a common link to Lewis Woodson. The conversation intensified. Adrenaline rushed into Mother's veins and her speech became more excited. Her eyes began to move rapidly, away from Norma's eyes, but then flicked into keen focus on Norma's inflections when key words were spoken. Norma then began to recite the Woodson oral history pertaining to Thomas Jefferson but stopped in mid-sentence, challenging Mother to finish it. When Mother said "Thomas Jefferson," both ladies knew a phenomenal event had occurred.

As it turned out, Norma was descended not from Lewis Woodson, but from his brother William, of whom our line of the family had no knowledge. Norma and Mother were each elated by the reconnection of family lines that had been long separated. Mother would spend a great deal of the balance of her life finishing sentences, pages, chapters, and books pertaining to the same history.

Another event heightened family pride in 1972. A new high school was built in the neighborhood where Mother, Dad, Jon, and I were raised. Named the Howard Dilworth Woodson Senior High School, it was dedicated on December 9. Normally referred to in the Washington, D.C., area as "H. D. Woodson," it is a testament to Pop's community leadership. It is rare that a high school is named after a community leader; most are named after communities or presidents.

To attend the dedication I took time off from my job at Philadelphia National Bank, where I had begun working after leaving Lincoln University. I attended Temple University in the evenings, working toward an M.B.A. Jon began working toward a doctorate at Brown University and did not make the trip from Rhode Island. Lewis Woodson attended the dedication, looking unusually solemn. I later realized that he and his wife had separated.

MOTHER PLUNGES INTO THE PAST

Energized by her encounter with Norma Woodson McDaniel, the dedication of Woodson High School, and her retirement, Mother threw herself into genealogical exploration. Through historian Floyd Miller, Mother learned that Lewis (b. 1806) wrote under the pen name Augustine. As Augustine, Lewis wrote that his father lived in Jackson County, Ohio. Previously, she knew that Lewis' father was Thomas but had no idea where Thomas had lived. She soon began to speak with family members and others in Ohio who knew of the state's frontier history.

Late in 1972, Mother and Uncle Granville drove his Subaru to Pittsburgh and Jackson County, Ohio, in pursuit of family history. They met with Floyd Miller in Oberlin, Ohio, where he taught history. They uncovered an avalanche of information about Lewis Woodson. They were then able to distinguish between the lives of Lewis Woodson and Thomas Woodson, realizing that Thomas Woodson never lived in Pittsburgh, as they had once thought. Knowledge of Lewis Woodson had been lost over the years, so the oral history known by Pop's descendants had blended the lives of Thomas and Lewis, father and son.

In the Jackson County hamlet known simply as Roads, Mother and Uncle Granville visited a small cemetery that contained the graves of ten Woodsons. Lewis Woodson left Ohio in 1831; his descendants had no knowledge of this cemetery. Mother percolated with excitement over this phenomenal discovery. An arch over the cemetery entrance that once identified it as Woodson Cemetery had collapsed years before. With reverence and amazement, they approached, studied, and deciphered a badly worn gray tombstone. The stone leaned slightly backward as if to escape any ill intentions. It marked the burial site of Jemima Woodson, wife of Thomas Woodson. She was born May 12, 1783, and died March 18, 1868, more than a hundred years before.

While in Ohio, Mother and Uncle Granville learned even more about Lewis (b. 1806). They discovered his role with the A.M.E. Church in Chillicothe, Ohio, beginning in 1821 and a record of his marriage to Caroline. They found that two of his brothers also became A.M.E. ministers.

The discovery of the cemetery and, in particular, of Jemima Woodson's existence proved to be particularly fortuitous. It was not long before Mother became obsessed with Jemima's origin, how she and Thomas met, and more. Mother noted the names of other families buried in the cemetery. Aside from the Woodsons, several Cassel, Wilson, and Leach graves lie in the peaceful seclusion afforded by its rural setting. Mother surmised that those families were connected; she would later learn the relationships.

After returning from Ohio, Mother found documentation on all of Lewis' brothers and sisters and uncovered information on the adult lives of most of them. Mother spent days and weeks poring over U.S. Census data at the National Archives in Washington, finding dozens of Woodsons who lived through the end of the nineteenth century. She found Thomas Woodson listed in the 1830 census for Jackson County, Ohio. There was still a twenty-eight year gap from 1802 when he left Monticello, but the information advanced the family genealogy light-years from the point when there was no documentation of Thomas Woodson's life.

The personal computer was then only a few years away from development, but Mother didn't know that then and couldn't have waited for the marvelous invention that would have made her pursuit much easier. She established contact with members representing six of the ten family lines (the eleventh child, Sarah Jane, had no children), encouraging others to join her research efforts. She found a few apostles. Uncle Granville, however, developed emphysema; he could no longer match Mother's pace.

NOTES

1. Geoffrey Barraclough, *The Times Atlas of World History* (London: Times Books, 1979), 88–89: map of the Roman Empire indicates that the Romans occupied all of southern Europe and these portions of northern Europe: France, the Low Countries, England, and western Germany; Frances Gies and Joseph Gies, *Marriage and the Family in the Middle Ages* (New York: Harper and Row, 1987), 45. The Gieses note that "the European countryside was dominated by great slave-manned plantations (latifundia)." The areas of Europe not occupied by the Roman Empire, such as present-day Poland, Russia, and Scandinavia, were very sparsely populated by peoples whom historians consider to have been barbarian.

2. Gies and Gies, *Marriage and the Family*, 166: study of surnames at medieval abbey.

3. A substantial amount of material contained in this chapter was drawn from interviews with John S. Woodson (b. 1918) conducted in person and by phone during 1999.

CHAPTER NINE

The Third Heart:
The Brilliance of
Dr. Fawn Brodie

The function of various forms of oppression . . . is to accomplish this
division by offering different groups of the oppressed various advantages
over other groups and thus pit them one against the other.
—Gerda Lerner, 1997[1]

Elated with the newly uncovered genealogical trail and fascinated with Lewis
Woodson's accomplishments, Mother shifted her mission to connecting all
of the living descendants of Thomas and Jemima Woodson and to pushing
back into the early life of Thomas Woodson. The Woodson genealogy com-
peted successfully with other endeavors. She taught at Trinity College in
Washington, D.C., and became an advocate for improved public education.
Mother also devoted time to Dad's pursuits. Aided by her earnings from
Trinity, they bought a twenty-six-foot wood-hulled sailboat from Uncle
Granville. It was docked in Annapolis for easy access to the Chesapeake Bay.

In 1974 Mother learned of a new biography of Thomas Jefferson that
acknowledged the liaison with Sally Hemings. She was stunned. She purchased the book and read it with exhilaration. Her life was again immersed
in the saga of Thomas Woodson's life. *Thomas Jefferson, an Intimate History*
was a stupendous piece of historical research, furnishing enormously helpful
insights into Jefferson's life and the long-hidden realities of life at Monticello.
It answered so many of Mother's questions about the Jeffersons and the Hem-

inges. Yet the author, Fawn Brodie, had not researched the lives of the offspring of the Jefferson/Hemings liaison.

There was more work ahead. Mother sought to record Thomas Woodson's whereabouts between 1802 when he left Monticello and 1830, when he was know to be in Jackson County, Ohio, as that time span was to us then mostly a blank page. Without knowing much about Dr. Brodie, Mother developed a deep respect for her. While Mother unearthed the long buried trial of the Woodson family genealogy with a minimum of interpretation, Brodie had delved into the psyche of Thomas Jefferson, into the possibilities of his sexual passion, and into the pain of slavery. Brodie hunted in the quagmire of American racial taboos, a place seldom approached by academicians even now. The floor of the jungle was richly endowed with an acidic soil known for supporting hypocrisy, intolerance, and related species of parasites, all feeding on the soul of civilization.

The great American racial taboo has evolved from the paradigm that refused to view Africans outside of the context of slavery and rejected their capacity to survive and prosper in freedom. Now mutated into the proposition that American institutions are free of prejudice and discrimination, that opportunity in America is accessed on a color-blind basis, the taboo continues to twist reality as much as ever. The American slave taboo looks back at enslaved African Americans, finding one-dimensional features and purely functional definitions of their lives. This taboo fails to find humanity in the histories of those who were enslaved. The American miscegenation taboo prevents discussion of the sexual intermingling of races. Though the number of mulattos in America before the Civil War exceeded the number of male slaveholders, no recognition is afforded the practice and its effects on American history. White families very seldom acknowledge blood relations of a darker hue. Many blacks have more interest in creating cultural links to Africa than exploring their American genealogical roots. The great Jefferson taboo, as Brodie called it, prevented historians from probing Jefferson's widowhood, the intricacies of slave life at Monticello, or the assertions that Jefferson fathered the children of Sally Hemings.

Taboos survive only when fed. The story of George Wythe's death, which will follow, belies the ardent appetite of the American miscegenation taboo. Miscegenation was considered a sin by white Americans before the Civil War, and miscegenation remained illegal in some states after the Civil War. It was illegal in Virginia until 1967, when the U.S. Supreme Court declared state bans on miscegenation unconstitutional. Many Americans today believe people of each race should "stay to their own." In 1999 Jeffersonian historians finally accepted the reality of the Hemings/Jefferson liaison, yet some resist further exploration and understanding. In a 1999 essay historian Jan Lewis proclaimed, "It is not clear, however, why questions about Jefferson's private behavior should be of concern to us as either historians or citizens." Similar comments by academicians did not follow the publication of Andrew Burstein's *Inner Jefferson* (1995) or Joseph Ellis' *American Sphinx: The Character of Thomas Jefferson* (1997). Both books denied the Jefferson/Hemings liaison. Academicians selectively seek to close doors on scholarly exploration. For decades Winthrop Jordan repeated his assessment that it did "not matter" if the Jefferson/Hemings liaison was a reality. The trouble with this selective anti-intellectualism is that it is more effective than many would admit in sustaining the racial taboos mentioned here.[2]

George Wythe was a Virginia delegate to the Continental Congress and a signer of the Declaration of Independence. He was a law professor at the College of William and Mary while Thomas Jefferson studied there. Seventeen years older, Wythe was Jefferson's mentor. Wythe's draft of the Virginia protest against the proposed Stamp Act in 1764 was his earliest notable contribution. Working together, he and Jefferson revised Virginia law after the Revolution.

Wythe died after being poisoned in June 1806. He was not married at the time. He had married twice; each wife had died without giving birth. Wythe produced a son, Michael Brown, by his mulatto housekeeper, Lydia Broadnax. Separately, Wythe befriended a grandnephew, George Sweney, as if the latter were also a son. On April 20, 1803, Wythe made out a will, leaving some property to Lydia and another former slave named Benjamin. He left half of his bank stock to Michael Brown and the other half to Sweney. Wythe appointed President Thomas Jefferson as executor in charge of the "maintenance, education and other benefit" of Michael Brown. The will indicated that Sweney should receive all of the bank stock if Brown predeceased him.[3]

Wythe did not die immediately from the poisoning. Before dying, he asserted that Sweney was the culprit and cut Sweney out of his will. Michael Brown also died from this poisoning, but Lydia survived. Arsenic, placed in strawberries and coffee, was discovered.

Sweney's trial was sensational. The will was an obvious affirmation of Wythe's paternity of Michael Brown. Moreover, Wythe had asked the president of the United States to oversee the culmination of his parental commitment to his mulatto son. The leading citizens of Richmond were appalled at the openness with which Wythe handled his commitment to his mulatto son's well-being. Edmund Randolph, who served as the first attorney general of the United States, and William Wirt took up Sweney's defense.[4]

Under Virginia law, a black could not testify against a white person, so Lydia's testimony was prohibited. Sweney was thus acquitted of murdering

George Wythe and upon appeal was acquitted of forging checks in his uncle's name. The murder of Michael Brown did not ever reach trial. The murderer of a signer of the Declaration of Independence was acquitted in order to reinforce American racial taboos! Blacks were to have no rights in the Virginia legal system. The obvious reality of miscegenation would not be acknowledged. Virginia ensured that the offspring of miscegenation would not openly inherit the personal property of their fathers. Racial taboos were held above the law.

What gave Dr. Brodie the courage to hunt in such a jungle? Her talent was extraordinary. Mother set out to discover the origins of Pop Woodson. Fawn Brodie and Mother began to correspond and exchange information. I was moved by this exchange, as both women deserved the recognition each offered to the other. After reading *Thomas Jefferson, an Intimate History*, I wanted to know something about the author. But, bound by my responsibilities as a young father and various personal missions, I did not pursue my interest in Dr. Brodie while she was alive, and I was disheartened by her death. Years later events would put me in touch with her son, Bruce, in an effort to discover more about her. Dr. Bruce Brodie steered me to Newell Bringhurst, a California historian from whose work most of the following information is drawn.

THE PROMISE OF FAWN MCKAY BRODIE

Fawn McKay was born September 15, 1915, in Ogden, Utah. Her parents, Thomas E. and Fawn Brimhall McKay, were born into the elite of the Church of Jesus Christ of Latter-day Saints. David O. McKay, Fawn's uncle, was a member of the Council of Twelve Apostles, the Mormon Church's highest ranking panel, at the time of her birth. Later, her uncle became the president of the church. Her mother's father served as president of Brigham Young University from 1904 to 1921. He was a fine educator, an open-minded man who outwardly appeared to be devout. Her paternal grandfather helped found the town of Huntsville, a farming community ten miles east of Ogden. Fawn McKay was raised in that picturesque town.[5]

Fawn's father became active in Utah politics. Thomas E. McKay was elected president of the Utah Senate and later became the state utilities commissioner. He was also involved with the church hierarchy in support roles. He never expected his children to question the tenets of the church. When Fawn reached adulthood and began to search deeper into church traditions, her father offered stiff resistance. He told his daughter simply, "You've got to believe." Fawn and her father found it impossible to communicate on matters of religion and philosophy. They avoided any discussion that was "unpleasant." Fawn's mother outwardly adhered to Mormon tenets but was more apt to question some aspects of the religion's foundation. Fawn's sister, Louise, said of her mother's objectivity, "The greatest thing she gave us was a need for intellectual honesty." Fawn took cues from her mother, whom she later described as a "quiet heretic." Fawn wrote, "Her heresy took the form mostly of encouraging me to be on my own."[6]

Fawn's childhood had all the markings of an idyllic reflection of Mormon righteousness, American manifest destiny, and pre-Depression economic success. This was, by and large, the case. Early on, Fawn's superior intellect became apparent. Her older sister recounted this intimate tale:

When I was five and Fawn three, I remember mother trying to teach me to repeat the poem "Little Orphan Annie." I was struggling to just learn the first verse. One morning . . . mother asked me to say the poem. I just barely got past the first verse and stopped. Fawn piped up. "Let me say it mother." And she went through all three verses without one mistake.[7]

At the age of four, Fawn was reading fourth grade books. When Fawn formally entered school, it was clear that an evaluation was needed to direct her placement. At the age of six she was placed in the third grade.

The previous year, 1920, American women gained voting rights. Fawn never felt the restraint on her development which was prevalent in previous generations. She excelled in spelling, writing, public speaking, and debate. She graduated from Weber High School in Ogden as class salutatorian in 1930 at the age of fourteen. At the University of Utah in Salt Lake City, she read quantities of Shakespeare, Sophocles, and Euripides and developed a taste for Russian novels. Graduating in 1934 with high honors and membership in Phi Beta Kappa, she returned to Ogden to teach at Weber College, a two-year institution operated under the auspices of the Mormon Church.

THE EMANCIPATION OF FAWN BRODIE

After a year of teaching, Fawn left Utah in the fall of 1935 for graduate school. She later explained, "It was not really until I went away to graduate school at the University of Chicago that I understood how much of a liberation the university experience in Salt Lake City had been . . . the sense of liberation I had at the University of Chicago was enormously exhilarating. I felt very quickly that I never could go back to the old life, and I never did." At work in a school cafeteria she met Bernard Brodie, also a student. Bernard was a Chicago native; his ancestry was Latvian-Jewish. Like Fawn he was very bright and articulate. They were married on August 25, 1936. Fawn Brodie was twenty years old. This was not just a marriage. It was a profound break with her past and her heritage.[8]

Though Fawn envisioned herself as a writer of fiction, she discovered that her talent for fiction fell short. Bernard was fascinated by the origins of the Mormon Church. As Fawn answered her husband's questions, she was stimulated to delve further into the revelations of Joseph Smith, the church's founder. Researching those origins at the University of Chicago Library, she was unable to find a good biography of Joseph Smith. She found that her assessment hinged solely on Smith's credibility. Intending to write an article about the sources of the Book of Mormon, Fawn continued research that would last seven years and culminate in the publication of her biography of Joseph Smith, *No Man Knows My History*. Brodie was thrilled: "It was a piece of detective work that I found absolutely compelling. It was fantastic! I was gripped by it. I spent seven years doing the research and writing and I was fascinated the whole time. I was baffled by the complexities of this man and remained somewhat baffled even after the book was finished."[9]

Fawn Brodie was convinced that Joseph Smith was not a "true prophet" even before she began writing. Research convinced her that the Book of Mormon was fraudulently conceived. She had not been a devout believer since her years at the University of Utah and knew that devout Mormons would defend their creed and brand her work as heresy. Still, she believed her work would benefit younger "Jack Mormons," people who aligned themselves with the Mormon Church but did not literally accept the Book of Mormon. She believed that Jack Mormons deserved to examine for themselves the evidence regarding the origins of the church, but felt the truth would not cause them to separate from it.

She also knew that the book would create difficulties within her family. Officials of the Mormon Church voted to excommunicate Fawn Brodie, charging her with apostasy on May 23, 1946. She anticipated the excommunication and did not protest, thinking it was justified. Her mother and sisters thought the excommunication was neither justified nor just. Her father was particularly hurt by his daughter's work. He never read the book, which caused Fawn Brodie great emotional pain. By revealing the shocking and fascinating life of Joseph Smith, Fawn Brodie established her talent and her courage as fixtures in the field of biography. The stature she accrued eventually led her to write her famous biography of Thomas Jefferson. As she finished *No Man Knows My History*, little did she know that she had already prepared for a second round of fame and recrimination.

JOSEPH THE PROPHET

Joseph Smith was born in Vermont into a family that migrated to the Green Mountains after living in more densely settled parts of New England in previous generations. Because the rocky terrain of Vermont was not particularly accommodating to farming, Smith's family moved to Palmyra, New York, in 1817, the same year that the state of New York sanctioned the Erie Canal. The family bought land at a price inflated by the advent of the canal and suffered for years as result of the overpayment.

Smith spurned the drudgery and monotony of farming, preferring mystical pursuits. He was an imaginative boy who dreamed of finding buried treasures. He was captured by stories of buried Spanish gold and Indian mounds with beaten silver lying among bones of the dead. Tales of mineral rods and clairvoyant talents also gripped him. Histories of the Mound Builders, an imagined tribe of Indians who once lived in the western New York and Ohio area, enhanced the local folklore. Local newspapers regularly carried embellishments of this "history." Smith ultimately created a religious movement out of such folklore. He claimed to have discovered a set of golden plates that had been inscribed by a wayward tribe which had migrated to America from Jerusalem over a thousand years before. Divine inspiration allowed him to translate the inscriptions into English.[10]

Fawn Brodie surmised that Smith incorporated the work of two authors into his legend. The first was *View of the Hebrews; or the Ten Lost Tribes of Israel*, by a Vermont minister, Ethan Smith, who was not related. The second was a manuscript Solomon Spaulding had written on the history of the American Indian. Today it is commonly acknowledged that the entire Book of Mormon was not written by Joseph Smith, as the style reveals the strong probability of another author, but the notion was rejected at that time. Fawn Brodie postulated that Sidney Rigdon, an early convert to Mormonism, obtained Spaulding's work, gave it to Smith, and kept his transmittal secret.

Fawn Brodie uncovered several documents that exposed the wanderings of Smith's imagination in his youth. She uncovered doubt, which was created by early defectors from the Mormon Church who took measures to expose the true origins of Joseph Smith's legend. *No Man Knows My History* reveals a tightly drawn pattern between Smith's youthful exploration of local folklore and the creation of the Book of Mormon.

Smith drew converts to the faith, structured upon the Book of Mormon, in 1831. He and his followers migrated to Kirtland, Ohio, near Cleveland, where many local residents joined the movement. Smith underpinned his revelations with the statements of witnesses. At first, three witnesses testified to the creation of the Book of Mormon. Later, eight witnesses testified as to the same matter. An insular hierarchy grew from these beginnings, including the Council of Twelve Apostles, which remains today as the high order of the church.

Rumors of Smith's adulterous exploits began in the early 1830s. Smith seduced an attractive seventeen-year-old girl in 1836, and the transgression became known in the inner circle of the church. Smith not only prevailed in his denial, but his accuser was later excommunicated. The girl, Fannie Alger, moved to Indiana and married, never exposing Smith. The pattern continued and intensified. Smith secretly began to marry the targets of his sexual pleasure, many of whom were already legally married. This introduced polygamy to the church, as he convinced himself and collaborators that Joseph the Prophet, as he was known, did not commit adultery in the eyes of the Mormon Church because it recognized "secret marriage." Scandals threatened the cohesiveness of the church, but Smith was able to survive every crisis. Polygamy remained a part of Mormon life even after Smith's death. It was not until 1890 that the church renounced the practice.

Polygamy in the Mormon Church was a widely known phenomenon before the publication of Fawn Brodie's biography of Joseph Smith, yet its origins were not well understood. She placed its origin in the personality of Joseph Smith. He used his religious stature and personal charisma to devise new rules of social behavior, exploiting circumstances that were not of his making. For instance, because his church was not recognized by local political authorities, marriages he performed were not recognized. Nevertheless, he continued to marry couples, proclaiming his denominational authority superior to secular law. He then successfully used the same authority to sanction multiple marriages.

No Man Knows My History was an extraordinary biographical work. Brodie's case was thorough and compellingly presented. She reconstructed a history of the beginnings of the Mormon Church, one that it certainly did not want to recognize.

LIFE TO THE FULLEST

Bernard Brodie earned a Ph.D. from the University of Chicago in 1940. The family moved several times as Bernard pursued his career. Fawn Brodie raised three children while continuing research in biography and history. At first she stayed uncommitted to publication deadlines, but when her oldest child entered school Fawn returned to biography.[11]

Her next book treated the life of Thaddeus Stevens, a Republican leader in Congress during the Reconstruction era who had championed the rights of emancipated African Americans. Stevens also fought for public education. He led the attempt to impeach President Andrew Johnson and took on other causes that lacked organized constituencies. In stark contrast to her first biography, which humanized an icon and bared his imperfections and his misdeeds, the Stevens endeavor enhanced the prevailing image of her biographical subject.

Fawn Brodie's mother attempted suicide in the 1950s; her father suffered a heart attack. Thomas E. McKay died in 1958 after years of ill health. Her mother then succeeded in a suicide attempt. Fawn Brodie saw a psychoanalyst for two and a half years in the 1950s, attempting to come to terms with her tremendous pain. The therapy led to new approaches in her biographical work. She explored psychology and psychoanalysis and developed friendships with several psychoanalysts as a result.[12]

Fawn Brodie began to teach history at the University of Southern California. The turmoil of the 1960s opened a new vista, as contemporary politics captured her attention. The assassination of Robert Kennedy, riots in the Watts section of Los Angeles, the Manson murders, and the Patty Hearst kidnapping were all electrifying events. The world seemed to be turned on its edge. Every day arrived with such exhilaration that the past then seemed lost. If you weren't "relevant" during those days, you were pronounced dead. Fawn Brodie made a speech in Salt Lake City, urging Mormons to allow African Americans to become priests. She pointed out that Joseph Smith's ideas had evolved during his life. Originally a firm anti-abolitionist, he later favored the equality of blacks in every respect except intermarriage. She found the real point of resistance in "quiet decisions made by Mormon leaders in the past." She concluded her speech by saying, "The past should not control the decisions we make today, especially if they are decisions reinforcing injustice."[13]

Despite her fame as a biographer, Fawn Brodie had to struggle to gain a full professorship in the history department at UCLA. The department head, an undistinguished male historian, claimed to be troubled by the fact that Brodie's degrees were earned in literature, not history. She was, however, eventually awarded the professorship.

AN INTIMATE HISTORY

Historian Winthrop Jordan's work, *White over Black: Attitudes Towards the Negro, 1550–1812*, captured Brodie's attention. In it Jordan acknowledged that Jefferson may have had a sexual liaison with Sally Hemings; but

Jordan did not pursue the evidence to Brodie's satisfaction, and she decided to take a look for herself.[14]

As with *No Man Knows My History*, Brodie's work on Jefferson represents a fusion; the parts are clearly defined, yet they fit well together. Brodie's biography combined various pieces of information to support her conclusion that the liaison was entirely plausible. The most potent evidence came from newspaper accounts, including that of James Callender. Brodie revived the statement Madison Hemings had given to a newspaperman in 1873. The three-page "memoir" gave a vivid account of three generations of miscegenation in the Hemings family. Madison Hemings explained that Thomas Jefferson was the father of all of the children of his mother, Sally Hemings. Madison Hemings' remembrance, ignored for one hundred years, was never widely circulated before the publication of Brodie's biography.[15]

Brodie also must have been strongly swayed by the Wright/Trollope account, referred to in Chapter Six, which kept alive rumors of Jefferson's mulatto children leaving Monticello at will. The account did not offer names and other specifics, but it represented more independent corroboration. Brodie found the Wright/Trollope account through the work of Pearl Graham, a writer who stumbled upon the Hemings/Jefferson controversy but who was unable to perform the detective work Fawn Brodie was by then used to doing. Brodie cited references to Sally Hemings' attractiveness and the physical likeness of her children to Thomas Jefferson. Brodie brought historical evidence to bear against the story that Jefferson's nephews fathered Sally Hemings' children. Her exhaustive research accumulated more and more evidence supporting the liaison.

Thomas Jefferson, an Intimate History triggered whirlwinds of denial, surprise, and adulation. The book became a best-seller and inspired other literary works about the Jefferson/Hemings liaison. For Minnie S. Woodson this work was a megawatt floodlight exposing a history that other historians held no desire to reveal.

NOTES

1. Gerda Lerner, *Why History Matters* (Oxford: Oxford University Press, 1997), 137–38.

2. Jan E. Lewis, "The White Jeffersons," in *Sally Hemings and Thomas Jefferson*, ed. Jan E. Lewis and Peter S. Onuf (Charlottesville: University Press of Virginia, 1999), 153; and Newell G. Bringhurst, *Fawn McKay Brodie: A Biographer's Life* (Norman: University of Oklahoma Press, 1999), 218: Jordan quote.

3. Fawn M. Brodie, *Thomas Jefferson, an Intimate History* (New York: W. W. Norton, 1974), 390.

4. Ibid., 391.

5. Bringhurst, *Fawn McKay Brodie*, 7–12: early childhood.

6. Ibid., 20: "quite heretic."

7. Newell G. Bringhurst, "Fawn McKay Brodie: Her Biographies as Autobiography," *Pacific Historical Review*, vol. 203–30 (May 1990), 205, from unpublished recollections of Flora McKay Crawford, "Flora on Fawn."

8. Bringhurst, *Fawn McKay Brodie*, 59: marriage.

9. Ibid., 116–20.

10. Fawn Brodie, *No Man Knows My History* (New York: Knopf, 1945), 27–36.

11. Bringhurst, *Fawn McKay Brodie*, 116–20.

12. Bringhurst, "Fawn McKay Brodie," 220.

13. Bringhurst, *Fawn McKay Brodie*, 191.

14. Ibid., 218.

15. Brodie, *Thomas Jefferson*, 471–76.

CHAPTER TEN

Minnie S. Woodson Strikes Genealogical Gold

If the school, pulpit, and the press be natural and legitimate means for our moral elevation, . . . [a]ll that is requisite to effect it, is the will.

—Lewis Woodson, 1873

Mother and Dad drove to Ohio in September 1975, visiting places neither had previously been. My father later described his involvement by saying, "I was the chauffeur." His interest, however, went well beyond staying on the correct side of the road. They visited local historian Beverly J. Gray in Chillicothe, Ohio. Ms. Gray is descended from a family of mulattos who came to southern Ohio early in the nineteenth century and stayed there. Some descendents of Joe Fossett, one of Betty Hemings' grandsons, still live in Chillicothe, and Gray had known the families all her life. She also knows descendents of Madison Hemings who live in Ohio. She gave Mother information about the Woodsons' early years in Ohio and about the history of the A.M.E. Church in Chillicothe. My parents also called on George Woodson in Wilberforce, where a tornado had struck a few months before their arrival. I had met George Woodson during my rambling trip to St. Louis with Lewis Woodson (b. 1933). Wilberforce University was badly damaged by the tornado, but George Woodson's house was spared.

My parents searched historical libraries in Columbus and Chillicothe, the county seat of Ross County. The Thomas Woodson family lived there for eight years before buying the farm in Jackson County. In Chillicothe and in Jackson County, Mother collected deeds, wills, and marriage licenses, documenting lives of dozens of Woodsons born in the nineteenth century. She obtained a copy of Thomas Woodson's will and news articles about the early days of Berlin Crossroads. Documentation confirmed the oral history, which indicated that coal was found on Thomas Woodson's property and that he sold land for a significant profit. A map dating from the 1870s indicates that land adjacent to Thomas Woodson's remaining property belonged to the Jackson County Coal and Iron Company.[1]

While in Jackson County, they located Ronald Wilson. The Wilson surname marked several stones in the little cemetery in Roads. Ronald Wilson and his brother were sitting on their porch when Mother and Dad drove up to their house. The two little old white men did not seem surprised at all that someone was poking around Jackson County digging into the past. Fawn Brodie's book had stirred conversations about times long gone in seemingly unconnected places.

Ronald Wilson told them that the Woodson and Leach families were related, as Jemima Woodson and Fanny Leach were sisters. This was vital oral history because no document ever existed in Ohio linking Fanny and Jemima, who lived and died there, as sisters. The Wilsons are descended from Fanny Leach Wilson (b. 1815), a daughter of Fanny Leach (b. circa 1778). Further, Ronald Wilson said that as a child of six he had seen Thomas Woodson (b. 1790). My parents were astounded and amazed. Wilson asked Mother and Dad, "Was Tom Woodson a white man?" Months later Mother assured me that Ronald Wilson was indeed 103 years old and looked the part. (He had to have been that old to have seen Thomas Woodson.) Mother often had to overcome my cautious nature, as I found her discoveries too good to be true. Wilson said that the Leach and Woodson families had come to Jackson County from "Greensboro," indicating that "Greensboro" was somewhere to the east. Mother and Dad later surmised that this place was actually Greenbriar, West Virginia, which was part of Virginia before the Civil War. Mother would later repeat the conversation with Ronald Wilson many times, stretching to imitate Wilson's twang in pronouncing "Greensboro."

Next, they drove to Lewisburg, seat of Greenbriar County, located just west of the Allegheny Mountains. The Greenbriar River runs through the county, pouring into the New River. The New River empties into the Kanawha River, which flows into the Ohio. Greenbriar was located on the Midland Trail, which was used during the post–Revolutionary War westward migration. Once across the Alleghenies, the path through Greenbriar to the Ohio River was obstacle-free.

Mother and Dad dug into county courthouse records, not knowing what, if anything, could be found. They found that Fanny Leach had sold her land to William Renick in 1824 before relocating to Ohio. The discovery confirmed Ronald Wilson's oral history by connecting Fanny to Greenbriar County through documentation. Mother began to look at documents of the Renick family, having temporarily hit a dead end looking for a trail of the Woodsons and Leaches. An article in a genealogical magazine listed Fanny Leach as a daughter of William Renick. This turned out to be a mistake. Fanny's name appeared in a will next to but not in William Renick's will. Trying to sort out the history and the mistake, Mother looked at the will next to William Renick's will and made a remarkable discovery! The will of Hannah Grant contained the names of Fanny Leach, Marmer Woodson, Thomas Woodson, and Louis Woodson of Ohio! This was a genealogical gold strike, a mother lode. Clearly, the will was an astounding discovery, but who in the world was Hannah Grant? Fanny Leach and Marmer Woodson were cited in the will as her children. Spelled correctly, Marmer Woodson was Jemima Woodson, and thus Hannah Grant was the mother of the two sisters! Lewis Woodson's name is commonly misspelled. Though Lewis Woodson was in Pittsburgh by the date of the will, June 10, 1834, Hannah was not aware of this, or it was simply not important to her declining condition. The combination of the will and Ronald Wilson's oral history placed the Woodson family in Greenbriar County, closer in time and location to Monticello than the Jackson County chronicles.[2]

Hannah Grant's will and the deed that documented the sale of Leach land not only placed the Leaches and the Woodsons in Greenbriar County but began to expose the family origins of Jemima Woodson. As Mother explained these deeper roots to Dad, her eyes sparkled and her eyelids and eyebrows bounced with glee, as if she were a schoolgirl again reveling over a good report card. She would later return to the cemetery at Roads and to Wilberforce, and next began treks to the courthouses in several Virginia counties. This would be the only visit to Greenbriar County.

When Mother started on the trail in 1972, she was ready to follow it "wherever it may lead." Intellectually, she was not sure if the oral history she had heard from the Woodson men was valid because there were no tangible links to Thomas Jefferson and Monticello. After finding Hannah Grant's will, Mother was certain beyond doubt that Thomas Woodson was the son of Thomas Jefferson. At every turn the oral history was being confirmed by documentation. The picture of Thomas Woodson's early life was becoming clearer. Mother knew that Greenbriar County was a way station for the family and that the family had come from Virginia, and she became certain

Know all men by these presents that I Hannah Grant a free woman of _color_ of the county of Greenbrier and State of Virginia being weakly in body but of sound & perfect mind do hereby make and publish this my last will and testament

Revoking all others heretofore made in manner and form following Viz it.. item first I do hereby will and bequeath unto Shelton Brock a bound boy now living with me one half quarter of section of land in the state of Ohio to be bought with my money and I do hereby appoint Thomas Woodson a freeman of _color_ in Ohio as his guardian to see that he gets said land and has the benefit of it. Item second I also will and bequeath unto the heirs of Matilda Woodson of Ohio ten dollars in cash. Item third I also will and bequeath unto Lewis Woodson of Ohio ten dollars in cash I also will and wish that at my death my property of all sorts be sold and after my Funeral expenses and just debts be paid that the remainder be equally divided amongst my children Viz Fanny Leach, Marmer Woodson, Moses Grant Nelson Grant Richard Grant Rachel Grant Odd Grant I likewise wish and hereby appoint my trusty friend John Burr as my lawful Executor of this my last will and testament in testimony whereof I hereunto set my hand and seal this 10 day of May 1834

Teste
Ephraim G Howe
Michael Bright

Hannah + Grant {Seal}
her
mark

Hannah Grant's will.

that if any older connection were to be found it would lead to a Jefferson/ Monticello connection. No information surfaced which challenged the oral history; but, if it had, beyond this point Mother would have questioned its validity. She was not certain that the trail would keep yielding documentation, as she feared that any earlier evidence, if it had ever existed, would have been destroyed. Yet the trail had yielded so much that further pursuit was in order.

The time was rich with discovery. Though Fawn Brodie's book inspired Mother to continue on the trail, this was not her only focus of discovery. Lewis Woodson's institution-building during the early years of African American settlement in the Midwest was another source of fascination. Mother gathered information on such ancestors as Sarah Jane Woodson Early, youngest daughter of Thomas Woodson. After Sarah Jane retired from a career in education, she wrote a biography of her husband, the Reverend Jordan Early. Mother discovered this biography in the Moreland-Spingarn Collection at Howard University in Washington, D.C.

Mother began to correspond with Fawn Brodie. She informed Brodie of the Woodson oral history and of her recent discoveries. Brodie was in touch with the descendants of Madison Hemings and Eston Hemings Jefferson. While Brodie met with descendants of Eston Hemings, she never met Mother in person. In 1977, Brodie published an article in *American Heritage*, revealing information she had gathered from the descendants of Thomas Woodson, Madison Hemings, and Eston Hemings Jefferson.

Trips to the National Archives building on Constitution Avenue in Washington, D.C., became a regular part of Mother's regimen. She found Thomas Woodson and his family listed in the U.S. Census of 1820 in Greenbriar County. Thomas Woodson, Hannah Grant, and Fanny Leach were three of six "free colored" persons listed in the 1820 Greenbriar census as heads of households. The Greenbriar County census for 1810 has been lost. The U.S. Census recorded Thomas Woodson in a time and place consistent with the Woodson oral history, which linked Thomas Woodson and Thomas Jefferson.

Before Mother started her search, the oldest point of history which was documented by the Woodsons of Washington was the birth of Pop's father, Granville Sharp Woodson in 1840 in Pittsburgh. At the outset there was no proof that Thomas Woodson even existed. With the deaths of Thomas Woodson, Lewis Woodson, and Granville Woodson in or between 1878 and 1880, our family lost its link to the past until Mother began her remarkable search. She discovered dozens of documents pertaining to Thomas Woodson's life. She then stretched the confirmed history back to 1820 in Greenbriar County West Virginia (then Virginia). In 1975 the gap between Tom's departure from Monticello in 1802 and Thomas Woodson's documented residence in Greenbriar County was eighteen years.

During her search, possibly on another trip to Ohio, Mother found a notation submitted by the Reverend Thomas Wesley Woodson (1853–1946) to the editors of an A.M.E. Church encyclopedia published in 1912. The biographical sketch he submitted included the information that he was the grandson of Thomas Woodson, who was the son of Thomas Jefferson.

This notation prompts the question, Why wasn't this written down sooner? Blacks have endured centuries of abuse in this land. African languages were torn away from our ancestors. Especially in the South, blacks were abused if they did something as simple as look in a white person's eyes. During Reverend Thomas Wesley Woodson's life, lynchings were "the rule of law" though whites paid lip-service to a proper system. Blacks kept their history and genealogy alive within their own communities, where the oral history was sufficient and safer. There was no expectation that whites would believe their history or admit it if they did. In addition to Thomas Wesley Woodson's notation, Mother found instances of hints other Woodsons left linking their heritage to Thomas Jefferson. In the Augustine letters Lewis Woodson made reference to a pair of Parisian eyeglasses. Among the personal papers of Jesse Moreland and Lucy Woodson Moreland in the Moreland-Spingarn Library at Howard University is a large piece of brown paper covered with writing, most it unintelligible. In the middle of the paper is the name Thos. Jefferson. These odd clues were perhaps adopted by the Woodsons to keep their history alive.

The discovery was rich with links. Mother uncovered history that would have been unimaginable years or even months before. Still a gap existed. She wondered about finding links to further complete the life story of Thomas Woodson and confirm the Woodson oral history. The path seemed to be a dead end. Efforts to locate Thomas Woodson among slave records of the white Virginia Woodsons living in the counties near Monticello in the years 1795–1810 proved fruitless. She began to realize that pursuing the roots of Jemima, Thomas' wife, might yield information that could then place Thomas in an earlier time. She decided to assume that Jemima arrived in Greenbriar from a Woodson plantation located relatively close to Monticello. The oral history placed Thomas on a Woodson farm. Further, she assumed, until information was found to the contrary, that Thomas adopted the surname Woodson not only because he lived for a time on a Woodson plantation but also because it was Jemima's surname. She would attempt to find a path that led in that direction.

PUSHING INTO THE EIGHTEENTH CENTURY

Mother continued to research white Woodsons living in the counties near Monticello. Now, instead of looking for Tom, she looked for Jemima. Within a couple of months it seemed as though she was personally acquainted with every Woodson that lived in Virginia from 1619 to 1820. When I visited my parents in Washington during this time, Mother would recite the names and vital information of dozens of white Woodsons from the period. I usually listened to this genealogical litany while Mother cooked dinner and I sat on a favored stool. The Woodsons she sought were slave owners among a great number of Woodsons in Virginia who were descendants of the John Woodson who had come to the Virginia colony from England in 1619.

Mother followed John Woodson's history in a book of genealogy by Henry Morton Woodson. A copy was housed at the Library of Congress. Mother spent days there reading it. She was particularly interested in Dorothea Randolph Woodson's family. Dorothea was Jefferson's mother's sister and had married Colonel John Woodson.[3]

The next major discoveries were in the will of Drury Woodson and his tax records of the early and mid-1780s, which listed names of adult slaves. Mother discovered that Drury Woodson had been the owner of Jemima and Jemima's mother and sister, Hannah and Fanny! Drury Woodson lived and died in Cumberland County, located on the Piedmont Plateau, on the south bank of the James River. Mother confirmed that the names listed in the will were actually the Hannah, Fanny and Jemima she sought by sifting through the tax records of Drury Woodson. The 1781 property tax record listed only one child with Hannah, as Jemima was not then born. This meant that the ages of the three slaves listed in the Drury Woodson will matched the ages of Hannah Grant and her two daughters.[4]

Though this still did not directly place Thomas Woodson on the Drury Woodson plantation, it closed the gap further. It placed Thomas Woodson's wife, as a child, twenty-five miles from Monticello. Mother believed that Thomas was not sent to Drury Woodson's plantation. She thought it more likely that Thomas was sent to the Goochland County farm of either John or Josiah Woodson, sons of Colonel John Woodson, who died in 1790. The oral history handed down in my family stated that Thomas was sent to John Woodson's farm. John and Josiah were Thomas Jefferson's first cousins. She did not discover precisely how Thomas and Jemima met or how Jemima became free. Those questions remain as challenges.

I have discovered that a John Woodson operated a ferry across the James River under sanction of the state of Virginia. The ferry operated near the

Drury Woodson farm. Certainly the frequency of contact between the Woodsons of Goochland and Cumberland Counties was intensified by this enterprise. Thomas Jefferson used this ferry several times. Drury Woodson's will mentioned a John Woodson; Drury did not have a son named John. I discovered several white John Woodsons and determined a likelihood that Thomas Woodson had contact with more than one of them. However, only the one from Goochland County migrated west, and he is certainly the one noted in my family's oral history. Yet they were related and connected. This series of links gives credence to the likelihood that the encounter and union between Thomas and Jemima was an offshoot of the interchange between the white Woodsons.[5]

Alone, this assemblage of connections did not "prove" that Thomas Woodson came from Monticello. "Proof" lay in the interpretation of assembled pieces of evidence. As a separate body of evidence, the white Woodson connections with both Thomas and Jemima appreciably strengthened the likelihood of Thomas' biological connection to Thomas Jefferson. Mother was ecstatic but not completely satisfied. Her new pursuit became discovering the circumstances under which Thomas, Hannah, Fanny and Jemima gained freedom and reached Greenbriar County.

In 1979 the Jefferson/Hemings controversy took another turn. Barbara Chase-Riboud, a Philadelphian transplanted to France, wrote a fictional account, *Sally Hemings*, based on Fawn Brodie's book. Chase-Riboud's book was very popular, selling over a million copies. Jeffersonians were horrified. *The Jefferson Scandals: A Rebuttal* by Virginius Dabney was one of many attempts to maintain past illusions. *Sally Hemings* painted a credible picture of Hemings' life. In particular, the kinship between John Wayles' daughters, Martha Wayles Jefferson (Thomas Jefferson's wife) and Sally Hemings, was soundly accepted by the public. No longer were historians able to push the half-sister relationship into a closet.

LIFE IN THE PRESENT TENSE

Mother and Dad's retirement activity was not directed exclusively to genealogical research. Mother served on the Washington, D.C., school board. Dad was the skeptic. Although he worked to help her win election to the board, he did not think the position would allow her to accomplish much. With more time on her hands, Mother also began to paint again. I joined them for weekend sails on the Chesapeake Bay on the wooden-hulled sailboat. Dad was playing catch-up, as Mother and I were already accomplished sailors. During the time my Uncle Granville had owned the boat, Dad was often at sea or in a far-off land working for the Naval Oceanographic Office. Uncle Granville's wife, Herta, was not fond of sailing, thus Mother grabbed the opportunity to sail with him. A new sail mate was Trena Parker Woodson, a beautiful brown beach bum from Atlantic City, New Jersey. We married in 1973. Not yet having achieved her dream of a leisurely life of sun and surf, she resigned herself to the excruciatingly painful life of an airline hostess, flying the world over, staying in Hilton Intercontinental Hotels and occasionally bringing home a duty-free trinket or two hundred.

In the summer of 1975, Dad sold that boat and bought a larger one, a thirty-six-foot fiberglass sloop named *Sweet Pea*. I sailed as much as I could. Mother enjoyed *Sweet Pea* but was kept busy by her school board duties and other projects. I worked a regular workweek; Dad's workweek avocations were golf and tennis. On weekends, Dad and I set off to explore the Chesapeake Bay.

Sailing adventures moved into high gear in October 1975, not long after Mother and Dad returned from Ohio. Dad planned to sail to Haiti, where he and Mother had lived in 1943. One of his former co-workers had retired to the Florida Keys; the plan was to take two boats to Haiti. I helped ferry *Sweet Pea* on the first leg of the trip. We left Annapolis on a cloudy, windy Saturday. The problem was that the wind blew from the south, which was where we wished to go. Progress for the first thirty-six hours down the Chesapeake Bay was very slow. When we finally made our way south of the Potomac River, the wind failed to blow from any direction. Greatly disappointed, we motored into Portsmouth, Virginia.

The next day, we motored further south, first through the harbor, then through canals leading to the sounds of the North Carolina coastline. We had passed by dozens of mothballed navy ships, all of which had seen better days, when an unmistakable shape appeared on the horizon. It was the S.S. *United States*, which had carried Mother, Dad, Jon, and me home from Europe after Dad finished his tour of duty in Germany! I was too young to remember having the run of the ship while my parents suffered seasickness, yet I knew it well from family pictures. Ocean liners doubled as troop carriers in times of need. The S.S. *United States* was the fastest ocean liner ever built. Its top speed was classified information. On our voyage home from Germany, we passed the Statue of Liberty a day early. Dad had told me that at least a dozen times over the years.

Mother's eyes were tearful, and her speech was altered by occasional quivering. Dad was stunned into an uncommon silence. I had never seen my parents become so emotional. This outpouring was over a large hunk of scrap metal! After passing it, we each looked back at least a half dozen times.

Witnessing Mother and Dad's reaction was as unforgettable for me as the voyage across the Atlantic in 1953 had been for them. Dad broke the silence by telling us that the ship's top speed had been classified information and a dozen other facts about it we had heard many times before. Along with Bob Seaton, a retired Air Force officer who was also along for the trip, I disembarked in North Carolina and returned to Philadelphia. Mother and Dad continued south.

My parents left *Sweet Pea* in the South for the winter, but returned for the final push to Haiti in the early spring. Bob Seaton again joined them. The trip was challenging, as the party sailed the entire distance beating into the wind. They never reached Haiti. The farthest point was Georgetown, a town in the Bahamas, south of Nassau. They ran out of time to fight their way farther south.

I flew to Nassau to meet Mother and Dad that spring. I wanted to help with the trip back to Florida and to experience blue water sailing. After a cab ride to the marina, I asked the guys in the marina office if they knew the whereabouts of two Americans on a thirty-six-foot sloop. They had no difficulty making the connection. As I walked toward *Sweet Pea*, I saw that the canopy was up, a good sign that someone was aboard.

I found the quintessential John Woodson setting. Dad was serving midafternoon rum colas. In addition to Mother and Dad, Frank and Frank's exwife were aboard. Frank, one of Dad's former co-workers whose last name will remain a mystery here, married his ex-wife when he was about thirty and she was a stunning beautiful nineteen-year-old college student at American University. They divorced after ten years; Frank married another nineteen-year-old college student. That marriage was allegedly on the skids also. Frank and his first wife had come to the warm shores and cool breezes of the Caribbean to "discuss their child's education." Dad had another good story to embellish and tell. Meanwhile, he was happy to share Bacardi's best rum, Anejo, with the best of friends.

The sail to Florida was idyllic. We were pushed along by trade winds; nights were moonlit. *Sweet Pea* was in her element, gliding across the Gulf Stream like a paper airplane. During a twenty-four-hour period, we did not see another boat, a plane, or any sign of mankind beyond *Sweet Pea's* lifelines. The trip exceeded my expectations. Though the sail was a true thrill, Mother told me that she knew I was also there because I was not about to let my parents sail on blue water alone. She read me perfectly. Fifty hours after slipping out of Nassau, we were docked in Vero Beach, Florida. During the next few days the dolphins escorted us north in the Intercoastal Waterway.

I am told that Resolution 238 of the United Marital Commission decrees that wives enjoy shared vacation time in matching proportions to parents, otherwise said husband shall forfeit quiet enjoyment of his castle until compensation of a value equal to his sanity is paid in full with compounded hourly interest. I have this by the authority of the Beach Goddess. I met Trena, the Beach Goddess, in San Juan, Puerto, Rico, after I left Mother and Dad in Florida. Trena never met a Hilton she didn't like, but the Caribe Hilton is especially beautiful. Fortunately, Trena was still working for Trans World Airways, enjoying massive hotel discounts.

To my surprise, the nightclub act at the El San Juan Hotel got my adrenaline pumping faster than the trip across the Gulf Stream. In addition to dancing girls and magic acts, a rather large Bengal tiger made an appearance on stage. Trena and I were no longer pleased with our second row seats. In fact I calculated that the first row would have been a safer position since any leap into the audience would have taken our feline friend over the heads of those seated there. The tiger commanded strict attention even though it (I didn't inspect for gender) did not say much. Hotel patrons were expected to gamble afterwards. We were on excitement overload, so the casino visit lasted only ten minutes.

I have been in the vicinity of the El San Juan Hotel a couple of times since being "entertained" by the tiger. I always check the nightclub roster, not in hopes of catching the show again but to ensure that there are no large pussy-cats nearby that might spring loose and visit me while I'm napping on the beach.

Then a father of two sons, John (born in 1975) and Byron (born in 1977), I continued to visit my parents frequently on weekends. There was more to talk about than ever and a lot of catching-up to do. If there was one subject that drew the most attention over time, it was the Woodson family legacy and Mother's ongoing genealogical research. Not only was the subject inescapably fascinating, but Mother had absorbed a massive amount of data and had a very natural need to talk about it. These encounters all had the drama of a volcanic eruption. As soon as she began to speak, the researched information spewed out as fast as she could talk with a prevailing sense of endlessness.

At times I felt uneasy about Mother's quest. I often played devil's advocate, forcing her to cite layer upon layer of evidence to prove each point. Her research and its depth were stupendous, and I was constantly amazed. I knew the collision with institutional forces that refused to recognize the true and intimate life of Thomas Jefferson was coming closer. I had no time to support Mother's endeavor, yet I knew that when she went public with her research she would need my support. When we first read Fawn Brodie's biography, we thought that the landscape of the Jefferson/Hemings controversy had been forever altered. However, it slowly became clear that a gang of good old boys who were then invisible to us had, figuratively, poured motor oil on the road, sending Dr. Brodie's shiny new Mercedes sliding off the road.

In 1977 Mother and Dad produced the first *Woodson Source Book*. It was a phenomenal leap from the one-page family tree created in 1969. The names and lives of hundreds of Woodsons were now chronicled and interconnected. Fifty copies of 290-page book were mailed to relatives throughout the country. Mother and Dad created the source book to inform the Woodsons of the legacy of Thomas Woodson and to encourage them to join the effort to uncover additional information. In effect, the copies were seeds produced expressly to generate new pools of energy to recapture and extend the legacy of Thomas and Jemima Woodson and to link that legacy to an even earlier one. This original source book contained only brief mention of the oral history linking the family to Thomas Jefferson. Later versions of the *Woodson Source Book* delved a little further into this family linkage.

Mother and Dad spoke with cousins in Pittsburgh about a reunion, and that discussion led to talk of a family association. The Thomas Woodson Family Association held its first reunion in Pittsburgh in 1978. The family met at the Hilton overlooking Point State Park at the convergence of the Allegheny, Monongahela, and Ohio Rivers. The location was fitting. In the mid-nineteenth century, Lewis Woodson lived only a few steps away from the hotel site. The majority of those present were from the Lewis Woodson line, but a few members of other family lines also attended. Norma Woodson McDaniel, the teacher Mother fatefully met in 1972, John Quill Taylor King, and his mother, Alice Woodson King Johnson, came. They were descendants of the William Woodson line. Edgar P. Woodson of Marysville, Ohio, arrived. He was a member of the James Woodson line. Absent were the descendants of Jemima Woodson Nukes and two other known Woodson lines. Connections with those relatives had yet to be made. Only a few descendants of Rachel Woodson Cassell attended, but that line would provide strong contingents at future reunions.

For the next few years reunions were held on regularly. Family members hosted reunions in places as far apart as Austin, Texas, and Washington, D.C. The Association was incorporated and the presidency was judiciously passed among the family leaders. Dad served as the second president. Jane Faithful of Ohio, a Frances Woodson Cassell descendent, was its first female president.

MORE RECONNECTIONS

Trena and I, by then blessed with three delightful children, combined a trip to the 1984 reunion with a vacation. We decided to travel from Philadelphia to Kentucky by train. Trips to Washington were like trips to the dry cleaners for me, so the vacation seemed to start only when my son Byron, then seven years old, met another youngster after we rolled out of Union Station and crossed the Potomac River. The youngster from West Virginia was on his way home from visiting his father, stationed in Germany with the army. As the train approached Charlottesville, Virginia, I became apprehensive. I knew that once we crossed the Allegheny Mountains my long-anticipated rendezvous with the past would soon be upon me. I thought of my family's 200-year-old genealogical controversy, which began in Charlottesville.

Rolling through the Blue Ridge Mountain passes toward the Alleghenies, Byron and his new friend enticed my oldest son, John, to join them in setting up a Monopoly board in the café car. Having lived on an army base in Germany during my early childhood in the 1950s I saw a bit of my own childhood in the young West Virginian, who relished his camouflage-colored mock fatigues, complete with cap and black boots. Our five-year-old daughter Kellie, undisturbed by her brothers' relocation to another rail car, controlled a more valuable monopoly, the attention of Mom and Dad. She didn't flaunt her bounty but celebrated as she floated between our seats and hers, touching the floor sparingly. Trena remained uncharacteristically serene during the twelve-hour trip, so I enjoyed a treat as well. The Monopoly game disbanded when the slender, blond-haired kid departed with his grandparents. We detrained in Huntingdon, a town on the Ohio River, late that night.

In a rented Dodge station wagon, we headed across Kentucky for Mammoth Cave National Park the next day. We slept in a tent I had lugged along. Trena was delighted to see a doe with her trailing fawn near our campsite the next morning but was otherwise unimpressed with the wooded experience. Trena's definition of vacation included far-off island beaches, Hilton Hotels, Boeing 727s, Paris, Cairo, and the high adventure of a guided tour of the Pyramids. Gazing at the fawn, Kellie expressed her rapture with numerous tender variations of "Ooo." She was thoroughly impressed with the "little baby deer." Animals in a natural habitat were novelties to us. We are city folk; this was a new experience. Later in the morning we explored the Mammoth Caves. Kellie's bliss was dashed for the balance of the day when the tour guide turned out the lights in a very large cave, lighting a small candle for effect.

We next took in Abe Lincoln's boyhood home and the lush, gorgeous horse country northeast of Lexington, Kentucky. Traveling north that Friday afternoon, accommodations became a matter of dispute. The itinerary, planned two months before, called for a second night in the tent. Mutiny was at hand, and the boys sided with the person who usually did the cooking! We crossed the Ohio River and spent the night at Brown's Motel in Aberdeen, Ohio. As the Beach Goddess declared the motel bathtub a luxury of heretofore unimaginable refinement, I briefly contemplated pitching the tent roadside and making my return to Brown's when the bubbly bath oil ran out. A sunny Saturday morning ride through southern Ohio found a hardscrabble land of little hills on a road that twisted and turned without pattern.

In the hamlet of Roads we joined the 1984 Thomas Woodson Family Reunion. My parents were there along with about one hundred other Woodson descendants, with more arriving by the minute. Walking past the one-room cinderblock building that had replaced the Rachel Cassell Educational Center, we entered the sacred ground that had some years ago lost the arched sign that designated it the " Woodson Cemetery." I had anticipated a trek to the cemetery during the dozen years following Mother's discovery. The African American families gathered that day had lost track of each other over the generations. My mother reconnected the family by researching the Woodson genealogy, then contacted families by phone. Since the first reunion had been held in Pittsburgh, more family lines had been located. Some lines had parted 140 years and four generations earlier.

An awesome sense of humility and pride came over me as I first set eyes on the badly worn gravestone of Jemima Woodson. To think that my grandfather and his father had never seen this sacred site! I was stunned. Mother circulated among relatives, matching faces with voices she recognized. It wasn't obvious to everyone, but she continued her mission, absorbing more genealogy on that day than most people absorb in a lifetime.

Since Mother's discovery of the cemetery, I had gained an understanding of the interrelations between the families buried there. Woodson, Leach, Cassell, Wilson, and other names marked the gravestones. I learned from Mother that no Leaches or Woodsons lived in Jackson County any longer. Wilsons, who were descended from Fanny Leach Wilson, did remain in the area. A few Wilsons stopped by the cemetery that day to greet us, including a fellow who smiled the entire time Mother spoke with him. He looked to be about ten years my senior. I said hello to the man but was stymied at further conversation. I asked Mother in a soft tone but one loud enough to be heard, "Mother, do the Wilsons consider themselves white or black?" She didn't answer. I thought she heard me, but she was soon at another end of the cemetery. Mother was not prone to ignore people, especially me. Before asking her again, as I tend to be persistent, I realized that I had asked a question she considered inane and contrary to her mission. Mother not only considered racial divisiveness offensive, she considered racial identification itself offensive, especially between family members. The Wilson man certainly came in friendship if not kinship. I certainly wanted to converse with him, but felt at a loss as to how to launch the conversation.

Blacks habitually talk to whites in a certain conversational style and talk to blacks in another. Whites do the same. When I attended Western High School during the mid-1960s in Washington, D.C., it was racially integrated. I had black, white, and Asian friends, but there were two or three students whose racial identity I was never able or motivated to determine. I avoided them. I never had a problem being friendly to whites who returned a like degree of respect or friendliness. I didn't have a problem with mixed-race people who did not identify themselves as African Americans. Still, I found it difficult when I did not know someone's racial identity.

I did not converse with the Wilson man. My inability to handle the situation made me feel inept. Trena and the kids were occupied and didn't seem to need my attention. I wandered out of the cemetery trying to fathom all that had transpired among the Woodsons since they first walked on that ground 150 years before then.

Three cars with Minnesota plates rolled to a stop at the bottom of the sloping entrance. Emerging from the cars were descendants of Frances Woodson Cassell (b. 1814), whom I knew only from Mother's research papers; they had come heavy. I absorbed the wonder of the moment, as if these beautiful, robust people had found their way out of a huge dust storm that had lasted one hundred years. As my thoughts shifted from who would come next to what would come next, the significance of this gathering overcame me; I began to choke. I fought back the tears and turned around. I was indescribably proud of my family and knew that the force bringing us together would provide benefits far beyond the confines of the family. Frances' descendants from Detroit and elsewhere had arrived earlier. One came from New Zealand. My great-great grandfather, Lewis Woodson (b. 1806), Frances' oldest brother, fathered ten children who lived to maturity. Frances also produced ten and, from what I was witnessing, equal portions of Woodson tenacity and pride. I was ecstatic to be a part of the magnetism that pulled this family together, but more than others I realized that we were moving toward a collision with larger and more complex forces.

For the next few hours, I retreated into the warm beautiful smiles, keenly attentive ears, and happy chatter of my cousin Madelyn. She is, like me, a member of the Lewis line of the family. The reunion continued later that afternoon with supper in a nearby state park and a banquet dinner at the reunion hotel in Columbus the following day. In Columbus, relatives were able to purchase the latest version of the *Woodson Source Book*, which then comprised 450 pages. While the reunion concluded at the Wilberforce, Ohio, home of George Woodson on Monday, Trena, the kids, and I boarded a Greyhound bus for Philadelphia. Our intricately planned vacation was over; the quest for roots was not.

CONVERGENCE AT MONTICELLO

In early 1986, Mother learned that cancer had invaded her body. Walter Reed Medical Center diagnosed her condition, saying that it was hopeless. She was sent home by doctors who predicted that she had only a few months to live. Mother had other ideas! She read a book by a cancer survivor and talked to her multidisciplined (an M.D. was buried in there somewhere) brother in California. She adopted a macrobiotic diet and practiced Do-In, a derivative of acupuncture. She educated herself about time-honored Oriental healing techniques as well as the high-tech discoveries of modern Western medicine. The cancer team at Howard University operated. In a few months she had rid her body of cancer! She had things to do, and dying wasn't on the list. Nevertheless, she did miss the 1986 Woodson family reunion in Minneapolis.

In 1987, Mother finished *The Sable Curtain*, a novel based on the life of Thomas Woodson. It followed the format of Barbara Chase-Riboud's novel *Sally Hemings*, fiction based on a historical platform. After failing to attract a publisher Mother self-published *The Sable Curtain*, selling all 500 copies. Its story line did not start in Paris with Tom's conception but in 1802 with his banishment from Monticello. The story vividly developed the strong bonds that must have helped the family flourish in Greenbriar County. This time, technology made Mother's task a little easier. She bought and used an Apple II E computer. Word processing programs for personal computers were just then arriving in the marketplace. Though all the copies printed were sold, *The Sable Curtain* did not have a significant impact on the Jefferson/Hemings controversy.

During the 1992 reunion, which convened in Richmond, Virginia, the Woodsons began their destined encounter with the Jefferson/Hemings controversy. From Richmond, a group of 200 Woodsons traveled to Monticello. From babies to ladies in wheelchairs, they assembled to make a statement about their heritage. The Thomas Woodson Family Association presented a copy of the *Woodson Source Book* to the Thomas Jefferson Memorial Foundation. Lucia "Cinder" Stanton, a historian who worked for the Foundation, took the work seriously. NBC News covered the family's trip to Monticello, and the family portrait taken on this occasion would later appear in *Ebony* magazine in July 1993 along with an article about the Woodson link to Thomas Jefferson.[6]

Excited by the success of the reunion, Robert Cooley, a cousin from Virginia, attended a seminar entitled *Jefferson, Race and Slavery* at the University of Virginia in October 1992. After listening to scholarly discourse for a couple of hours, he stood up to inform the audience that he knew of the existence and history of the first son of Sally Hemings and Thomas Jefferson. He explained that he knew of that son's life because he, Robert Cooley, was a descendant of that son. The room was silenced! The press covered his announcement. Most historians present that day recoiled at the notion that Cooley's oral history would receive any attention.[7]

Reverberations of this event echoed throughout Virginia and among the historical community throughout the nation. A hundred African Americans, claiming to be descendants of Thomas Jefferson, took a group picture on the steps of Monticello. Would this be accepted or challenged?

Thomas Jefferson's legacy was celebrated within the historical and academic communities in 1993, the 250th anniversary of his birth. Documentary films were produced, including one by Martin Dolbeare, who filmed an interview with Mother and Dad. Mother's research was beginning to have an impact beyond the family. The Thomas Jefferson Memorial Foundation produced an exhibit about the slaves who lived and worked at Monticello. A footnote was added to a listing of the Hemings family members recognizing the strong oral history of the Thomas Woodson family. Later the Foundation established a permanent exhibit in the Visitors Center at Monticello, that identified Thomas Woodson as a son of Sally Hemings. This was an important beginning for the mainstream recognition of Thomas Woodson's origin as the son of Sally Hemings and Thomas Jefferson. At the urging of Cinder Stanton, research historian for the Foundation, plaques were placed on Mulberry Row to tell some of its history, which had been ignored since the Foundation acquired Monticello in 1923. Most of the people who lived on, worked on, and built the Monticello plantation were African Americans, but the Foundation made virtually no effort to recognize or tell that history until 1994. Since then more progress has been made in this respect, but the effort still falls far short of its potential.

THE FINAL QUESTION

Mother died in the spring of 1994. She fought the scourge of cancer for eight years, ridding herself of it twice. She seemed to create life after life. Only her will and intellect kept her alive during those years. I never understood why Mother returned to a conventional diet, but I was not about to give advice to someone so full of wisdom. The cancer did not slow her down entirely until her last two months. The last piece of wisdom she imparted to me was, "Have some fun, honey." This was an attempt in her last weeks and days to push me toward my father's version of enjoyment, emphasizing sports and hearty friendships rather than her own version, driven by passionate curiosity. She wanted me to live beyond her seventy-three years. To be fully convinced, I would have had to forget all of the fun she had in her quest. That was impossible.

Mother followed the Woodson oral history where it was logical to journey, as one piece of information led to another. She learned to trust the oral history, as she found its path delightful. Mother's work with the Woodson family legacy brought her great joy. Likewise, Madison Hemings must have been gratified in 1873 to recount his family history and childhood memories. Madison knew that his words could be twisted and ridiculed, but found peace within by exposing the truth to those who sought it. Mother performed one amazing feat after another in her genealogical search. Her discovery of Jemima Woodson's gravestone in Ohio, Hannah Grant's will in Lewisburg, West Virginia, and Drury Woodson's will were remarkable accomplishments.

She continued to search because there was still a gap; the Woodson oral history was still not "proven." Mother held onto the idea that if the evidence was compelling enough, historians would have to recognize Thomas Woodson as a son of Thomas Jefferson. Even in my youth I was not as trusting. I never assumed that historians sought objective truth. Mother sought proof, but what was that? Videotape of intimacy between Thomas Jefferson and Sally Hemings did not exist. Even if it was possible for such a thing to exist, the authenticity of the tape would certainly be questioned. Some people would deny the liaison of Thomas Jefferson and Sally Hemings beyond all reason.

Mother was quick to discuss the details of her research, but not the potential impact. She knew that acceptance of the liaison between Sally Hemings and Thomas Jefferson created difficulties for the American social paradigm. Prejudices based on race and skin tone had troubled her throughout her life. She was never at ease discussing the racial divisions within our society. She

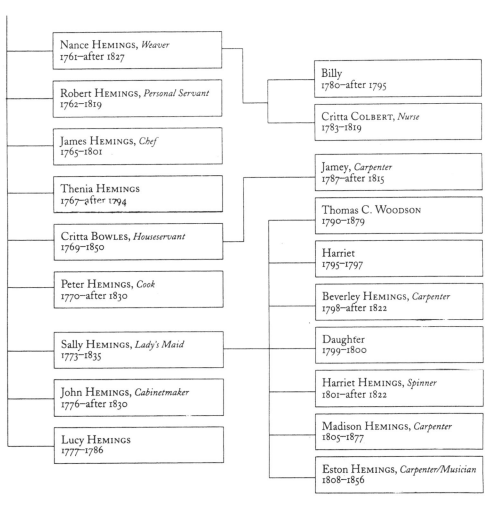

Nance HEMINGS, *Weaver* 1761–after 1827	Billy 1780–after 1795
Robert HEMINGS, *Personal Servant* 1762–1819	Critta COLBERT, *Nurse* 1783–1819
James HEMINGS, *Chef* 1765–1801	Jamey, *Carpenter* 1787–after 1815
Thenia HEMINGS 1767–after 1794	Thomas C. WOODSON 1790–1879
Critta BOWLES, *Houseservant* 1769–1850	Harriet 1795–1797
Peter HEMINGS, *Cook* 1770–after 1830	Beverley HEMINGS, *Carpenter* 1798–after 1822
Sally HEMINGS, *Lady's Maid* 1773–1835	Daughter 1799–1800
John HEMINGS, *Cabinetmaker* 1776–after 1830	Harriet HEMINGS, *Spinner* 1801–after 1822
Lucy HEMINGS 1777–1786	Madison HEMINGS, *Carpenter* 1805–1877
	Eston HEMINGS, *Carpenter/Musician* 1808–1856

A portion of the genealogical chart from Lucia A. Stanton's monograph, *Slavery at Monticello* (1996). Reproduced courtesy of the Thomas Jefferson Memorial Foundation.

was the product of a mixed-race marriage. Such discussions would leave her feeling torn apart.

NOTES

1. Minnie S. Woodson, *Woodson Source Book* (Washington, D.C.: Privately printed, 1984), 26: Lick Township, Jackson County, Ohio, map from D. J. Lake, *Atlas of Jackson, Ohio* (Philadelphia: Titus, Sims, & Titus, 1875).

2. Minnie S. Woodson, *The Sable Curtain* (Washington, D.C.: Privately printed, 1987), appendix: deed of land sale, Fanny Leach to William Renick, Greenbriar County Deed Book #6, and will of Hannah Grant, Greenbriar County Will Book #3, 160–61.

3. Henry Morton Woodson, *Historical Genealogy of the Woodsons and Their Connections* (Columbia: E. W. Stephens, 1915).

4. Woodson, *Sable Curtain*, appendix: Personal Property Tax Records for Goochland, Cumberland, Hanover, and Buckingham Counties for 1783, located at the Virginia Historical Library and Archives, Richmond, Virginia.

5. Julian Boyd, *The Papers of Thomas Jefferson*, vol. II (Princeton: Princeton University Press, 1950–   ), 458: location of ferries; ownership and will of Drury Woodson, Cumberland County (VA) Will Book; James A. Bear and Lucia C. Stanton, eds., *Jefferson's Memorandum Books*, vol. 1 (Princeton: Princeton University Press, 1997), 211, 353, 390: Jefferson's use of John Woodson's ferry.

6. Laura Randolph, "Thomas Jefferson's Black and White Descendents Debate His Lineage and Legacy," *Ebony*, July 1993, 25–29.

7. Ibid., 25.

CHAPTER ELEVEN

Search for Truth?

Who controls the past controls the future: Who controls the present
controls the past.

—George Orwell[1]

During the summer of 1997, I received a call from Eugene Foster, a retired
pathologist from Charlottesville, Virginia. Dr. Foster was organizing a DNA
test with the stated intent of settling the Jefferson/Hemings paternity controversy. The notion of a DNA test for the Jefferson/Hemings controversy
first came my way while reading Judith Justus' book, *Down from the Mountain*. I even looked forward to the test. Still, my first telephone contact with
Foster concerned me. He seemed a little befuddled. He had mailed a letter
to me, but it was returned to him as he used the wrong address. He actually
sent the letter a second time to another incorrect address and shared his
frustration with me. Our subsequent conversations went well. After we
spoke, he talked with Dad and subsequently called other family members.
Dad did not initially call him back, as he had no interest in a DNA test.
Other family members were not inclined to cooperate with the test either;
they assumed the test was a ruse.

Though Mother had invested seven years of her life researching the family
history and was convinced at her death that the liaison of Jefferson and Hemings was a reality, my initial disposition was to adopt Mother's original mis-

sion: "Let's prove the oral history to be correct or prove it wrong." I wanted my family's oral history to be substantiated, but I also wished to prevent the controversy from haunting me for the rest of my life. I wanted to accept whatever seemed to be the truth and hoped for a credible process.

Dr. Foster, dressed as he often is, in a dark blue blazer, traveled to Philadelphia in mid-October to obtain my blood sample, arriving on a sunny Sunday morning with his wife, Jane. Trena, who was dressing for church, had to that point paid scant attention to my conversations with Foster. Once she saw the Fosters and the Continental breakfast of sorts I'd prepared, however, curiosity got the best of her. Eugene Foster was staid and focused. Jane, who wore a bright red cardigan over her white blouse, was lively and engaging. Dr. Foster explained that a friend had convinced him to organize the DNA test. He had researched opportunities genetic procedures could offer, then contacted Chris Tyler-Smith, a leading genetics researcher from Oxford University in England who had recently developed a method of performing the test without the need to exhume Thomas Jefferson's body. Dr. Tyler-Smith had agreed to conduct the test. Blood samples of descendants from an entirely male line could be used; descendants fitting the criteria were available among the Woodsons and among the descendants of Thomas Jefferson's uncle, Field Jefferson. Additionally, one descendant of Eston Hemings Jefferson was from an all-male family line.

The conversation floated among DNA testing, eating habits, the Jefferson/Hemings controversy, children, and vacation travel. I proudly offered some knowledge of Lewis Woodson's life due to a recent discovery. While in Pittsburgh for an NAACP convention during the summer, I wandered into the John Heinz History Center while Trena was busy at the Convention Center marketing her business. There I discovered that information on my great-great-grandfather's influence as an abolitionist had been made part of the museum's permanent display. Though this part of my family's history had nothing to do with the Jefferson/Hemings controversy, Dr. Foster seemed to be interested. I was pleased with his willingness to probe into the experiences and accomplishments of my family through the generations. It was certainly ironic that a scientist would appreciate a segment of history many historians avoided like the plague.

Dr. Foster wanted to "lift this from the hands of the historians to create objective evidence." The words were music to my ears. My lack of faith in Jeffersonian historians was total; in my opinion evidence based on DNA tests would be credible only if they were excluded from the process. Foster hoped to establish independent evidence to "throw back to historians." He did not maintain that the tests in themselves would prove anything; instead they would provide objective evidence that could sway the historians one way or the other. Foster did not appreciate that the Sally Hemings descendants might care to comment on the results; he envisioned our role only as blood donors. His view didn't surprise me, but I was mystified by it. Jeffersonian historians were unified in their denial; if the matter were left only to them, there would be no controversy. There seemed to be no recognition that after Fawn Brodie died, the controversy was kept alive by the Woodson family. It was the Woodsons whom NBC had filmed at Monticello, and it was the Woodsons who appeared in *Ebony* in 1993. It was Bob Cooley who stood up to correct the historians at their conference. Yet, in the tradition Ralph Ellison described in *Invisible Man*, the Woodsons and other Sally Hemings descendants and their thoughts didn't register with Dr. Foster and others from Charlottesville. Our affirmations lived detached from our humanity.

Foster said that the results would be released in a scientific journal. Though I signed an agreement relieving Foster of the obligation to notify me of the results before the public release, he verbally promised to call me before such release. He made a similar promise to my cousin Robert Golden, who was by then president of the Thomas Woodson Family Association.

Later I sent Dr. Foster a copy of the *Woodson Source Book* along with a copy of the "Pittsburgh Memorial," the document written by Lewis Woodson and other blacks in Pittsburgh to defend their right to vote. I put Dr. Foster in touch with my first cousin Granville, as he needed more blood samples. Foster contacted my third cousin in Pittsburgh. I encouraged him to obtain a sample from outside of the Lewis Woodson family line. He was already on that track and in touch with William Woodson of Atlanta. I emphasized that descendants of the James line of the family lived in Ohio.

Geneticists agreed to oversee the DNA analysis and to arrange for the use of laboratory facilities without cost to Dr. Foster. He took blood samples to England for analysis. Dr. Foster and Dr. Tyler-Smith had agreed to publish the results in a scientific journal once they were available.

This new method was made possible because geneticists had further improved DNA mapping, which involved looking among Y-chromosomes of test participants for matches. Y-chromosomes are supposedly passed on from father to son with very little change. Samples were collected from five Woodsons, one descendant of Eston Hemings Jefferson, five descendants of Field Jefferson, three descendants of the Carr brothers, and five controls. The controls are men descended from old Virginia families but not from the Jefferson, Hemings, or Wayles lines. They are the equivalent of reference points. Simply put, matches between the Woodson and the Field Jefferson descendants would throw the weight of the scientific evidence in favor of validating the liaison between Sally Hemings and Thomas Jefferson. If no matches existed between these groups, then the weight of the scientific evidence would be thrown against the possibility of a liaison.

The Prevalence of Denial

In 1998, historians Joseph Ellis, Alf Mapp, Jr., and others proclaimed that the DNA test would prove nothing. They held that, if matches appeared between the Woodson and the Field Jefferson descendants, the best that could be said was that the children of Sally Hemings were fathered by *a* Jefferson, not Thomas Jefferson. These historians believed that there were other Jeffersons who could have fathered Sally Hemings' children. They did not offer to explain why the other Jeffersons were able to impregnate Sally Hemings only when Thomas Jefferson was in residence at Monticello.[2]

The testing did, however, promise uncontested evidence as it relates to some participants. The Carr brothers story, then favored by Jeffersonians such as Andrew Burstein, would lose weight if a match between the Hemings descendants and the Carr descendants were not found. The most effective defense constructed for Thomas Jefferson against the charge of miscegenation was the assertion that one or both of Jefferson's nephews, Peter or Samuel Carr, fathered Sally Hemings' children. This story originated 150 years ago with Thomas Jefferson's grandchildren through Martha Jefferson Randolph, Thomas Jefferson Randolph (T. J. Randolph), and Ellen Randolph Coolidge. The story emerged not long after the death of Samuel Carr in 1855. Peter died first, in 1815. A letter dated June 1, 1868, from one Jefferson biographer, Henry S. Randall, to another, James Parton, delivered a lively assurance of Peter Carr's siring of Sally Hemings' children. The primary source of the account was a conversation between Henry Randall and T. J. Randolph. Curiously, T. J. Randolph's sister Ellen, in a letter to her husband, identified Samuel Carr as the father of Sally's children. Instead of treating these conflicting accounts with caution, twentieth-century historians have cited Peter or Samuel Carr or both as the father(s) of Sally Hemings' children. When in doubt, punt?[3]

Historian Douglass Adair defended the idea that one of the Carr brothers fathered Sally Hemings' children with characteristic aplomb. He not only contended that Peter Carr and Sally Hemings were bound by affection, but he described the affair with the zest of a romantic novelist, telling of a remarkable love: "We can only assume that when Peter Carr became her lover he must have wooed her. And apparently he won her heart for once and for all, for there is no evidence of Sally Hemings' attachment ever to any other man." Adair's romanticism would play well on daytime television, but it never belonged in the historical record. It would have been more logical for this fiery affair to begin in 1791 rather than in 1795, when Sally Hemings began to conceive children again, if it were to happen at all. Peter Carr spent parts of 1791, 1792, and 1793 alternating between Monticello and his mother's plantation. Sally bore no children in those years. She did give birth in October 1795. Peter studied law and began to practice. He married in 1797 and had a son by 1799. Even if one accepts Adair's contention that an affair could have continued after Carr's marriage, why did those tender hearts not explode with passion in 1791 when Sally was eighteen years old, or the year after, or the one after that?[4]

After a 150-year life, the Carr brothers story has recently been abandoned by establishment historians, but it is appropriate here to place in perspective the statements of T. J. Randolph and his siblings, which proved to be misleading. According to Henry Randall, Martha Jefferson Randolph instructed two of her sons to "always defend the character of their grandfather." Their love for their mother and grandfather and their attempts to abide by Martha's wishes should be appreciated for what they were. Their contrivance was predictable and is forgivable. Martha Randolph lost her mother and had to share her father with the demands of revolution. She married a poor provider and bore eleven children. She cannot be chastised for reacting as historians reported that she did to the situation left by her father. Jefferson's silence on the charges lodged by Callender and whispered by others exacerbated her heavy burden.

It is not clear however, how historians could have accepted the Randolph misstatements when the validity of many of them was obviously questionable. Neither can attacks by historians on the character and reliability of James Callender be justified. Jeffersonians created and still maintain a double standard whereby evidence is ignored if it does not prove their theory and other obviously tainted evidence is accepted. The adoption of the oral statements of the Randolphs and others as fact, while every statement of the slaves who lived and labored at Monticello is categorically labeled as unreliable "oral history," was a blatantly biased process. Do double standards persist?

Notwithstanding other skirmishes, the credibility of James Callender has been the most contentious aspect of the 200-year-old controversy. As late as 1999 the spirit of the attack on Callender seemed to have passed unaltered from the muddy streets of Richmond in the late summer of 1803. In *Wolf by the Ears* (1977), ostensibly a book about Jefferson and slavery, John Chester Miller devoted a chapter to James Callender, whom Jefferson once called "a man of genius." Further, Jefferson said that Callender edited "the best

205

newspaper in America." Despite acknowledging Jefferson's praise of Callender, Miller claimed that Callender "never made the slightest effort to verify the 'facts' he so stridently proclaimed. It was 'journalism' at its most reckless, wildly irresponsible and scurrilous. . . . For him the story, especially if it reeked of scandal, was everything; truth, if it stood in his way, was summarily mowed down."[5]

How could Jefferson and his defender disagree so completely on the professionalism of Jefferson's accuser? Clearly one answer is that Jefferson praised Callender when the two were political collaborators. That aside, when did Callender lose his genius and professional acumen?

In *The Inner Jefferson* (1995) Andrew Burstein quickly glossed over the events leading to Callender's infamous exposé, painting him as "a political refugee . . . found guilty of sedition . . . a heavy drinking journalist." Burstein, Miller, and the others failed to mention Callender's defense of the free press during the time when our Founding Fathers habitually jailed reporters who were members of the opposition party. Was this "scandalmonger" not a courageous and effective opponent of the terribly anti-democratic Alien and Sedition Acts?[6]

Douglass Adair created a new defense against Callender's charges in his published article "The Jefferson Scandals." Adair concluded that Callender's assertion was wrong because Sally Hemings did not bear a child in 1790. He found that Callender made up "Tom" out of the clear blue sky and that Madison Hemings was wrong when he stated that his mother Sally was pregnant when she returned from France in 1789. Yet Adair and others failed to explain why, if Tom never existed, Jefferson's defenders and operatives did not point this out. It would certainly have been in their interests to do so. There were a million people in Virginia at the time, and no one came forth with that information as scandal about the president's sex life whirled about his home state. Garry Wills, Merrill Peterson, and others have enlisted in the "Tom didn't exist" school of thought.[7]

The "Tom didn't exist" school of thought has moved into the new millennium, albeit in a modified version. A new generation of Jeffersonians, including Dianne Swann-Wright and Joshua Rothman claim that Tom didn't exist, but most of them take the position that, while Sally Hemings did give birth to a son in 1790, the baby died in childhood. In the 1999 book *Sally Hemings and Thomas Jefferson*, Rothman attempts to accredit this posture by invoking the stature of Sally Hemings, the woman now raised from the depths of degradation: "Hemings herself claimed this child died shortly after being born." In fact no document exists written by Sally Hemings, nor does any document written in her lifetime quoting her saying as much as one word.

The theoretical support for Rothman's postulation came from a man named S. F. Whetmore, whom Rothman fails to cite in his endnotes and whom the book's editors, Jan Lewis and Peter Onuf, fail to credit for his article, which appears in the appendix of *Sally Hemings and Thomas Jefferson*. Peter Onuf is the Thomas Jefferson Memorial Foundation Professor of History at the University of Virginia. Whetmore was the editor of the *Pike County Republican* in 1873 when Madison Hemings's reminiscences were published. Any mistakes in Whetmore's article should be attributed to him. Rothman fails to mention in his account that Madison Hemings, who was interviewed by Whetmore, was not alive during the time Tom (Thomas) lived at Monticello or when the baby allegedly died and, therefore, may not be a reliable source. James Callender, a legion of other news reporters, and about one million other Virginians were certainly alive then and none denied Callender's account or other accounts recording Tom as the son of Sally Hemings. Rothman failed to mention the evidence of Thomas Woodson's bent for anonymity and the possible reasons for it. Madison Hemings may have simply honored his brother's quest for anonymity. Generation after generation of Jeffersonian historians have at a minimum failed to weigh all of the evidence available. Claims such as Rothman's continue the 150-year old tradition of Jeffersonian historians who abuse the historical record and show disrespect for the African American community who lived and worked at Monticello. If Mr. Rothman does not like the historical record he should be careful not create one in its stead.[8]

Historian Willard Sterne Randall was in a hurry to finish his Jefferson biography for the 250th anniversary of Thomas Jefferson's birth. In it he says that Nelson Jones, described as a white carpenter at Monticello, was probably Sally Hemings' father (Randall provided no evidence that Nelson Jones and Betty Hemings ever met). This contention belies the evidence that Sally Hemings was conceived and born at John Wayles' plantation, The Forest, not at Monticello, and ignores Madison Hemings's statement that Wayles was the father of Sally Hemings and five of her siblings. Randall criticized Fawn Brodie's work, claiming that the association Brodie drew between thoughts Jefferson recorded on his trip through the Rhine River Valley and his feelings toward Sally Hemings was spurious because Sally Hemings had not then come to France and Jefferson therefore had not seen her in years. Yet even a quick turn through George Green Shackelford's marvelous account of Jefferson's European travels reveals that the trip through the Rhine River Valley took place in 1788 after Sally Hemings and Maria Jefferson had arrived in France.[9]

Thomas Jefferson and Sally Hemings: An American Controversy (1997) by Annette Gordon-Reed, a Harvard Law School graduate who teaches at New York Law School, provides a road map for the debate and discredits the assertions of many traditional historians regarding the Jefferson/Hemings controversy. The preface provides an excellent viewpoint:

Consider the nature of evidence and the nature of proof. Evidence goes toward establishing proof. By way of analogy, evidence can be described as the bricks that go into making up a wall of proof. Some scholars and commentators, who almost invariably approach the subject of Thomas Jefferson and Sally Hemings in a defensive posture, have demanded that every brick of evidence that the two might have had a relationship amount to its own individual wall of proof. If the item of evidence offered does not itself add up to proof, they deem it to be "no evidence" or alternatively never mention it at all. Demanding that individual items of evidence amount to proof sets a standard that only can be met in the rarest of circumstances, either in history or law. There are, no doubt, many things that have been designated historical truths on the basis of far less evidence than exists in this matter. . . . Of course, at this time, whether Thomas Jefferson and Sally Hemings had a sexual liaison is, not a legal, but a historical question. The principles that demand a consistent standard for assessing evidence should apply, nevertheless. The consistency has been utterly lacking in the scholarly writing on this question, and that is cause for concern.[10]

Gordon-Reed's book, which failed to assert the reality of the Jefferson/Hemings liaison, was well received by the academic community, which, fifteen or so years after Fawn Brodie's death, had formulated almost unanimous denial of the liaison. Indignation reigned among them in 1996 when the Hollywood production company Merchant Ivory released a film, *Jefferson in Paris*, that used Jefferson's sex life as its theme.

REPORTING HISTORY

After the blood samples were collected, we anticipated press coverage of the DNA test soon thereafter, despite Dr. Foster's commitment to nonsensationalism. I suspected that someone would find the subject too tantalizing to keep away from the press. I was rather surprised that there appeared to have been no press coverage of the test by year's end. In February 1998, I finally received a call from Fox News' Washington, D.C. affiliate, inviting me to join the production of a news spot announcing the results of the DNA test.

Trena made the trip to Monticello with me. Cousin Bob Cooley was scheduled for the shoot along with two cousins from Pittsburgh, Robert Woodson and Robert Golden. When we arrived at the visitors' parking area, I spotted Bob Cooley sitting in a dark green Jaguar sedan, poised to climb to the crest of the Monticello mountain. We had spoken to Bob by phone a few days prior but had not seen him in fifteen years. The Jaguar was pointed into an unmarked road that was obviously not used by regular visitors. I yelled, "Hello, counselor." Bob, yelled back, "Follow me." He had obviously used the road before. The Jaguar took off like a rocket, climbing straight up the mountain. I pushed Trena's dark green Lexus into hot pursuit. After a short blast, we arrived at the rear of the gift shop and parked among the employees' cars.

The Fox TV shoot went well. Some of the camera shoot took place near the South Dependencies, a row of rooms just below the mansion. Sally Hemings' yet to be marked room was there, next to the kitchen. The lawn just beyond the Dependencies provided a lovely camera backdrop. I was comfortable giving my spiel. Whitney Espich, the public relations representative for the Thomas Jefferson Monticello Foundation, warned me that I should not be surprised by the perspective presented in the news spot. I appreciated her candor. I knew newsrooms could create whatever story they chose to tell, regardless of what the interviewee said. After the shoot, I caught the last half of a standard Monticello house tour. I thought that the guide, Jamie, was skillful with his presentation to the point of being entertaining. At the tour's end, Jamie asked if there was anything in particular I wanted to see or know. I opted only to view Jefferson's bedroom and hear his standard presentation in that room.

My cousins from Pittsburgh left for home. Trena and Bob Cooley had not taken the tour but were still somewhere on the mountaintop. I went to the administration office in search of them and found Trena in a room just beyond the receptionist's desk. After declining a soda or tea, I walked into the room, which was the director's office. Bob, Trena, and Dan Jordan, the director of Monticello, were engaged in a jovial interchange. Jordan, a lively, handsome, and gracious man, welcomed me in. He spoke warmly of Mother and Dad. The chat went on for quite a while and established an enduring relationship.

Trena and I learned from Bob Cooley that *U.S. News & World Report* had printed an article about the DNA test in December 1997. While waiting for the release of the DNA test results, Trena and I devoured a dozen biographies of Thomas Jefferson along with books related to the history of slavery in America. The Sally Hemings/Thomas Jefferson controversy was dominating our household conversation.[11]

In March, a reporter from the *Virginia Pilot*, Warren Fiske, called to interview me about the Woodson family history and the DNA test, and he called repeatedly over a two week period. The article's release was delayed for a week or so, but it seemed like a month to me. When I finally learned the date of its printing, I called the paper for a copy. I received it along with a $4 invoice. It occurred to me that a big city paper would never have trusted me for that much money. When I opened that Sunday *Virginia Pilot*, I saw a picture of Thomas Jefferson and another of my Woodson family heading an enormous news article! I was ecstatic. The article contained quotes from historians but devoted more space to the unacknowledged and acknowledged descendants, descendants of Sally Hemings and of the two daughters of Martha Wayles Jefferson, respectively. At least some Woodson family history was finally reported to the public![12]

Late in April 1998, I learned that the *Washington Post* had published an article about the DNA tests. I was in Washington at the time and made a point of purchasing the morning paper. When I read the article, I was overcome with disappointment. It contained quotes from two members of the acknowledged family and none from the unacknowledged family. It quoted historian Joseph Ellis, who declared that the DNA test would prove nothing. Ellis, the author of *American Sphinx: The Character of Thomas Jefferson*, labeled those who believed they "held the key" to the controversy "liars and fools." The article also contained comments from Annette Gordon-Reed. No hint was provided as to the thoughts of the descendants of Sally Hemings. The blood donors themselves were invisible and inconsequential as far as the *Washington Post* was concerned. The blood samples had somehow been separated from our humanity and very existence.[13]

I was devastated. I had believed the DNA test would give the Hemings/ Jefferson/Woodson families a platform from which we could all tell our side of the story. After all, had we not participated, there would have been no test. The *Washington Post* is read by network television newsrooms, NPR, and the rest of the journalistic world. I knew others would follow the lead of the *Washington Post* and the *New York Times*. Had I known we would be ignored by the newspapers of record, I would not have provided a blood sample.

In frustration, I called the *Washington Post* reporter, Leef Smith. She had a Virginia telephone number, so I assumed that she worked in the Virginia bureau of the newspaper and that her work followed the lead of the recent *Virginia Pilot* article. First, I asked why she had not called any Woodsons for comment. She said that she had called Bob Cooley and John King, who were quoted in the *Virginia Pilot* article, but they had not called her back. I told her that there were lots of Woodson relatives in the D.C. area, and she asked whether "she was supposed to call every Woodson in the phone book," correctly intimating that not every Woodson in the phone book was my relative. When I asked if she had read the *Virginia Pilot* article, she said that she had and that she had called everyone who was quoted in it. I corrected her, noting that my name appeared with a quote in that article. She said nothing in response to my clarification. Further, I pointed out that the *Virginia Pilot* article identified me as a Philadelphian; my phone number had not changed in twenty-four years; I was not hard to find.

Disturbed at the responses, I asked how she was able to reach two members of the acknowledged family and none from the unacknowledged family. She said that she had called Monticello for the names of the white family members. She quipped, "They have an association!" I was too insulted to ask her what she thought the Thomas Woodson Family Association Inc. is. Our association's name also appeared in the *Virginia Pilot* article. Obviously, she missed it. I did ask, however, why she did not ask the folks at Monticello for the names of additional Woodson family members or for my phone number. She did not answer. She obviously assumed that the folks that run Monticello would have no relationship with the African Americans who claimed to be descended from Thomas Jefferson. I was certain most reporters had ways of finding people that I could not imagine.

Ms. Smith indicated that she found the controversy "fascinating." This was a clear attempt at nonconfrontational conversation, and I accepted it as such. I wanted the press to reverse 200 years of misrepresentation of my family's history, so I struggled to find a thread of agreement. Leef Smith complained she was given only three days to write the article. Knowing the complexity of the controversy, I certainly appreciated the consequence of that constraint. I told her that the *Virginia Pilot* reporter called over a two week period and that her editors should have given her more time.

I tried to explain why we were certain that Thomas Jefferson fathered Sally Hemings' children. After a few seconds she pulled the Carr brothers story into the conversation. I explained that Sally Hemings did not conceive children during the years that the Carr brothers spent the most time at Monticello. I asked Smith why historians were allowed to put forth the prospect that either Peter or Sam Carr or both fathered Sally's children without identifying which one was the father or whether there was any evidence that Sally

211

actually may have had a sexual liaison with both. Smith seemed to discern no need for substantiation, nor did she appear at all curious about which one may have been the father. One Randolph descendant identified Peter Carr as the father, and another Randolph descendant identified Samuel Carr as such. Smith easily accepted the idea that anyone and everyone could have or did have sex with Sally Hemings. I found it appalling that a woman would accept this position. Annette Gordon-Reed not only sharply discounted the Carr brothers story based on the evidence, but she seemed to be offended by its sexist tone.

I asked Leef Smith why she had not asked Joseph Ellis which Carr fathered Sally's children. She replied that she was merely a reporter, not a historian. She "didn't have to figure out the history, just report it." I found the conversation extremely offensive. I was disturbed that Smith, paid to explore and report, challenged every word I uttered as soon as it was spoken, while she explicitly denied the need to question any of the loose ends the "experts" presented.

I told Leef Smith that I was offended that Joseph Ellis had called my family "liars and fools" and that the *Washington Post* would print the disparaging remark. Joseph Ellis actually had called anyone who thought they had the key to the controversy "liars and fools." Ms. Smith gibed, "He wasn't talking about your family." I shot back, "If he was not talking about my family, then who was he talking about?" There was no answer.

Early in the conversation we discussed Annette Gordon-Reed's book, which found historians inappropriately discounting the oral histories of African Americans. Smith seemed to feel that the quotes from Gordon-Reed gave her article "balance." I pointed out that Gordon-Reed had not affirmed a belief in the liaison, so the viewpoint of those who believed it took place was still missing. I charged that the article lacked balance, an elemental aspect of good journalism.

I asked Ms. Smith if she had read Fawn Brodie's book. Brodie's position would have represented balance, in my view. "She died," Smith quickly assured me. For Leef Smith, it seems, death not only ended life but wiped away the past as well. Earlier I had explained that the Carr brothers could not have fathered Tom (Thomas) since he was conceived in Paris, France, where Sally Hemings lived at the time. She followed the point. Referring to Tom, she said, "Yeah, the one that died!" She said it as though we had finally found a rare point of agreement. It felt like a kick in the stomach, and I did not respond, thinking, "If he died, then where the hell did I come from?" I was too outdone to protest. This lethal scenario, that Tom died in infancy, had ostensibly traveled from Madison, who was born after Tom left Monticello, to Fawn Brodie to Annette Gordon-Reed to Leef Smith. By then I had learned the futility of providing Smith with a counter scenario. If I made a point, I would only encounter silence, then contradiction on the next point, not agreement.

The conversation did end on a positive note. Smith was to appear on television with the story in a few days. She wanted to be fair and get it right. I could only think, "Lord, help us." Still, I was glad I had called her. Maybe the short-term pain would yield a long-term gain. I was sure that she would give the issue more thought; the conversation was too exhausting to forget.

I did not sleep well for the next two nights. What bothered me most was not the *Washington Post*'s lopsided journalism but Professor Ellis' comments in the article. Ellis said of Jefferson's capacity for affection that "his deepest sensual urges were directed at buildings rather than women." Yet Martha Wayles Jefferson bore seven children in ten years of marriage. How could the *Washington Post* waste space on such nonsense and completely ignore the subjects of the DNA test, when the article's headline promised to report on the DNA tests?

Is it customary for history professors to label their intellectual opponents "liars and fool"? Why would a history professor publicly air such an emotional and harsh comment? Who was the target of this anger? If atypical, then why would Professor Ellis make a distinction in this case? What was different about the people who disagreed with Ellis' view of this history?

The *Washington Post*'s role in printing his vicious comment also bothered me. Ms. Smith had told me at one point in our conversation that if I had a problem with what Ellis said then I should take it up with Ellis. I understood her point, but was it appropriate to apply her principle in this instance? If a pattern of similar comments appeared in the paper, then I would have no grounds for displeasure with the *Washington Post*. For instance, if I found an article on page 6 by reporter Jones quoting a Mr. Doe calling someone a "pig" and an article on page 12 by reporter Peterson quoting Mr. Carter calling Ms. Brown an "idiot," then my feeling of injury would be better viewed as oversensitivity. So I started to read articles in the *Washington Post* more closely, particularly those written by Leef Smith. There was no pattern whatsoever of this sort of language in the *Washington Post*. Vile comments, which I imagine reporters frequently hear in courtrooms and at crime scenes, are not repeated in the newspaper. Why did the Jefferson/Hemings story deserve such exceptional emphasis?

THE VANISHING HISTORY OF MONTICELLO

Trena read everything that I brought home from the library while trying to become as knowledgeable about Jefferson and the controversy as possible. It was easy to find distortions in the works written by Jeffersonian historians on the matter of Sally Hemings. Everything they wrote on the matter seemed nonsensical. It was clear to us that Annette Gordon-Reed, as a member of the academic community, was very polite and forgiving in her criticism of the mostly male historians who all denied Jefferson's paternity of Sally Hemings' children. Trena took on the task of making more copies of the *Woodson Source Book*, as none had been printed in fifteen years. Many family members wanted copies. Some cousins lent their copies to others who never returned them. Older cousins wanted them as gifts for their children. Trena also dug deeper into the Jefferson/Hemings controversy, finding new revelations.

We always assumed that historians had destroyed documents and artifacts to hide the real history of Monticello. Fawn Brodie reported the journal of Thomas Jefferson's letters for the year 1788 as missing. This year was the only full year Sally Hemings lived in Paris and the year during which she likely became more than an incidental part of the statesman's life.

I told Trena about another violation of the historic record. The steps in Thomas Jefferson's bedroom were abruptly removed in 1979! These steps had led to the space over Jefferson's bed, which he referred to as a "closet."[14] Mother had been very disturbed when she learned of the removal, as it signified to her that historians and curators would stop at nothing to hide the true history of the Monticello plantation and would destroy any hint of the role African Americans played in American history. Mother was not the only person upset by the removal. Barbara Chase-Riboud, author of *Sally Hemings*, was infuriated by it:

Three months after the [first] publication of *Sally Hemings*, on the night of July 3, 1979, the stairway at the foot of Thomas Jefferson's bed was removed. . . . I was ardently assured that it had not been removed because it was mentioned in *Sally Hemings* and tourists were asking to see it. The book itself had gotten the Jeffersonian scholars and enthusiasts up in arms, now they were roiled by the news that God forbid *Sally Hemings* was going to be a movie.[15]

Historians were, however, able to delay the movie for twenty years.

Management at Monticello claims that the steps were not the original ones that led to the closet during Jefferson's life, but were constructed by the Levy family, which later owned Monticello. Management removed the steps in an attempt to achieve "purification," so it claimed. By this logic the mansion would be in serious jeopardy if anyone were ever to break a windowpane. The removal of the steps diverts the attention of Monticello visitors away from the space above the bed, to which light is furnished by three exquisite portals. The dismantled steps may well not have been the original ones but their removal certainly destroyed the opportunity for visitors to gain full appreciation of spaces within Jefferson's bedroom.

The removal also helped to destroy possible linkages visitors might have made between the room and Sally Hemings. The folklore among African Americans in Charlottesville was that "Sally Hemings slept in the space above Jefferson's bed." While I do not accept that interpretation literally, the existence of the "closet" above the bed would have been helpful to Sally Hemings at times when she chose to deny the knowledge of her presence to others. The removal did not take place in 1924, 1943, or 1976 but shortly after the release of Chase-Riboud's book.

The intention of the removal is obvious. The lack of shame shown by the stewards of the mansion is not of consequence, but the restoration of the steps is of real and symbolic importance.

Trena's research soon focused our attention on even more disturbing revelations. We were first offended to learn of a mutilation of the *Farm Book*, the record Thomas Jefferson left of events on the Monticello plantation. The *Farm Book* is certainly an unparalleled national treasure and a priceless piece of American heritage. Nevertheless, a historian or curator ripped out two pages that revealed aspects of Jefferson's treatment of his slaves. Pages 25 and 26 of the *Farm Book* are detached from the book, which is now held by the Massachusetts Historical Society. The two pages are owned by the David Library of the American Revolution, located in Washington Crossing, Pennsylvania. The David Library has no record of how the pages were acquired, and its founder, Sol Feinstone, who purchased and preserved the pages, died in 1980. Feinstone acquired many documents in the 1960s. Until recent decades historians made no reference to Jefferson ever selling slaves. I suspect that historians endeavored to shield Jefferson from the label of slave trader by removing this record of sales of slaves. The existence of the pages was reported in Cinder Stanton's *Slavery at Monticello*.[16]

Next, an erasure in the *Farm Book* captured Trena's attention. We would have been absolutely shocked if we had not by that time grown immune to the offenses of the Jeffersonians. Beginning in 1774, Jefferson recorded information about his slaves such as birth dates, distribution of food and blankets, along with records of crops production, construction purchases, and the like in the *Farm Book*. Page 31 contains a register of slaves. The page

Register of births. B. denotes Bedford

Males	Females
85. Brown. Bet Br's. Davy. Abby's. B. [erasure] John. Dinah's. B.	
86. Bartlet. Molly's. Ned. Jenny's Kit. Judy Hix's. Philip. Cate's B.	Sarah. Lucinda's.
87. Jamey. Critta's.	Melinda. Bet Br's. I.E. Edy. Isabel's Ursula. Minerva's.
88. Lewis. Jenny's.	~~Clarinda~~. Molly's. I.E. Fanny. Jenny's. Mary. Minerva's. Sarah. Cate's. B. Fanny. Abby's. B. Cate. Suck's. B.
89. ~~Sandy~~. Lucinda's I.E.	Aggey. Isabel's. [erasure] Aggy. Dinah's B.
90. Jesse. Lewis's. Dick. Jenny's. [erasure] Daniel. Suck's. B.	~~Rachael~~. Thamar's I.E.

From *The Garden and Farm Books of Thomas Jefferson*, edited by Robert C. Baron (Golden: Fulcrum, 1986), 247. Reproduced by permission of Fulcrum Books. The heading from page 246 has been moved to the top of this column for clarity.

organizes names into male and female columns and by year of birth. Astoundingly, three names and an erasure appear under the male column for the year 1790!

In the volumes written to rebut the Jefferson/Hemings liaison, historians never reported the existence of an erasure precisely where Thomas' name would have appeared in the *Farm Book* had it not been mutilated. Historians such as John Chester Miller raised the absence of Thomas' name in the *Farm Book* as if it were the Holy Grail. The report issued by the Thomas Jefferson Memorial Foundation in January 2000 emphasizes "If a child born in 1790 survived infancy, its absence from the Farm Book in 1794 and succeeding years is hard to explain," but does not mention the erasure. Certainly the Foundation, which employs a legion of historians with Ph.D.s, cannot plead ignorance. How could they possibly place such a statement on their Web site when the specificity of the statement shows that they knew exactly where to find the answer to the problem at hand?[17]

The erasure is not the work of the book's author, as Jefferson's habit was to draw a line through errors. The lack of comment on the erasure again calls into question the reliability of Jeffersonian historians and makes me wonder where the rest of the secrets are buried. It should be further noted that all of the other slave lists in the *Farm Book* were compiled before 1790, when Thomas (Tom) was born, or after 1802, when he left Monticello. The absence of his name or evidence of an erasure from those lists is meaningless.

For Trena and me, the missing steps, missing documents, and the erasure were only logical extensions of the tactics used by Jeffersonian historians. We found their presentations preposterous, but far from surprising. Their depiction of American history falls well within the paradigm which has kept and continues to keep the past, present, and future of white and black Americans as separate as possible.

CONVERSATION ON THE MOUNTAIN TOP

In July 1998, Trena and I drove to Monticello to attend a "conversation." The topic was "Thomas Jefferson and Today's African Americans." We expected Bob Cooley to be there as well and looked forward to seeing him. Bob, uncharacteristically, did not attend, slowed by an injury received while visiting New York City two months prior. Two weeks after our trip, a blood clot or stroke caused Bob's death. The Woodson family's most outspoken proponent of the Woodson/Jefferson connection was gone.

Trena and I were invited to lunch at the Foster home the day of the conversation. Their Charlottesville home is comfortable and inviting, set upon a pretty hillside. We met Jane's charmingly feisty sister, a Californian. Over Mexican corn soup we talked about our children and travel plans. Trena had taken our sons to Egypt after the oldest, John, graduated from the University of Pittsburgh that April. Dr. Foster kept the test results secret in anticipation of their publication in a scientific journal. Publication had been delayed beyond the anticipated date, as a commitment to publish had not yet been secured. Later, Trena and I talked about possible inferences from our lunch conversation that might reflect on the test results, but there was little to go on. We stopped next at the Visitors Center at Monticello, located at the foot of the mountain, about a mile from the mansion. The center contained numerous displays, including depictions of the lives and histories of slaves of Monticello. A display on the descendants of Monticello slaves, where Woodson descendants were well represented was certainly a bold step forward and a tribute to Cinder Stanton's professional drive and integrity. Despondency and consternation, brought on by the manner in which the *Washington Post* and the *New York Times* handled the announcement of the DNA testing, were certainly cured by this trip to Monticello. I felt like I was among friends and could see progress in the way the story of the Monticello plantation was being portrayed. I wondered, though, if any of the venerable University of Virginia historians would attend the "conversation."

We also visited the research center, located in an old gatehouse on the mountain, to examine the book collection available there. While we were there, Cinder Stanton popped in to say hello. I had not seen Cinder since the 1994 Woodson reunion in Ohio. Trena had spoken to Cinder often by phone in prior months, but had never met her. They hugged like old high school classmates.

Once upon the top of the mountain that evening, the first familiar face we saw was that of the Foundation's president, Dan Jordan. Standing at the base of the East Portico steps, he invited guests to tour the mansion. Tour guides were on hand. We wandered around a bit. The mansion was becoming familiar. Monticello never reached its current pristine condition while Jefferson lived, but who could quibble about programmatic purity when faced with the enchanting beauty of Monticello?

Before the conversation began, I went for refreshments on the North Terrace. I spoke with a cheerfully robust man from Charlottesville who, after brief chatter, asked me what connection I had to Monticello. I told him that I am a descendant of Thomas Jefferson and Sally Hemings. He replied, "Oh, you are a descendant of Sally Hemings." I continued, "I am descended from Thomas Jefferson *and* Sally Hemings; I don't claim to be descended from Sally Hemings unless I am descended from Thomas Jefferson; either I am descended from both of them or my ancestors dropped from the heavens." He quickly blurted out something about immaculate conception which induced me to join him in a hearty laugh.

Dr. Roger Wilkins, a professor of history at George Mason University, gave a talk about Jefferson, Jefferson's views toward slavery, and how we might judge Jefferson on the issue today. The audience was seated in a tent, an unnecessary precaution, as the weather was perfect. The beauty of the West Portico of Monticello formed a backdrop as the audience watched the speaker. Quoting the icon, Professor Wilkins often cited the contradictions between Jefferson's early efforts to mitigate the expansion of slavery and his later silence on the issue. He drew his audience's attention to Jefferson's doubt that African Americans were capable of caring for themselves in freedom. He spoke of the possibility that Thomas Jefferson may have fathered the children of Sally Hemings, but only in the context that we do not really know much about the relationship between the icon and the attractive young slave girl. The presentation certainly did not break new ground. I found none of the exalted Jeffersonian historians, creators of the "chaste and pure" Jefferson, in attendance.

We then returned to the North Terrace for a final round of mixing and refreshments. Dan Jordan asked about Dad's welfare and whereabouts. Dad is an avid traveler, so I gave Dan an update. Becky, Jane Foster's zesty sister, and I became better acquainted. One of Jane's delightful friends swerved toward me in a flash and exclaimed with a drawl that must have started somewhere south of Richmond, "Well, you must be the real McCoy!" I was stunned by this new identification, but I responded, "Well, I think I am." Stretching "am" to its limit, I let her have all the drawl I could muster. She told me that I was better looking than Jefferson. This was southern seduction at its best. How could I do anything but like this lady?

Another woman came over to share a joke that played on the given name of the widely-praised Jeffersonian historian Dumas Malone, principally by separating it into two syllables. Trena told me later that she had spent her time immersed in historical debate. While exchanging repartee on the Carr brothers story, Trena had jumped to the misstatements of overseer Edmund Bacon. Dr. Foster had then come over to weigh into the conversation in Trena's support.

Giddy chatter marked our drive to Washington late that night. The day and evening had been a blast! We gained great satisfaction from absorbing the true history of the Monticello plantation, and we were becoming increasingly confident that it would finally reach the American people and deepen their understanding of their and our heritage.

NOTES

1. Quoted in Robert Andrews, ed., *Famous Lines* (New York: Columbia University Press, 1997), 359.

2. Warren Fiske, "Jefferson's Other Legacy," *Virginia Pilot*, April 12, 1998: Mapp's comments.

3. Judith Justus, *Down from the Mountain: The Oral History of the Hemings Family* (Perrysville: Privately printed, 1990), 162: deaths of Peter and Samuel Carr.

4. Douglass Adair, "The Jefferson Scandals," in *Fame and the Founding Fathers* (New York: W. W. Norton, 1974), 175: Peter Carr and Sally Hemings; Fawn M. Brodie, *Thomas Jefferson, an Intimate History* (New York: W. W. Norton, 1974), 493: dates pertaining to Carr brothers.

5. John Chester Miller, *Wolf by the Ears: Thomas Jefferson and Slavery* (1977; Charlottesville: University Press of Virginia, 1991), 149: "genius" and "reckless journalism."

6. Andrew Burstein, *The Inner Jefferson* (Charlottesville: University Press of Virginia, 1996), 228.

7. Adair, "Jefferson Scandals," 188.

8. Joshua Rothman, "James Callender and Social Knowledge of Interracial Sex in Antebellum Virginia," in *Sally Hemings and Thomas Jefferson*, ed. Jan E. Lewis and Peter S. Onuf (Charlottesville: University Press of Virginia, 1999), 102.

9. Willard Sterne Randall, *Thomas Jefferson, a Life* (New York: Henry Holt & Co., 1993), 180: Nelson Jones, Monticello carpenter; 476: Randall on Brodie.

10. Annette Gordon-Reed, *Thomas Jefferson and Sally Hemings: An American Controversy* (Charlottesville: University Press of Virginia, 1997), xv–xvii.

11. Barbara Murray, "Clearing the Heirs," *U.S. News & World Report*, December 22, 1997, 54–56.

12. Fiske, "Jefferson's Other Legacy?"

13. Leef Smith, "Jeffersonian Genes," *Washington Post*, April 28, 1998.

14. Edwin Betts and James Bear, eds., *The Family Letters of Thomas Jefferson* (Charlottesville: University Press of Virginia, 1986), 411: mention of closet in Thomas Jefferson's letter to Martha Jefferson Randolph, November 4, 1815.

15. Barbara Chase-Riboud, *Sally Hemings* (New York: Ballantine, 1994), 347 (pictures showing a portion of the steps before their removal appear in *National Geographic*, February 1976, and *Reader's Digest* 1974; the later picture appears in *Down from the Mountain* by Judith Justus).

16. Lucia C. Stanton, *Slavery at Monticello* (Charlottesville: Thomas Jefferson Memorial Foundation, 1996), 16.

17. Robert C. Barron, ed., *The Garden and Farm Books of Thomas Jefferson* (Golden: Fulcrum, 1986) 247; "Thomas Jefferson Memorial Foundation's New Position on Thomas C. Woodson," from the Thomas Jefferson Memorial Foundation Web site: www.monticello.org.

CHAPTER TWELVE

Stop and Look Both Ways

I hear that melting-pot stuff a lot, and all I can say is that we haven't melted.

—Jesse Jackson[1]

On the last Friday in October 1998, I was working in the office of North Capitol Neighborhood Development, Inc., in Washington, D.C., when I received a call from Leef Smith of the *Washington Post*. The news was shocking and disappointing. Smith told me that *Nature*, a leading scientific magazine, had released the content of an article reporting the results of the DNA test to the all major media outlets. She informed me that *Nature* would publish its article the following week. Smith believed the content of the article had been leaked and thus *Nature* was compelled to release its article earlier than planned. She also told me that a match was found between the DNA of the Eston Hemings Jefferson descendant and the Field Jefferson descendants but not between the Field Jefferson descendants and the Woodsons. I was shocked and surprised by both the reported result and the manner in which the release was unfolding. When Ms. Smith asked me why Dr. Foster had not informed me of the results, I told her I did not know. Dr. Foster had promised to inform me of the results before the public release, but I had heard nothing from him.

Leef Smith wanted me to comment on the results, but I indicated that I wanted to collect my thoughts and call her back. I did so within two minutes. The conversation was relatively short. I told her I was pleased that the family's assertion of the reality of the Hemings/Jefferson liaison was affirmed by the DNA test. I asked Ms. Smith if she would fax a copy of the *Nature* article to me. She declined to do so, and asked if I was disappointed that a match was not found between the Woodsons and the Field Jefferson descendants. I answered, "Yes."

I was surprised and disturbed by the results. My belief that Thomas Woodson and his descendants were descendants of Thomas Jefferson was unshaken. Yet I wondered how I could put the nightmare behind me, since I had long sought finality to the family controversy. I then thought the test must have been a ruse. Based on the vast historical record, I could not fathom how Eston could be the son of Thomas Jefferson and not Tom (Thomas Woodson). The controversy started in 1802 with Tom. If the test was a ruse, however, then the force of deceit was stronger than I was willing or able to fight. Those were my initial thoughts.

Trena was in Washington on business; we went to lunch. I didn't mention the phone call from Leef Smith during lunch, but afterwards I told her. We returned to my office. Trena decided to obtain a copy of the *Nature* article. Though the journal is published in London, she discovered that *Nature* had a downtown Washington office; she called and asked for the article. Within minutes, we had a copy. It was easier than I expected. Trena read the article while I tried to get some work done.

SURPRISE ENTRY

As Trena commented on the reported test results, it became clear that was not one article but two. One was written by Eugene Foster and Chris Tyler-Smith. That was no surprise. Then I looked at the other pages and saw Joseph Ellis' name at the top in bold letters. *Nature*, ostensibly an objective scientific magazine, had distributed an article by historian Ellis to the press corps! This was an absolute surprise. I was outraged, disgusted, and repulsed by the connection between a Jeffersonian historian and *Nature* before the scientific results were released to the public! The connection was in my view a violation of *Nature*'s alleged objectivity. (Indicted suspects are not allowed in the jury room, are they?) Professor Ellis was certainly not an objective observer of the controversy. How could the results meet objective standards if the parties reporting the results represented the antithesis of them?

Trena reached Dr. Foster by phone and asked why the test results had been dumped into the media instead of first being printed in *Nature*. His answer matched Leef Smith's; an alleged leak had caused the information to be released prematurely. He did not give a cogent explanation for not calling us before the media got hold of the reported results, but he expressed sorrow for not calling. I asked Dr. Foster if he knew how Joseph Ellis was selected for the peer review role, as I assumed that his article was a conclusion of a peer review process. Dr. Foster pointed out that Ellis was not a part of the peer review, which was performed by geneticists. Ellis' role was included to provide historical interpretation. It became clear that Foster, who had organized the project, had not brought Ellis into the picture, nor did he know when Ellis entered the picture or what influence he may or may not have exerted. How could Ellis constructively add historical interpretation when historians of his ilk had muddied the waters for over one hundred years? Of course I viewed Dr. Foster's explanation of Ellis' role as a farce. For me, all he brought to the situation was an element of mistrust.

I called Leef Smith. I wanted to go on the record with a protest. As I expected, Smith saw nothing inappropriate in Ellis' role as a contributor to *Nature*. Directing my frustration toward Leef Smith was unfair to her; she had not dragged Ellis into the picture. But I needed to create some memory of my protest and disgust.

We returned to Philadelphia that evening. The next day we received a call from Kristen Moore of the Washington Bureau of NBC. Moore had already produced a news clip about the Woodson family's assertion of its connection to Thomas Jefferson. The news clip, which aired in September 1998 on the *Today* show, featured an interview with me. Ms. Moore now arranged for a camera crew to visit our Philadelphia home to tape my reaction to the reported DNA test results. The crew was scheduled to arrive the following day, Sunday.

The front page of the Sunday *Philadelphia Inquirer* featured an article about the test results. We learned that all the other major dailies, including the *New York Times, Washington Post, Los Angeles Times*, and *Chicago Tribune*, also ran front-page articles. The articles quoted Joseph Ellis, Annette Gordon-Reed, and Eugene Foster heavily, though most of the Foster quotes were derived from the *Nature* article, not from interviews. The *New York Times* printed Ellis' message on its front page: "Our heroes—and especially presidents—are not gods or saints, but flesh and blood humans." This message was outed in spectacular form two days before the congressional election, the results of which were expected to influence President Clinton's ability to survive the Monica Lewinsky scandal. Professor Joseph Ellis was an avid Clinton supporter, and the president's operatives were pulling out all the stops to save the president's job and their own as well. The

Jefferson/Hemings controversy was being used for that end. I found the entire scenario repugnant.[2]

The camera crew arrived Sunday afternoon. Kristen Moore stayed in Washington, interviewing me via a speakerphone placed on my living room floor. The camera crew lit up my living room like the sun. None of this helped me relax. A media novice, I made the mistake of trying to memorize a short statement. I froze on camera and wasn't able to get out more than six words at a time. Kristen was very patient and gracious. I was thankful to her and to NBC but otherwise disgusted. I felt like a pawn in a game that someone had orchestrated. I wanted out of the nightmare.

On Monday, I traveled to Washington, D.C., and purchased a copy of *U.S. News & World Report* in Union Station as soon as I stepped off my train, knowing that the magazine featured an article about the DNA test results. The front cover revealed another surprise. Not only was "Jefferson and Sally" printed boldly on the cover, but the headline banner on the front cover offered "Jefferson's Legacy by Joseph J. Ellis." With one glance I was saturated with disgust. It seemed as if history professor Joseph Ellis had taken control of the public release of the DNA test results.[3]

Predictably, Ellis' article tied the Lewinsky scandal into the Jefferson/Hemings DNA test results. Ellis suggested Jefferson as a "character witness" for President Clinton, adding, "The dominant effect of this news will be to make Clinton's sins seem less aberrant." After finally acknowledging the Jefferson/Hemings liaison, then declaring a new line of resistance by calling Jefferson "too human," Ellis ended his article: "So now Jefferson surfaces again, not only offering aid to an embattled President Clinton but also making himself useful as a most potent guide into a fresh round of more candid conversations about the way we truly were and are one people."[4]

The title of Ellis' article was "When a Saint Becomes a Sinner." Americans have revered and paid homage to Jefferson; but, knowing his status as a slave owner, they have never regarded him as a saint. Why would the acknowledgment of the Jefferson/Hemings liaison characterize Jefferson as a sinner? Why? We knew him as a slave owner. Slaveholding is a sin, but this label was applied long, long ago. Martha Jefferson died before Sally Hemings' children were conceived. Adultery does not apply. Surely, thirty years after the sexual revolution, Ellis did not hope to use Jefferson and Clinton to reinstate fornication as a rallying point for sexual counterrevolution. No. Ellis looks at miscegenation as the sin in question. The U.S. Supreme Court rejected state laws against miscegenation in 1967 (not 1867); nevertheless, some Americans continue to believe the races should "stay to their own." I resented Professor Ellis' continued barrage of nasty labels, this time directed at Thomas Jefferson.

Television newsrooms blasted the DNA test results onto the American body politic the day before the congressional election. Joseph Ellis and Annette Gordon-Reed were in virtually every living room in America along with comments linking Jefferson, Lewinsky, Hemings, and Clinton. The day after the congressional election, television networks aired snips of a press conference hastily called so that Dr. Foster could recount the highlights of his *Nature* article. The broadcast gave the impression of Foster chasing the story, when in reality he had initiated the process.

Follow-up reports oversimplified the test result reports. "Scientific" tests are supposed to create absolute results, or so people think. *Time* reported that "Jefferson was not Thomas Woodson's father," though the *Nature* articles never stated that. The *Nature* articles qualified the statement, distinguishing between scientific evidence and historical evidence, effectively indicating that both needed to be evaluated to make a determination in this case. Later *Nature* would back off of the oversimplified headline it used.

RETREAT

Trena and I retreated to a planned vacation in Las Vegas and the Grand Canyon. The canyon was my treat; Las Vegas was Trena's. Not long after our arrival we heard from our son, Byron, who had received a call in Pittsburgh from the *Oprah* show. Oprah's staff picked up my name from NBC's *Today* show after Kristen managed to air a dozen or so of my nervous words. Accepting my frazzled state, and reluctant to cut the vacation short, I suggested that my cousin Michele Cooley-Quille would represent the Woodson family much better than I. When Michele's father died, she attempted to have him buried in the Monticello graveyard. The Monticello Association, descendants of the acknowledged family, rejected the request. A member of the Monticello Association, Lucian Truscott IV, made the graveyard an issue of public debate. Upon missing an all-expense-paid trip to Chicago and a chance to meet Oprah, Trena became literally ill. She called back to the East Coast to be consoled by her lifelong friends, Linda and Denise. The rented minivan I drove to the Grand Canyon served as a rudimentary ambulance.

I started down Bright Angel Trail alone the morning after our arrival at the South Rim. After fifteen minutes or so, I met a couple from Tucson, Arizona. I decided to match Paul and Nancy's pace, which was nearly as fast as mine. They were good company. They took pictures of me with my camera. I had descended into the canyon once before, thirty-six years prior, at the age of fifteen. In November, the ranks of tourists become thin, so the canyon looked and felt very much like it did years before in August. My pace was much faster than I planned the day before. My excitement was indescribable. The canyon is rugged and majestic. I was free and careless, absorbing the most stunning sight on earth. There were no ghosts, telephones, or video cameras following me down the winding trail. I soon reached Indian Garden, a campsite, which was as far as I had journeyed on my previous trip.

After a very short respite and self-inspection, I broke out on the trail to Plateau Point. The surroundings were dry, lacking any vegetation over a foot tall. I was the only customer the two-mile trail attracted. When I reached Plateau Point, four people were there. I approached the railing at the far side of a flat rock expanse very slowly. Beyond the railing was the Colorado River, 1,300 feet straight down and barely a ribbon from my vantage point! It was awesome. The river looked tiny and innocent from Plateau Point, but over many years it had carved the absolutely immense ditch in which I was standing. I looked back and up to the South Rim and wondered if I was insane for leaving it. I knew the walk back was feasible within a span of five or six hours, but it sure didn't look possible! I was in good company. Exchanging cameras, I found that I was out of film. Unbelievable! A guy from Florida quickly offered me a new roll. Really un . . . believable! A German named Hans took my picture.

Hans and I left from Plateau Point and walked more than half way up the canyon together. He was much younger than I, but not much stronger. He was mature and deliberate; though we recognized our difference in age, we had a lot in common. I told Hans I had lived in Germany as a small boy. He wasn't surprised, having perceived that I had experienced a good deal of what the world had to offer. I returned to the South Rim a stunning two hours before my predicted arrival. After lunch and a second cup of hot tea at Angel Lodge, I could feel no effects from the climb. I made the trip on sheer tenacity, not bodily strength. If my body made the trip, it merely followed along.

WEAPONS OF MASS DISTRACTION

The trip to the Grand Canyon was a wonderful diversion. In the "real world" President Clinton, Special Prosecutor Kenneth Starr, Republicans on the House Judiciary Committee, and Monica Lewinsky's former friend, Linda Tripp, competed for the title "Most Contemptuous." The day before the congressional election, *New York Times* columnist William Safire suggested that the release of the Jefferson DNA test reports was timed to help President Clinton, noting that Joseph Ellis' name had appeared along with those of other historians opposed to the president's impeachment in a full-page paid advertisement in the *New York Times*. Ellis had been scrambling to save Clinton's presidency, and he wasn't alone. On January 16, 1999, an article appeared on the *Philadelphia Inquirer*'s front page reporting the firing of the editor of the *Journal of the American Medical Association (JAMA)*. Like *Nature*, *JAMA* printed an article favorable to Clinton. George Lundberg, the fired editor, left his post after seventeen years without mounting a defense. Were Clinton operatives using the scientific community, in particular its journals, to further their cause? American Medical Association executive vice president E. Ratcliffe Anderson, Jr. indicated that Lunderg was fired for "inexcusably interjecting *JAMA* into the middle of a debate that has nothing to do with science or medicine." Anderson said that it appeared that the *JAMA* article release was timed to coincide with Clinton's impeachment trial. When *Philadelphia Inquirer* reporter Marie McCullough called *Nature,* to see if there was a pattern to this she was met with denial. Laura Garwin, North American editor for *Nature*, declared that the release of its article, which preceded publication of its magazine and appeared just in time for Sunday pre-election newspaper coverage and the election itself, was a coincidence.[5]

By some accounts, manipulation of scientific news would be the most tame of tricks the Clinton operatives performed during the months when Clinton's fate hung in the wind. *Vanity Fair* printed an article by Christopher Hitchens entitled "Weapons of Mass Distraction." Hitchens found no justification for the August 20, 1998 missile attacks on Sudan and Afghanistan, which were alleged to be retaliations directed at an Islamic fanatic named Osama bin Laden. Hitchens argued, forcefully, that the only purpose for the missile that destroyed a Sudanese pharmaceutical plant was to distract the press corps from Monica Lewinsky's return to grand jury testimony. The U.S. government's alleged justifications for the attack evaporated shortly after they were articulated. The government claimed that the plant did not make medicines but later retracted that statement. It also claimed to have a soil sample containing a chemical used to make nerve gas, but the sample failed to appear as a CIA informant who had fabricated evidence was fired. No proof of bin Laden's connection to the pharmaceutical plant emerged. If proof existed, it should have been grounds for discussion with the Sudanese government, not grounds for a missle attack. Hitchens found the justification for the sorties that hit Afghanistan lacked substance also.[6]

I am certainly not an expert on White House intrigue, but I do know a few things about a possible connection between the Lewinsky and Hemings scandals. President Clinton was not taking long walks on the beach with his dog, Buddy, while Kenneth Starr and fanatical Republicans were scrounging to remove him from office. The allegations that Clinton operatives manipulated and distracted the press corps seem to form patterns and in combination are compelling. The Lewinsky and Hemings scandals were in fact tied together in newspapers and on television at a time and in a manner that yielded maximum benefit to President Clinton, however that benefit is judged and measured. The possible political benefit is debatable, yet what other scheme could have possibly been devised to aid the president? I think they went with what they could get their hands on and Buddy missed the beach.

In January 1999 the God and Country Foundation held a press conference to announce that *Nature* had agreed to clarify the headline of Dr. Foster's article, "Jefferson fathered slave's last child." *Nature* composed the headline, not Foster, who had always carefully avoided the claim that the tests proved anything. To claim that a match or lack of match in genetic material through seven generations constituted proof would demand complete fidelity in each marital union, the lack of adoptions, and so on, and there was no proof of those circumstances. The God and Country Foundation used yet another argument to oppose the assertion that Thomas Jefferson fathered any of Sally Hemings' children, claiming that other Jeffersons could have fathered them. It did not explain why these other Jeffersons were only able to impregnate Sally Hemings when Thomas Jefferson was nearby, and the reporters attending the announcement apparently did not think to ask. Faced with the foundation's challenge and Foster's exactness, *Nature* clarified its position, attempting to distinguish between clarification and retraction.[7]

I found additional fault with *Nature*'s presentation. The test allegedly did not find matches between the Woodsons and the Field Jefferson descendants, but it did find matches among the different Woodson lines. Foster was silent regarding the Woodsons' matches, and Ellis' article implied that Woodson matches had not been found, citing possible "non-paternities among Tom's offspring." Ellis' article in *Nature* misled rather than elucidated and caused some readers to wonder why *Nature* had broadened its coverage to what the magazine called "William Jefferson Clinton's sexual indiscretions." I wrote to *Nature* in protest, but no one responded. Dr. Foster's often stated goal was objectivity. *Nature* destroyed the prospect of objectivity by bringing Ellis into the sphere before the release of the scientific results. Dr. Foster told me he had sought out *Nature*, as a respected and objective scientific journal;

but *Nature* took Foster's quest and dove headlong into the murk of the Monica Lewinsky scandal seemingly in the president's corner. Was there no gatekeeper, like AMA's Anderson, to stop these or other antics?[8]

THE NO-BOOK TOUR

One of the reasons some reporters gave for not including the family in coverage of the controversy was that families are liable to be "unobjective." The press claimed that they could rely only on historians and other experts whose work had been published. Yet these experts seemed to lack any ability to distinguish fact from fiction; thus the press relied upon a meaningless standard. In February *Emerge* published an article I wrote about the Woodson legacy, and *Ebony* printed an article also. The *Emerge* article and the prospect of this book gave me the credentials necessary for public recognition. Newspapers and universities began to accept me as a person qualified to speak about my own genealogy. I was anxious to replace the denigration my family had suffered for decades with a genuine rather than a presumed or contrived knowledge of the family.[9]

The Race Relations Institute at Fisk University invited Trena and me to present a lecture on its Nashville, Tennessee, campus. It was my first lecture; my pace was slow and my demeanor was tense. I spoke again before students at Morehouse and Spelman Colleges in the Camille Cosby Center at Spelman. This lecture went well; I spoke fluidly and with more conviction. The "No-Book Tour" hit a fine stride. Still I found that people could not shake their focus on Jefferson. They lacked a vision of the treasure the real story of Monticello could reveal. I spoke about the Hemings family, the implications of the irresolvable controversy, and my mother's research. Questions remained focused on Jefferson and the liaison.

We then drove to Greenbriar County, West Virginia, where we attempted to extend the research done by my mother and Ronald Woodson. Ronald Woodson of Texas had documented Thomas Woodson's presence in Greenbriar County in 1807 through county records, an important contribution, since the earliest documentation my mother found of his presence was the census of 1820. The Greenbriar County Historical Society helped me pinpoint Thomas Woodson's residence. We traveled to Brushy Ridge with a production crew from *Frontline*, which was filming a documentary. It was my first trip to Greenbriar County. I felt more connected than ever to Thomas Woodson's migratory life. I could feel and see the last skirmishes with Shawnee braves, whether my eyes were open or closed, and hear the movement of Conestoga wagons along the Midland Trail. It was still snowing in the sparsely populated highlands, though the March sunshine drove temperatures into the eighties upon our return to Nashville.

Another highlight of the tour was a presentation before staff members of the Thomas Jefferson Memorial Foundation, the current owner of Monticello. Trena and I were graciously welcomed, though many staffers were still in shock from recent revelations. I could tell from the faces that the group of forty or so ranged from naysayers to provocateurs to anarchists. The most entertaining were those sitting on the edge of their seats, wide-eyed and open-mouthed. They were in disbelief, not at what I was saying but for being there to witness an event no one had conceived of as being possible. The presentation was fun to do. Trena and I talked for only half an hour, then answered questions, so we only scratched the surface.

Before leaving Charlottesville, we dined with Cinder Stanton, an interesting mixture of zest and understatement. To me Cinder is the embodiment of the Jefferson quotation her boss, Daniel Jordan, repeats with regularity: "We shall follow the truth wherever it may lead." I consider Cinder to be the "Silent Sage of Monticello." We agreed on not having all of the answers. T. J. Randolph, we conceded, was particularly perplexing, as some his statements initially formed the bedrock of denial, while Fawn Brodie used other statements made by him to lift the cover and expose the truth. I told Cinder that Fawn Brodie's biographer was nearly finished with his work. I felt compelled to tell the women connected to the controversy as much as I could about Fawn Brodie, always feeling that the racial aspects of it were overemphasized at the expense of gender issues.

FAMILY REUNION

The annual reunion of the Monticello Association was held in May 1999 with events in Charlottesville and at Monticello. As a member of the Monticello Association, Lucian Truscott had invited the descendants of Madison Hemings, Eston Hemings Jefferson, and Thomas Woodson to the reunion during his appearance on the *Oprah* show the previous November. The invitation was rebellious and controversial, as the leadership of the Association was nowhere close to accepting the DNA test results as definitive or the Sally Hemings descendants as their cousins. To their dismay, inclusion of Sally Hemings' descendants in the Monticello Association and the burial of those family members in the Monticello graveyard became a focus of media attention.

The ride to Monticello reminded me of a much earlier trip. I thought of my arrival in Wilberforce, Ohio, in 1959 with cousin Lewis Woodson. I knew nothing then about the Ohio Woodsons. I didn't know if they would feel connected to me. Who feels the need to find all of their third cousins? That trip pushed me into a new level of family connections, and the trip to the 1999 Monticello Association Family Reunion did as well.

The first relative we met upon our arrival at Monticello was Lucian Truscott. Although this was our first meeting, we recognized him from his media appearances. The media, craving a focus, honed in on Lucian Truscott and Michele Cooley-Quille, a Woodson descendant. They were perfect. Trena gave Lucian a newly minted copy of the *Woodson Source Book*. Within minutes we met descendants of Madison Hemings and Eston Hemings Jefferson. Hugs and kisses were thicker than the grass on the West Lawn. Shay Banks-Young, a Madison Hemings descendant, was stunningly attired in an Afrocentric gown. Julia Westerinen, an Eston Hemings Jefferson descendant, opened her arms for me as soon as I saw her. My last step into her soft grasp ended over 150 years of separation and realized the complexity of America's past and present identities.

My Woodson cousins arrived and, with them, more embraces. Robert Golden, John King, and others were primarily from my father's generation. I was ecstatic that they were able to be present on this auspicious occasion. In contrast, my ever-so-beautiful cousin Michele arrived with a large belly and the effusive smile of an expectant mother. The recent death of Michele's father made her expectant motherhood seem simply divine.

Minutes flowed into hours, but at some point members of the Monticello Association walked onto the north side of the West Lawn. Daniel Jordan appeared momentarily as the arbiter, showman, and host extraordinaire. The president of the Monticello Association, Robert Gillespie, gave a speech, claiming that the Association needed more information to decide who should be considered a Jefferson descendant. Daniel Jordan spoke also.

A call went out for a group picture. A sea of photographers was on hand. At first the Sally Hemings descendants and Lucian Truscott were joined by few other members of the Monticello Association. One photographer, Jane Feldman, asked a Madison Hemings descendant, Shawn Lanier, to encourage everyone present to join in the photograph. Shawn, a student at Kent State University, launched an ebullient and effective series of pleas. The group nearly doubled in size, bolstered by Monticello Association members who did not share the skepticism of the Association's president. Many of those who then spread out on the lawn below the West Portico steps brought their children into the scene. Most Monticello Association members who abstained were childless and gray-haired. Lucian and Michele were in the front center position before the group grew larger. A Madison Hemings descendant took a position on the new front row, holding her baby, named, with enduring reverence, Madison. While the ranks grew, photographers were taking pictures. Jane Feldman called for a cheer. The assemblage was poised to celebrate, letting out the happy cheer of a winning team. Within seconds, the paparazzi earned a day's pay.

Photographers were ushered to the exit. The family had a few minutes to mingle before dinner was served at the historic Michie Tavern nearby. I turned to greet Robert Gillespie. He in turn indicated that he wished to meet "General King," as he called my cousin. I introduced him to General John King as well as Robert Golden, president of the Thomas Woodson Family Association.

Descending the steps, I found Trena greeting a young lady who stood near us on the steps during the picture-taking. Ann Duck's smile was delicate and infectious. She was a descendant of Maria Jefferson Eppes. I told her there were so many more Randolph descendants I wasn't sure I would meet any Eppes descendants. Maria Eppes' beauty was renowned in her day; I wondered whether it was legitimate to draw comparison between Maria and my newfound cousin, who was decidedly one of the prettiest among the group.

We also met "Nick" Coolidge, a resident of Washington, D.C. He and Trena discussed education at length, as he was dedicated to helping young people lift their horizons. He seemed a bit patronizing but otherwise genuine and delightful. Mr. Coolidge was an exception among his cousins. Many of the older Randolph descendants did not mingle or speak with descendants of Sally Hemings. He wasn't convinced we were his cousins, but Mr. Coolidge was out for a good time, mingling with good company. When we left on the bus that took us to the parking lot, Mr. Coolidge and Trena hugged. He smiled at us and said with anticipation, "I'll see you next year!"

The following morning we met a reporter from the *Philadelphia Inquirer* on Mulberry Row. Attention was finally directed to the Hemings family. Americans were increasingly curious about the history historians had kept hidden. Three years before, stones that had once formed the foundations of workshops and cabins on Mulberry Row were unearthed and placed to form the outlines of several foundations. Prior to the unearthing, the only surviving evidence of human life on Mulberry Row was the chimney of the joinery, which has stood alone for decades. Stone outlines are a start; I strongly favor restoration of a portion of Mulberry Row; the *Philadelphia Inquirer* reported my position.

The following day, the Monticello Association held a business meeting at the Omni Hotel in Charlottesville. Lunch was served before business began. We arrived late, so we were not able to chat with those at our table before business commenced. It quickly became apparent that business focused on the acceptance of Sally Hemings' descendants. Dr. Foster presented an explanation of the DNA test. He speaks deliberately, carefully qualifying statements as needed, with no inflection or exuberance. My guess is that many in the room who had not closely followed the intricacies of Y-chromosome testing and the consideration of "non-paternities" did not fully grasp Dr. Foster's explanation. People lead busy lives and look for simple explanations. John Works, Jr., who was clearly among those resisting the inclusion of Hemings descendants in the Monticello Association, stepped up to the microphone. He aggressively forged parameters for Dr. Foster's answer by citing a number of facts, all of which Dr. Foster had previously acknowledged, then asked, "These tests don't prove anything, do they?" Dr. Foster responded, "No, they don't prove anything. They don't prove a thing."

A few others asked questions of Dr. Foster. I was a little bored by the proceedings. I must have been looking at my dessert cup when I heard the voice of a kid at the microphone. I looked up at the chair across from me where Hunter, a young Randolph descendant, had sat through lunch. It was empty! Hunter was standing at the microphone. While Dr. Foster is surely a gentle and unimposing man, because of Hunter's comparatively small size the scene was reminiscent of David facing Goliath. Young Hunter ventured a question that was nearly coherent, but not quite clear enough. Billy Dalton, a Madison Hemings descendant, went to the microphone in Hunter's aid. Billy put his hand on Hunter's shoulder, suggesting that the boy repeat the question. Hunter did, but with little improvement. Billy, however, deciphered the essence of Hunter's frustration. Billy posed the question. "He wants to know if the tests were honest?" Hunter's head nodded slightly in affirmation. I was simply amazed. Dr. Foster, befuddled by the simplicity of the question, could only respond with a clear and simple response, "Why, yes. Of course they were honest."

John Works, who had pressed for Dr. Foster's "They don't prove anything" answer, made a motion to excuse guests from the room. Since the meeting was liable to become contentious, he argued, it should be closed to guests. News reporters had previously been banished. At that point the meeting did in fact become contentious. Guests were primarily Hemings descendants, and because the gentleman wanted them to leave, an increasingly lively debate began. Lucian Truscott queued for the microphone. When his turn arrived, Lucian blasted the motion with ridicule. He claimed that the motion was moot, because it could not achieve its aim of keeping the debate secret. A closed-door meeting could not be achieved, because Lucian promised to walk out into the hallway and tell the reporters everything that was said.

A formidable contingent of reporters was in fact in the hallway, poised with notepads, microphones, audiotape recorders, and video cameras. A bank of microphones had already been assembled. The *New York Times*, NPR, ABC, the *Chicago Tribune*, local television, and the local press were all represented. Leef Smith of the *Washington Post* was there. Lucian's grandfather was a famous World War II corps commander. Lucian had not fallen far from the tree; his tactics were impeccable.

Discussion got ahead of the agenda by moving for the inclusion of Hemings descendants in the Monticello Association. Mary Jefferson, an Eston Hemings Jefferson descendant, rose to explain to the association that she wasn't sure, just yet, if she wanted to join, saying she "came to check you out." The Monticello Association voted the motion down. Consequently guests remained in the room, except for Trena and Byron, who needed to start back to Philadelphia. After we left, a vote on the inclusion issue was blocked by the president, Robert Gillespie, who promised to convene a committee to study the matter.[10]

Thomas Jefferson and Robert Hemings traveled to Philadelphia in May 1776 in seven long, grueling days. We traveled home in five hours while listening to the music of Aretha Franklin and George Gershwin with the clarity of a live concert. Trena and I mentioned Nick Coolidge a few times during the drive. Inevitability was inherent in his parting message, "I'll see you next year."

NOTES

1. Quoted in Robert Andrews, ed., *Famous Lines* (New York: Columbia University Press, 1997), 325.

2. Dinitia Smith and Nicholas Wade, "DNA Test Finds Evidence of Jefferson Child by Slave," *New York Times*, November 1, 1998, A1.

3. Barbara Murray and Brian Duffy, "Jefferson's Secret Life," *U.S. News & World Report*, November 9, 1998, 58–66 (the issue was on newstands before that date).

4. Joseph Ellis, "When a Saint Becomes a Sinner," *U.S. News & World Report*, November 9, 1998, 67–69.

5. Richard Blow, "Sex Lives and Presidents," *George*, February 1999, 38; Marie McCullough, " 'Sex,' Politics Clash at a Medical Journal," *Philadelphia Inquirer*, January 14, 1999, A1, A14.

6. Christopher Hitchens, "Bill Clinton's Weapons of Mass Distraction," *Vanity Fair*, March 1999, 92–105.

7. Leef Smith, "Certainty of Jefferson-Hemings Affair Is Overstated, Critics Say," *Washington Post*, January 6, 1999.

8. Eugene A. Foster and C. Tyler-Smith, "Jefferson Fathered Slave's Last Child,"

Nature, November 5, 1998, 27–28; Eric S. Lander and Joseph J. Ellis, "Founding Father," *Nature*, November 5, 1998, 13–14. These articles were released to the press prior to publication on October 30, 1998, from the Washington, D.C., office of *Nature*.

9. Byron Woodson, "Blood for 'Truth,' " *Emerge*, February 1999; Laura Randolph, "The Thomas Jefferson/Sally Hemings Controversy," *Ebony*, February 1999.

10. As of the release date of this book, the Monticello Association has yet to decide upon opening the graveyard or the Association to those who are descended from Sally Hemings and Thomas Jefferson.

CHAPTER THIRTEEN

Calling All Cousins!

This is my family and we are one.
—Shay Banks-Young (Madison Hemings descendant),
February 5, 2000

After our oldest son, John, graduated from the University of Pittsburgh, Trena had taken our sons to Egypt for a celebration. John and Byron are interested in African culture and history, particularly in Nubia, an ancient culture from which Egyptian kingdoms drew part of their heritage. Mom and sons had a great time. They were amazed that many Egyptians looked like them. This was no surprise to me. Dad spent some time in Paris in the 1940s; Parisians had assumed he was Algerian. Many mixed-race people around the world look alike; social mores program us to find differences rather than likenesses, and we are often surprised when we take a closer look.

John reads Karl Marx, uses all the anti-capitalistic buzzwords, and styles his hair in braids. Some time ago he joined the campaign for the release of Mumia Abu-Jamal, a Philadelphia journalist once associated with the Black Panthers, now convicted of murdering a policeman. Once John moved home, I listened more closely to his assertions of Mumia's innocence and watched videotape pertaining to his conviction. I was intrigued with the depth of John's knowledge about the case and his growing knowledge of the law. The videotape particularly captured my attention. It explained that a man who was picked from a police lineup as the killer allegedly killed himself by way of a drug overdose the day of the infamous MOVE fire-bombing in Philadelphia which destroyed sixty-two homes. It made a complete picture for me. If the horrifying scenario is correct, the police disposed of the real killer and pointed the finger at a political antagonist. Those discussions drew me closer to John and helped me to appreciate his maturity. My long-held support of the death penalty began to wane.

Byron moved back to Philadelphia as well, after graduating from Pitt in 1999, precisely one hundred years after his great-grandfather, Howard D. Woodson. Byron is blessed with a buoyant personality like his mother's and with my father's disarming charm. He is well organized and disciplined, and I expect him to do things his old man never dreamed of doing.

We adopted our daughter Kellie when she was an itty-bitty baby. She enlivened our lives with a zesty attitude and rapid-fire speech that often resembled song more than conversation. She began to run away from home before she was allowed to cross the street. She packed a bag one day and ran off to a friend's house, down the alley to the next street over from ours. Progressively, she distanced herself from the family and ran away more often; it took more and more effort for us to find her. Life became nightmarish; she didn't respond well to tough love or to kindness. Beginning at age twelve she opted to live in a group home, then went from one such place to another. Kellie disowned us. Counseling did not help; she didn't bond with anyone. By 1999, Kellie had two daughters and a very unstable life.

Trena drove to Lancaster, Pennsylvania, to locate and reconnect with Kellie. Trena began to bring our youngest granddaughter to Philadelphia for a few days each month. The baby latched onto Trena like glue and treated me like a benchwarmer. Trena took the little tyke to the beach as part of each visit during the summer of 1999. The baby enlisted as a first-class Atlantic City Beach Bum. When winter arrived, we took her for a walk along the Schuylkill River, which she immediately mistook for the ocean. She didn't understand why she couldn't jump in; thankfully, a flock of geese soon caught her notice.

The family bond that began to disintegrate ten years before started to regenerate. Kellie has not enthusiastically welcomed us into her life. Yet, she has said enough and been warm enough to make me feel as though I have a daughter again. It's a wonderful gift. She knows we love her, and we know she loves and appreciates us. If acknowledgments do not extend far beyond that point, so be it.

While I focused more on events 200 years past, Dad flew to California to attend the wedding of my brother's son, Morgan. Morgan graduated from a well-respected Midwestern college and moved to Silicon Valley to join the future. His bride is a Virginian who relocated to California. After the wedding Dad visited cousins in Seattle, then returned east with wedding pictures and fortuitous stock tips on Silicon Valley technology firms. Morgan would have been a good candidate for the interviews Lise Funderburg conducted for her book, *Black, White, Other*. His appearance exhibits no trace of African ancestry, as his mother is of Scotch-Irish descent. He considers himself a biracial person in much the same way the singer Mariah Carey does. Morgan and his wife now have a hefty baby boy whose light hair emulates his mother's blonde hair, but whose blue eyes originate from a prior generation.[1]

I respect my brother Jon's courage in crossing the racial divide to marry the girl of his choice and my nephew's decision to become a father. Many biracial people stay single or, even if they marry, do not produce offspring, succumbing to real and perceived pressures. Morgan has scaled that wall and, by having a son, has done what his fervently family-oriented uncle considers to be a duty rather than a right. Following the lead of his sister Marnee, Morgan has stayed in touch with Dad since the wedding, which warms my heart immensely. The circuitous nature of the Hemings/Jefferson legacy plays out generation after generation; the past is surely not dead.

A BACKWARD STEP

In January 2000, news of the Thomas Jefferson Memorial Foundation's report on Thomas Jefferson and Sally Hemings caught us by surprise. We knew a report had been prepared, but its issuance was so long delayed we doubted it would ever be released. All the major news networks assembled camera crews on the West Lawn of Monticello to disseminate the Foundation's new position, which is that Eston Hemings Jefferson was probably the son of Thomas Jefferson, that Thomas Woodson was not the son of either Thomas Jefferson or Sally Hemings, and that the other children of Sally Hemings may have been Thomas Jefferson's children. Thus, the Foundation, established in 1923, has, after seventy-seven years of denial, finally acknowledged a portion of the liaison of Jefferson and Hemings. The *Washington Post*, whose coverage was carried in several newspapers around the nation, quoted the Foundation position that "a relationship over time led to the birth of one, and perhaps all, of the known children of Sally Hemings." The Foundation's report failed to determine whether the relationship "was love or lust, rape or romance."

The *Washington Post* coverage and nearly all other news reports referred to "Sally Hemings' six children," failing to explain that, the Foundation previously acknowledged that Hemings became pregnant seven times and that the Foundation had changed its position by dropping Thomas Woodson from its list of Hemings' children. The article made no mention of the Woodsons, the only people who five years before then were making public assertions of the Jefferson/Hemings liaison. Americans who saw the family on the *Oprah* show and read about the Woodsons and other family lines in their local newspapers assumed that all Sally Hemings' children, including Thomas, were being acknowledged as Jefferson's. The omission or failure to explain the previous posture effectively misled the public.

The Foundation posted a full report on its Web site explaining its new position with respect to Thomas Woodson. The very quiet denial of Thomas Woodson's Monticello origin cut off the opportunity for public discussion. Many of my friends and acquaintances, for instance, thought after reading the newspapers that the Foundation's report had agreed with the assertions of the Woodson family.

The evidence in support of Sally Hemings' motherhood of Thomas Woodson (Tom) is as follows:

1. James Callender reported in September 1802 that Sally was the concubine of Thomas Jefferson and that the boy named Tom was the son of Sally and Jefferson. Other newspapers including the *Virginia Gazette* authenticated Callender's reports by finding "nothing but proofs of their authenticity." The Republican paper, the *Richmond Examiner*, responding to Callender's accusation, acknowledged, "That this servant woman has a child is true." The comment appeared only days after Callender's article, thus the reference applied to Tom.

   A raucous scandal brewed throughout the United States, yet no one living during the period came forward to say that Tom or "a boy [of twelve]" did not exist or did not live at Monticello or was not the son of Sally Hemings. The lack of denial is very powerful evidence.

   Callender added to his original report two weeks afterwards by asserting that Sally Hemings had given birth to five children. The figure was accurate, as it counted Tom, Beverly, Harriet, and two children who died in infancy. Madison and Eston were born after Callender's assertion.

2. A letter written by a Mr. Gibbons, dated December 20, 1802, cites Tom, Beverly, and Harriet as children of Sally Hemings and Thomas Jefferson. The news reports of Callender and others did not mention children other than Tom, by name. Thus Gibbons must have obtained the names independently. This is strong evidence.

3. The Woodson family oral history was handed down for over 150 years through five lines of the family that had lost contact with one another over 120 years ago. For instance, my father, John Woodson, did not meet family members other than Lewis line members until 1972 at age fifty-four. Rev. Lewis Woodson moved from

Ohio to Pittsburgh in 1831. Lewis Woodson returned to Ohio for or after his mother's funeral in 1868. After 1868 contact between the several family lines was surely severed. Some family lines lost contact even before then. Minnie Woodson documented the life of Thomas Woodson in the *Woodson Source Book*, confirming the oral history and finding no documentation in conflict with the oral history. The family separation/migration proves that the oral history emanated directly from Thomas Woodson, and recognition of Lewis Woodson's unusual drive and his philosophies suggests that the oral history predates Thomas Jefferson's death. Moreover, the Jeffersonians' denials have changed so many times in hopes of survival that it is obvious, at least to the Hemings descendants, that their story, which has never been modified, is the real history.

4. This evidence was identified by Fawn Brodie. Ellen Randolph Coolidge indicated that four "yellow children," three boys and one girl, walked away and were left to their own. Two of these children were Sally's, Harriet and Beverly. The other boy was Critta's (Sally's sister) son, Jamie. The other has never been accounted for other than Tom.

5. At age sixty-eight, Madison Hemings told a news reporter that his mother was pregnant when she returned from France in 1790. Thomas Woodson was born in 1790, and Callender reported Tom's presence in 1802 and placed his age at "ten or twelve." If Tom was twelve then, he was born in 1790. The dates match.

6. Jeffersonian historians point out that Tom's name does not appear in the *Farm Book*. On page 31 of the *Farm Book*, where Tom's name would have appeared, identified by sex (male) and year of birth (1790), an erasure appears where Thomas Jefferson once wrote a name. Tom's (Thomas') name was there until someone removed it.

7. Two Frenchmen saw boys who were sons of enslaved women in 1796 who appeared as white as they were. Jamie and Thomas are the only possible candidates.

8. The given names of Sally Hemings' children were not derived from the Hemings family. All of the names, including Thomas', were connected to Thomas Jefferson. Evidence indicates that Thomas Jefferson called his son Thomas, not Tom, employing more formality than others. (For more information, please see endnote.[2])

The evidence that challenges Sally Hemings' motherhood of Thomas Woodson (Tom) is as follows:

1. The 1873 account of Madison Hemings' reminiscences indicates that the baby conceived in Paris (1789) died as an infant. Two other children born before Madison did die as infants.

The evidence is clearly and overwhelmingly in favor of Sally Hemings' motherhood of Thomas Woodson. A birth certificate does not exist and never did. If one did exist, at some point someone would have destroyed it.

The same supporting evidence favors Thomas Jefferson's fatherhood of Thomas Woodson. In addition to Madison Hemings' remark that the baby who was born in 1790 soon died, the other evidence challenging Thomas Jefferson's fatherhood of Thomas Woodson is the Y-chromosome DNA test. I assert that evaluation of those test results should be much more rigorous than that which experts have thus far been willing to undertake. There are issues pertaining to science, history, ethics, and reliability at stake.

The reason Thomas' name alone was erased from the *Farm Book* is that, until Fawn Brodie's book was published in 1974, Thomas' (Tom's) name was the only one involved in the public controversy. Madison Hemings' account was not widely distributed in 1873 and lay dormant until the publication of the Brodie book one hundred years later.

MISSING EVIDENCE

Fortunately, as a law professor Annette Gordon-Reed brought more objective standards of evaluating evidence to the Hemings/Jefferson debate. A look at how legal systems operate when there is cause to believe that evidence has been destroyed is therefore appropriate. To ignore such destruction only aids and condones the corrupt act. At the same time, determining what evidence has been destroyed may be difficult and risky. As I began to write this book, the murder trail precipitated by the disappearance of Anne Marie Fahey of Delaware gripped my attention. It is presented here for comparison.

Ms. Fahey's body was never found. Her wealthy boyfriend, Thomas Capano, a former Delaware prosecutor, was convicted of her murder. No forensic evidence whatsoever was collected by the police. The disappearance of Fahey's body delayed search warrants and indictment; in the meantime Capano removed and replaced all the furniture and carpeting in his living room, the probable crime scene. The other significant evidence seemed to be the testimony of Capano's brother that Thomas asked him to take his boat into the Atlantic Ocean and as he steered his boat the brother glanced in the direction of a splash caused by Thomas tossing an object overboard. The brother testified that he briefly saw a human leg in the water.

No body was produced, no forensic evidence was brought forth, and the brother could not be sure that the leg he saw was that of Ms. Fahey. Yet the jury convicted Thomas Capano, swayed by his effort to dispose of evidence. Not only did the jury convict; it came within two votes of imposing the death penalty. The public was so pleased with the conviction that the trial judge was drafted to run for governor. Awareness and recognition of the destruction of evidence can be used as a powerful tool in resolving a crime, controversy, or debate. A key ingredient seems to be the will to find the truth. The search for truth sometimes involves risk taking and/or a reevaluation of the prevailing paradigm. If the jury, for instance, had presumed that prosecutors such as Capano are committed to uphold the law and never break it, Thomas Capano would be a free man.

Traditionalist historians have embraced the Hemings/Jefferson DNA test. They bestow a presumption of integrity upon the process and claim ignorance of any need for examination. I participated in the DNA test and witnessed the transgression of historian Joseph Ellis far beyond the point which should have raised red flags. I witnessed *Nature*'s welcome of Ellis, signifying a bias toward the Jeffersonian historian as opposed to the descendants, whom Ellis labeled "liars and fools." I witnessed *Nature*'s publication of gossip about President Clinton's sex life and its linkage to the Hemings/Jefferson controversy, a shocking departure for a scientific journal. Along with *New York Times* columnist William Safire, I saw the DNA test results released not in a scientific journal but in a media dump "perfectly timed" to exert a hoped-for influence on the 1998 congressional election. I witnessed the release of the DNA results from a fax machine located two blocks from the White House. What's more, the assertions Dr. Foster made to me while standing in my dining room with respect to the integrity of the process were violated. Newspapers now refer to the test as "inconclusive," but that does not satisfy me. The test should be disregarded by those historians who use it to create one history for my white cousins and another for myself and my black cousins.

I did not give a blood sample for "inside the Beltway" political antics. Given what did happen, I fail to see how the DNA tests can be taken seriously.

ONE BI . . . GG FAMILY

In 1979, CBS began production of a miniseries about Sally Hemings soon after sales of Barbara Chase-Riboud's novel bounded past the 1-million-copy mark. In 1980 Pulitzer Prize–winner Dumas Malone and associates pounced on CBS executives to prevent the project's realization. The University of Virginia professor was successful; the miniseries was canned. In 1998, eighteen years later, CBS revived its interest in the project. *Sally Hemings, an American Scandal*, aired on the CBS network in February 2000. For the first time, acknowledgment of Jefferson's liaison with Sally Hemings reached the average American household. Racial mixture during America's early years finally emerged as a recognizable historical pattern.

Trena and I drove to Columbus, Ohio, for a preview of the TV movie *Sally Hemings*. The screening and reception took place on the campus of the Ohio State University. The screenwriter, Tina Andrews, was on hand along with 400 relatives and 300 or so friends of the family. Descendants of Sally Hemings were most prominent; lines from Tom, Madison, and Eston were well represented. Lucian Truscott IV and Marla Randolph Stevens, descendants of Martha Jefferson Randolph, were on hand. These two Randolph descendants are renegades from the acknowledged family and came to celebrate the movie and embrace their Hemings cousins. Was it ever festive! Smiles and cameras clicked without end. Tina Andrews was overwhelmed by the family's embrace. She cried. We cried with her.

For me, the movie had several highlights. The first was a tender scene where Sally Hemings taught a young male friend to read. It signified that Tina Andrews had captured one of the special qualities of the Hemings experience at Monticello. Interspersed with other action, the movie showed Sally Hemings leading a succession of red-haired little tykes around the Monticello grounds. Near the movie's end Thomas Woodson gallantly rode a fine horse across the West Lawn to greet and visit his mother, telling her and Thomas Jefferson of his marriage to Jemima. I yelled like a Phillies fan!

After the movie and the rousing applause, Shay Banks-Young (Madison) spoke and then asked Julia Westerinen (Eston), Lucian Truscott (Martha), and Robert Golden (Thomas) to come to the front to represent the family lines. "This is our family and we are one," Shay succinctly and sincerely announced to the audience.

A reception and gathering followed. In the food line I saw the nametag of a gorgeous little unassuming lady from Columbus, Rachel Blades. I knew the name because Trena had spoken with her by phone. She is descended from Delila Woodson Lucas, one of Thomas and Jemima's daughters. She was surprised that I knew who she was, as we had never before met. Mother had been unable to locate the Delila line, as she never identified any of Delila's children. The family association connected with the line in 1994, the same year connection was made with the line descended from Jemima, another daughter.

On the trip home, I thought about a small group of Woodsons from Connecticut. They recently made the connection also. They were descended from a William Woodson, but, as it turned out, not from Thomas' son William, but a third generation William, from Thomas' son Thomas. The Thomas line had also been a dead end for us. It then struck me that we were connected with living relatives of that line also. The Thomas Woodson Family Association can now identify living members of ten family lines. We also know that Sarah Jane Woodson Early was childless. We have them all! Reality continues to far exceed expectation.

What force brought all the family lines together after 150 years of separation? For me it is an awesome question to ponder. What force pushed us further to connect with the other Hemings lines and those descended from Martha Wayles Jefferson? I jumped for joy as a boy when cousin Lewis Woodson asked if I wanted to visit St. Louis, Missouri, and Wilberforce, Ohio. I was constantly flabbergasted by my mother's talent and tenacity and the richness of the story she uncovered. I didn't know the journey would be so long and so wonderful. I only knew I wanted to meet all the relatives I could possibly meet. Well, I have now met hundreds. It has been a blast. If it ever ends, I will certainly feel a void; the search is ingrained in me, part of my being and my joy.

When the Sally Hemings movie whirled across television screens, some Americans reeled at the sight of Sam Neil (Thomas Jefferson) holding actress Carmen Oguco (Sally Hemings) in his arms. She teased him; she scolded him. Some were aghast, and some cheered. In Charlottesville and elsewhere academicians cringed as Sally Hemings introduced Thomas Jefferson to his son, Thomas Woodson, but they found solace in their indignation. "It was a Hollywood movie," they scoffed, assured that it was not a "scholarly" venture. Yet there is good reason why the Brodie book and assertions of the Sally Hemings descendants have gained ground and moved across the new line the academics have drawn in the sand.

Jeffersonians faced, considerable challenge after Barbara Chase-Riboud's book sold over a million copies twenty years ago. They have been there before, stubbornly resisting. A new generation of Jeffersonian historians has reconstructed the history of the Monticello plantation instilled with confidence that James Callender saw a ghost, not Tom, that the orphan Thomas Woodson fell from a cloud, that no one will notice if they ignore Fawn Brodie's evidence.

More broadly, have these historians made a commitment to rebuild the shops and residences of Mulberry Row and educate visitors to Monticello about its history? A partial history is a false history; full disclosure is important. History should not burden the progressive spirit of Americans. History should only tell us how fast we can move forward without forgetting who we are.

NOTES

1. Lise Funderburg, *Black, White, Other* (New York: Quill, 1994).
2. James A. Bear and Lucia C. Stanton, eds., *Jefferson's Memorandum Books* vol.

2 (Princeton: Princeton University Press, 1997), 1031–37, 1050. Jefferson made notations of gifts of two dollars to a servant named Thomas in December 1800 and in February 1801, while in Washington, D.C. Thomas or Tom would have been ten years of age, an appropriate age for his father to have begun giving him money. Notations of a servant named Thomas do not appear before or after this two-month span. During the same stay in Washington, Jefferson gave five dollars to John. Tom (Thomas) and John Hemings most probably accompanied Jefferson to Washington as body servants. This time followed James Hemings' time as body servant and preceded Burwell's service as such. It would certainly not have been the first or only time Jefferson traveled with two members of the Hemings clan. This time precedes the Jefferson presidency, thus the servants Thomas and John were not servants of the President's House. Moreover, the monies for Thomas and John were disbursed as gifts, not payments.

Davy Bowles, a Monticello slave, accompanied Jefferson part of the way to Washington but returned to Monticello with the horses. It would have been uncharacteristic for Jefferson to travel without a body servant, and this trip was a particularly important one. Jefferson was elected president of the United States on February 17, 1801. On March 12, after being in Washington for two and a half months, Jefferson hired Edward Maher as a porter. This engagement was not intended for Jefferson's immediate needs, as Jefferson left Washington on April 1 for a trip to Monticello. Maher was engaged in anticipation of Jefferson's residence in the President's House.

Did this trip draw the attention of James Callender? Callender was released from jail on March 2, 1801. Callender held strongly racist views toward blacks. His references to blacks and descriptions of them were invariably nasty; his references to Sally Hemings were particularly vicious. Curiously, however, Callender referred to Tom as President Tom (not Monticello Tom) and spared him the usual blasphemy. Was Callender aware of Tom's trip to Washington, D.C.? Did that knowledge strike Callender's fancy and trigger a different journalistic treatment? Was the trip the reason why Callender mentioned Tom by name but not the two younger children then alive by name? Was Callender alerted by the trip?

Lastly, did someone in Washington ask Thomas, then a boy of ten years, who his mother was? And was the inquirer amazed to find that the mother of the boy, who looked white, was a slave?

Annotation—Trena Woodson identified Jefferson's notations of small gifts to "Thomas" as gifts to his son, Thomas (Tom). Months later, while writing the final manuscript, Byron Woodson read all the pages in *Jefferson's Memorandum Books* related to this particular trip to Washington, finding John's name, thus solidifying the connection.

Conclusion

The storm we have passed through proves our vessel indestructible.
—Thomas Jefferson, 1801

For nearly 200 years Jeffersonians denied the close relationship Thomas Jefferson maintained with Sally Hemings and the Hemings family. When Fawn Brodie proffered an alternative to the mysticism surrounding Monticello in 1974, the effort to purify its past grew more fierce and defensive. We know the Jeffersonian historians switched their stance in 1999, but the new stance is not valid either.

Historian Gerda Lerner assured us, "All human beings are practicing historians." History shapes our self-image, our standing in our community, and our nation. In *Why History Matters* Lerner explained, "The dominant system of ideas in Western societies for nearly four thousand years has been derived from and in turn supportive of the social system of patriarchy." In Lerner's view a system of dominance constructs "categories [of people] by which the unequal distribution of resources and power by small elites over large and diverse populations justified, explained and made acceptable to those exploited . . . the differences . . . based on race, class, sex, physical makeup." Eric Hobsbawm's writings reveal how dominance is perpetuated: "For the greater part of history we deal with societies and communities for which the past is essentially the pattern for the present." Many people have commented recently that the irresolvable persistence of the Hemings/Jefferson controversy says as much about America today as it says about eighteenth-century Virginia. Contradicting Lerner, Jeffersonian Winthrop Jordan maintained that "it does not much matter" whether Thomas Jefferson fathered Sally Hemings' children. It seems as though some history matters and some does not, at least to some people.[1]

According to Joseph Ellis, Jefferson was exposed as "a large and obvious target for those ideologically inspired historians and political pundits who went charging back into the American past in search of monstrous examples of racism, sexism and patriarchy to slay, then drag back into the present as trophies emblematic of how bad it was back then." Such wild conjecture is based on fear of the unfamiliar and an inability to envision harmony. Instead of openness to dialogue, attacks began. Instead of looking to the historic record for answers, Ellis called those with opposing views "liars and fools," severing any possibility of exchange. The reality Jeffersonian scholars harbor supposes that the icon is always under attack and depends on their protection. In a different reality, no attack has been planned; their suspicion is a menace, cement ready to patch the cracks in an aging system of caste.[2]

Traditionalist historians have composed the American civil religion through an unrelenting focus on icons. They clearly have little interest in the values of the "popular culture," either past or present. These historians are unable to evaluate the culture in which icons of old and the present live and thrive. Jeffersonian historians held no interest in understanding the realities of Mulberry Row. They would be delighted if they could tell us Jefferson lived alone. My reality is that, while I recognize that the magnificence of Jefferson's accomplishments set him apart and encourages passionate study and scrutiny, I find the Hemings family to be equally as fascinating, complex, and expressive as the Jeffersons. The personalities that leap from the historical record are strong, clear, and engaging. On the real mountaintop, the racial divide sometimes disappeared into a seamless quilt and at other times demanded adherence to the greatest injustices.[3]

After the Sage of Monticello retired and settled into new endeavors, establishing the University of Virginia, for instance, the Hemingses gained new skills and wove an infrastructure that enabled them to prosper beyond the foothills of Virginia in freedom. This preparation set a standard for thousands, then tens of thousands, who escaped enslavement by various means. To what extent did Jefferson aid this noble endeavor? It's an enchanting question, the answer to which I believe the most agile minds should stalk, enlightening us all.

Why Should Not the Laws of Nations (and Families) Go On Improving?

While honoring Nobel Prize winners in April 1962, President John F. Kennedy described the group as "the most extraordinary collection of talent, of human knowledge, that has ever been gathered at the White House, with the possible exception of when Thomas Jefferson dined alone." The genius that impressed Kennedy survived in the numerous writings Jefferson left for posterity. Jefferson's letters to his daughters Martha and Maria were meant to enrapture them as much as to transmit family news. In contrast, his political writings often exposed a chilling honesty. In one such passage Jefferson summed up the evolution of civilization in six sentences:

By the original Laws of Nations, war and extirpation were the punishment of injury. Humanizing by degrees, it admitted slavery instead of death. A further step was the exchange of prisoners instead of slavery. Another, to respect more the property of private persons under conquest, and be content with acquired dominion. Why should not this law of nations go on improving? Ages have intervened between its several steps; but as knowledge of late increases rapidly, why should not those steps be quickened?[4]

The placement of slavery as a foundation of civilization is a nasty notion to embrace. With those few words Jefferson opened the evolution of man's humanity and inhumanity for inspection. Greek city-states fought each other and enslaved the losing foe. Romans bureaucratized slavery, placing large slave-manned farms throughout their empire. Slavery was a prevalent aspect of African and Chinese history. As a student of the classics, Jefferson appreciated those cultures and did not shrink from their realities.

"Knowledge of late increas[ing] rapidly" did not pull large sections of populations appreciably away from the rigors of subsistence agriculture until after Jefferson's death. With the glorification of Greek and Roman cultures, which in reality exhibited some horrific practices, and by omissions such as the Armenian Holocaust, which took place less than a hundred years ago, the history of Western civilization has been appreciably sanitized. Jefferson left to others the task of filling in the smaller steps of civilization's progression. Gerda Lerner notes that "everywhere the first slaves known are women of foreign tribes." Enslavement of men was a further step. Jefferson grasped the march of social change with a lucidity few men have achieved. Yet his deeds extended far beyond his writings, as he, like his dear friend Lafayette, was a doer, a revolutionary, and a freedom fighter.[5]

The freedom fighter Martin Luther King, Jr., also grasped the same need for progression, saying "We will reach the goal of freedom because the goal of America is freedom." King challenged and cajoled fellow Americans to reach for higher ground by evoking the charge of the Founding Fathers. King's struggle made a difference, but Jefferson's charge was to "go on improving." Since the Civil War was *the* great war fought on our soil, Americans think of the freedom struggle of African Americans as if it were a unique experience. Yet, the Irish were dominated and abused by the English, the English were overrun and subjugated by the Normans, whose ancestors, the Gauls, were enslaved by Romans, and so on.[6]

We should consider the more recent horror in Bosnia, Ruwanda, and Kosovo to realize that the need to encourage peaceful and tolerant societies is ever-present and worldwide. History can help dissolve the differences, but only if that history is uncontaminated.

As descendants of Sally Hemings, we knew that Thomas Jefferson was our ancestor because our mothers and fathers told us of our heritage. When Fawn Brodie's book was published we learned about the life of Sally Hemings and learned that Jeffersonian historians had stretched to deny the liaison of Sally Hemings and Thomas Jefferson. The double standards employed by historians only strengthened the beliefs descendants held. The descendants of Sally Hemings did not ask for the DNA tests. Those who did organize and perform the tests should have conducted the process with dignity; our court systems demand decorum and etiquette for a reason. When Dr. Foster came to my home to take my blood sample, he gave me three assurances about how the test process would be handled. After those were all broken, how could he expect me to believe the reported results?

The erasure from the *Farm Book* of the name of a male slave born in 1790, written by Thomas Jefferson in his own hand, was never disclosed by Jeffersonians. The presence of Thomas' name, also written in Thomas Jefferson's own hand in *Jefferson's Memorandum Books*, was never disclosed. Except for Cinder Stanton, no Jeffersonian acknowledged the existence of the *Woodson Source Book*. When Trena learned of the erasure that appears in Jefferson's *Farm Book*, I was already full of distrust. I became more disgusted. Meanwhile, more mainstream journalists are beginning to report the Jefferson/Hemings controversy objectively. No longer can a tainted history be forced-fed to Americans. Hollywood screenwriters have adopted the version of this history Fawn Brodie and Minnie S. Woodson offered because scripts just do not make sense any other way.[7]

For centuries Sally Hemings was often called "Dusky Sally." Pulizter Prize–winning historian Garry Wills likened her to a "prostitute," and Jeffersonians quoted Wills for decades. Sally Hemings has now been raised from the degradation Jeffersonians once cast upon her. A new generation of Jeffersonians published *Sally Hemings and Thomas Jefferson* in 1999, after acknowledging the liaison as a reality. This book uses Sally Hemings' name nearly 200 times, but contains few references to her enslavement and repetitiously assures us that Sally's children would have been considered white under the Virginia law prevailing during her time. Rhys Isaac's essay "Monticello Stories Old and New" argues that Sally was Jefferson's wife, not his concubine, as her son Madison Hemings and the newsman James Callender called her. The book in fact makes as many references to Sally's whiteness as to her blackness. Jeffersonians are recasting Sally Hemings in their own frame of reference, focused exclusively on race, not the content of Sally's character or the vitality of Betty Hemings' clan. Jeffersonians are now inclined to dignify Sally Hemings and can only imagine doing this by expunging her blackness. This new generation of Jeffersonians does not plan to educate Americans about the rich history of the Monticello plantation. *Sally Hemings and Thomas Jefferson*, for instance, fails to identify exactly where Sally Hemings lived on the plantation or where she raised her children. It offers no description of the Hemings family. In 1839 the Reverend Lewis Woodson wrote, "Nature has no prejudice in her heart." He would not have recognized a need to disconnect his grandmother from her African roots.[8]

Ultimately, however, the Hemings/Jefferson controversy will not be resolved on the front page on the *Washington Post* or with a bogus headline in *Nature*, not at a press conference called by the Thomas Jefferson Memorial Foundation, not on CNN, and certainly not by the History Department at the University of Virginia. It was not resolved by the *Sally Hemings* TV miniseries that properly placed Thomas Woodson in the story line. It will be not be resolved by this book. It will be resolved by people with names like Michele, Lucian, Shay, Julia, Nick, Anne, Mary, Joy, Shack, Shannon, Marla, Colonel Truscott, and Colonel Woodson. It will be resolved by a family—my family.

NOTES

1. Gerda Lerner, *Why History Matters* (Oxford: Oxford University Press, 1997), dust cover, 146–47; Eric Hobsbawm, *On History* (New York: The New Press, 1997), 10; Jordan quoted in Newell G. Bringhurst, *Fawn McKay Brodie: A Biographer's Life* (Norman: University of Oklahoma Press, 1999), 218.

2. Joseph Ellis, *The American Sphinx: Thomas Jefferson* (New York: Vintage, 1998), 22. "target"; "Jeffersonian Genes," *Washington Post*, April 28, 1998: "liars and fools."

3. Historian Dumas Malone won a Pulitzer Prize for his massive six-volume biography, *Jefferson and His Time*. The work expunges the Hemings family from the life of Thomas Jefferson, ignoring the journals our Founding Father wrote. Malone handled the Hemings family in his footnotes, not in the text of his books, then only to deny the Hemings/Jefferson liaison. The Malone work promised to cover Jefferson "and his Time." The work virtually ignores the existence of African Americans in America. During much of Jefferson's life the number of African Americans in Virginia exceeded the number of whites. Jefferson tallied the black population of Virginia himself, but Malone ignored realities Jefferson appreciated and managed. The award of a Pulitzer Prize for Malone's work was a tragedy.

4. Kennedy quote from *Bartlett's Familiar Quotations*, 16th ed. (Boston: Little, Brown, 1992), 741; Jefferson quote from William Howard Adams, *The Paris Years of Thomas Jefferson* (New Haven: Yale University Press, 1997), 178.

5. Lerner, *Why History Matters*, 134: "first slaves."

6. Eric Foner, *The Story of American Freedom* (New York: W. W. Norton, 1999), 279: Martin Luther King, Jr., quote.

7. Minnie S. Woodson's work was acknowledged as a reference source for the 1995 movie *Jefferson in Paris* and she appeared in a documentary produced by Martin Dolbeare. Fawn Brodie's biography has served as the source for numerous films, commercial and documentary.

8. Adams, *The Paris Years of Thomas Jefferson* (New Haven: Yale University Press, 1997), 222: Wills quote; Lucia Stanton and Dianne Swann-Wright, "Bonds of Memory," *Sally Hemings and Thomas Jefferson*, ed. Jan Lewis and Peter Onuf (Charlottesville: University Press of Virginia, 1999), 164: Children of Sally Hemings would have been considered white by application of the law in Virginia and Ohio. The assertion is not disputed by this author. The timing and intent of this revelation is questioned here. Minnie S. Woodson, *Woodson Source Book* (Washington, D.C.: Privately printed, 1984), 133. From *The Colored American*, February 9, 1839: Lewis Woodson quote.

Mr. Jefferson's Will

I Thomas Jefferson of Monticello, in Albemarle, being of sound mind and in my ordinary state of health, make my last will and testament, in manner and form as follows.

I give to my grandson Francis Eppes, son of my dear deceased daughter Mary Eppes, in fee simple, all that part of my lands at Poplar Forest lying west of the following lines, to wit, Beginning at Radford's upper corner near the double branches of Bear creek and the public road, & running thence in a straight line to the fork of my private road, near the barn, thence along that private road (as it was changed in 1817.) to it's crossing of the main branch of North Tomahawk creek, and from that crossing, in a direct line over the main ridge which divides the North and South Tomahawk, to the South Tomahawk, at the confluence of two branches where the old road to the Waterlick crossed it, and from that confluence up the Northernmost branch (which separates McDaniel's and Perry's fields) to it's source, & thence by the shortest line to my Western boundary. And having, in a former correspondence with my deceased son in law John W. Eppes contemplated laying off for him with remainder to my grandson Francis, a certain portion in the Southern part of my lands in Bedford and Campbell, which I afterwards found to be generally more indifferent than I had supposed, & therefore determined to change it's location for the better; now to remove all doubt, if any could arise on a purpose merely voluntary & unexecuted, I hereby declare that what I have herein given to my sd. grandson Francis is instead of, and not additional to what I had formerly contemplated.

I subject all my other property to the payment of my debts in the first place.

Considering the insolvent state of the affairs of my friend & son in law Thomas

Mann Randolph, and that what will remain of my property will be the only resource against the want in which his family would otherwise be left, it must be his wish, as it is my duty, to guard that resource against all liability for his debts, engagements or purposes whatsoever, and to preclude the rights, powers and authorities over it which might result to him by operation of law, and which might, independently of his will, bring it within the power of the creditors, I do hereby devise and bequeath all the residue of my property real and personal, in possession or in action, whether held in my own right, or in that of my dear deceased wife, according to the powers vested in me by deed of settlement for that purpose, to my grandson Thomas J. Randolph, & my friends Nicholas P. Trist and Alexander Garret & their heirs during the life of my sd. son in law Thomas M. Randolph, to be held & administered by them, in trust, for the sole and separate use and behoof of my dear daughter Martha Randolph and her heirs. And, aware of the nice and difficult distinctions of the law in these cases, I will further explain by saying, that I understand and intend the effect of these limitations to be, that the legal estate and actual occupation shall be vested in my said trustees, and held by them in base fee, determinable on the death of my sd. son in law, and the remainder during the same time be vested in my sd. daughter and her heirs, and of course disposable by her last will, and that at the death of my sd. son in law, the particular estate of the sd. trustees shall be determined, and the remainder, in legal estate, possession and use become vested in my said daughter and her heirs, in absolute property forever.

In consequence of the variety and indescribableness of the articles of property within the house at Monticello, and the difficulty of inventorying and appraising them separately and specifically, and it's inutility, I dispense with having them inventoried and appraised; and it is my will that my executors be not held to give any security for the administration of my estate. I appoint my grandson Thomas Jefferson Randolph my sole executor during his life, and after his death, I constitute executors my friends Nicholas P. Trist and Alexander Garret joining to them my daughter Martha Randolph after the death of my sd. son in law Thomas M. Randolph.

Lastly I revoke all former wills by me heretofore made; and in witness that this is my will, I have written the whole with my own hand on two pages and have subscribed my name to each of them this 16th day of March one thousand eight hundred and twenty six

TH. JEFFERSON

I Thomas Jefferson of Monticello in Albemarle make and add the following Codicil to my will, controuling the same so far as it's provisions go.

I recommend to my daughter, Martha Randolph, the maintenance and care of my well-beloved sister Anne Scott Marks, and trust confidently that from affection to her, as well as for my sake, she will never let her want a comfort.

I have made no specific provision for the comfortable maintenance of my son in law Thomas M. Randolph, because of the difficulty and uncertainty of devising terms which shall vest any beneficial interest in him which the law will not transfer to the benefit of his creditors, to the destitution of my daughter and her family and disablement of her to supply him: whereas property placed under the exclusive control of my daughter and her independent will, as if she were a femme sole, considering the relation in which she stands both to him and his children, will be a certain resource against want for all.

I give to my friend James Madison of Montpellier my gold mounted walking staff of animal horn, as a token of the cordial and affectionate friendship which for nearly now an half century, has united us in the same principles and pursuits of what we have deemed for the greatest good of our country.

I give to the University of Virginia my library, except such particular books only, and of the same edition, as it may already possess, when this legacy shall take effect. The rest of my said library remaining after those given to the University shall have been taken out, I give to my two grandsons in law Nicholas P. Trist and Joseph Coolidge.

To my grandson Thomas Jefferson Randolph I give my silver watch in preference of the golden one, because of it's superior excellence. My papers of business going of course to him, as my executor, all others of a literary or other character I give to him as of his own property.

I give a gold watch to each of my grandchildren, who shall not have already recieved [*sic*] one from me, to be purchased and delivered by my executor, to my grandsons at the age of 21. and granddaughters at that of sixteen.

I give to my good, affectionate, and faithful servant Burwell his freedom, and the sum of three hundred Dollars to buy necessaries to commence his trade of painter and glazier, or to use otherwise as he pleases. I give also to my good servants John Hemings and Joe Fosset, their freedom at the end of one year after my death: and to each of them respectively all the tools of their respective shops or callings: and it is my will that a comfortable log-house be built for each of the three servants so emancipated on some part of my lands convenient to them with respect to the residence of their wives, and to Charlottesville and the University, where they will be mostly employed, and reasonably convenient also to the interests of the proprietor of the lands; of which houses I give the use of one, with a curtilage of an acre to each, during his life or personal occupation thereof.

I give also to John Hemings the service of his two apprentices, Madison and Eston Hemings, until their respective ages of twenty one years, at which period respectively, I give them their freedom. And I humbly and earnestly request of the legislature of Virginia a confirmation of the bequest of freedom to these servants, with permission to remain in this state where their families and connections are, as an additional instance of the favor, of which I have received so many other manifestations, in the course of my life, and for which I now give them my last, solemn, and dutiful thanks.

In testimony that this is a Codicil to my will of yesterday's date, and that it is to modify so far the provisions of that will, I have written it all with my own hand, in two pages, to each of which I subscribe my name this 17th. day of March one thousand eight hundred and twenty six.

Th. Jefferson

Reminiscences of Madison Hemings

I never knew of but one white man who bore the name of Hemings. He was an Englishman and my great grandfather. He was captain of an English whaling vessel which sailed between England and Williamsburg, Va., then quite a port. My [great-] grandmother was a fullblooded African, and possibly a native of that country. She was the property of John Wales, a Welchman. Capt. Hemings happened to be in the port of Williamsburg at the time my grandmother was born, and acknowledging her fatherhood he tried to purchase her of Mr. Wales who would not part with the child, though he was offered an extraordinarily large price for her. She was named Elizabeth Hemings. Being thwarted in the purchase, and determined to own his own flesh and blood he resolved to take the child by force or stealth, but the knowledge of his intention coming to John Wales' ears, through leaky fellow servants of the mother, she and the child were taken into the "great house" under their master's immediate care. I have been informed that it was not the extra value of that child over other slave children that induced Mr. Wales to refuse to sell it, for slave masters then, as in later days, had no compunctions of conscience which restrained them from parting mother and child of however tender age, but he was restrained by the fact that just about that time amalgamation began, and the child was so great a curiosity that its owner desired to raise it himself that he might see its outcome. Capt. Hemings soon afterwards sailed from Williamsburg, never to return. Such is the story that comes down to me.

Elizabeth Hemings grew to womanhood in the family of John Wales, whose wife dying she (Elizabeth) was taken by the widower Wales as his concubine, by whom she had six children—three sons and three daughters, viz: Robert, James, Peter, Critty, Sally and Thena. These children went by the name of Hemings.

Williamsburg was the capital of Virginia, and of course it was an aristocratic place, where the "bloods" of the Colony and the new State most did congregate. Thomas Jefferson, the author of the Declaration of Independence, was educated at William and Mary College, which had its seat at Williamsburg. He afterwards studied law with Geo. Wythe, and practiced law at the bar of the general court of the Colony. He was afterwards elected a member of the provincial legislature from Albemarle county. Thos. Jefferson was a visitor at the "great house" of John Wales, who had children about his own age. He formed the acquaintance of his daughter Martha (I believe that was her name, though I am not positively sure,) and an intimacy sprang up between them which ripened into love, and they were married. They afterwards went to live at his country seat Monticello, and in course of time had born to them a daughter whom they named Martha. About the time she was born my mother, the second daughter of John Wales and Elizabeth Hemings was born. On the death of John Wales, my grandmother, his concubine, and her children by him fell to Martha, Thomas Jefferson's wife, and consequently became the property of Thomas Jefferson, who in the course of time became famous, and was appointed minister to France during our revolutionary troubles, or soon after independence was gained. About the time of the appointment and before he was ready to leave the country his wife died, and as soon after her interment as he could attend to and arrange his domestic affairs in accordance with the changed circumstances of his family in consequence of this misfortune (I think not more than three weeks thereafter) he left for France, taking his eldest daughter with him. He had had sons born to him, but they died in early infancy, so he then had but two children—Martha and Maria. The latter was left at home, but was afterwards ordered to follow him to France. She was three years or so younger than Martha. My mother accompanied her as her body servant. When Mr. Jefferson went to France Martha was a young woman grown, my mother was about her age, and Maria was just budding into womanhood. Their stay (my mother's and Maria's) was about eighteen months. But during that time my mother became Mr. Jefferson's concubine, and when he was called back home she was *enciente* by him. He desired to bring my mother back to Virginia with him but she demurred. She was just beginning to understand the French language well, and in France she was free, while if she returned to Virginia she would be re-enslaved. So she refused to return with him. To induce her to do so he promised her extraordinary privileges, and made a solemn pledge that her children should be freed at the age of twenty-one years. In consequence of his promises, on which she implicitly replied [*sic*] she returned with him to Virginia. Soon after their arrival, she gave birth to a child, of whom Thomas Jefferson was the father. It lived but a short time. She gave birth to four others, and Jefferson was the father of all of them. Their names were Beverly, Harriet, Madison (myself), and Eston—three sons and one daughter. We all became free agreeably to the treaty entered into by our parents before we were born. We all married and have raised families.

Beverly left Monticello and went to Washington as a white man. He married a white woman in Maryland, and their only child, a daughter, was not known by the white folks to have any colored blood coursing in her veins. Beverly's wife's family were people in good circumstances.

Harriet married a white man in good standing in Washington City, whose name I could give, but will not, for prudential reasons. She raised a family of children, and so far as I know they were never suspected of being tainted with African blood in the community where she lived or lives. I have not heard from her for ten years, and do not know whether she is dead or alive. She thought it to her interest, on going to Washington, to assume the role of a white woman, and by her dress and conduct as such I am not aware that her identity as Harriet Hemings of Monticello has ever been discovered.

Eston married a colored woman in Virginia, and moved from there to Ohio, and lived in Chillicothe several years. In the fall of 1852 he removed to Wisconsin, where he died a year or two afterwards. He left three children.

As to myself, I was named Madison by the wife of James Madison, who was afterwards President of the United States. Mrs. Madison happened to be at Monticello at the time of my birth, and begged the privilege of naming me, promising my mother a fine present for the honor. She consented, and Mrs. Madison dubbed me by the name I now acknowledge, but like many promises of white folks to the slaves she never gave my mother anything. I was born at my father's seat of Monticello, in Albemarle county, Va., near Charlottesville, on the 19th day of January, 1805. My very earliest recollections are of my grandmother Elizabeth Hemings. That was when I was about three years old. She was sick and upon her death bed. I was eating a piece of bread and asked her if she would have some. She replied: "No; granny don't want bread any more." She shortly afterwards breathed her last. I have only a faint recollection of her.

Of my father, Thomas Jefferson, I knew more of his domestic than his public life during his life time. It is only since his death that I have learned much of the latter, except that he was considered as a foremost man in the land, and held many important trusts, including that of President. I learned to read by inducing the white children to teach me the letters and something more; what else I know of books I have picked up here and there till now I can read and write. I was almost 21 years of age when my father died on the 4th of July, 1826.

About his own home he was the quietest of men. He was hardly ever known to get angry, though sometimes he was irritated when matters went wrong, but even then he hardly ever allowed himself to be made unhappy any great length of time. Unlike Washington he had but little taste or care for agricultural pursuits. He left matters pertaining to his plantations mostly with his stewards and overseers. He always had mechanics at work for him, such as carpenters, blacksmiths, shoemakers, coopers, &c. It was his mechanics he seemed mostly to direct, and in their operations he took great interest. Almost every day of his later years he might have been seen among them. He occupied much of the time in his office engaged in correspondence and reading and writing. His general temperament was smooth and even; he was very undemonstrative. He was uniformly kind to all about him. He was not in the habit of showing partiality or fatherly affection to us children. We were the only children of his by a slave woman. He was affectionate toward his white grandchildren, of whom he had fourteen, twelve of whom lived to manhood and womanhood. His daughter Martha married Thomas Mann Randolph by whom she had thirteen children. Two died in infancy. The names of the living were Ann, Thomas Jefferson, Ellen, Cornelia, Virginia, Mary, James,[1] Benj. Franklin, Lewis Madison,[2] Septemia and Geo. Wythe. Thos. Jefferson Randolph was Chairman of the Democratic National Convention in Baltimore last spring which nominated Horace Greeley for the Presidency, and Geo. Wythe Randolph was Jeff. Davis' first Secretary of War in the late "unpleasantness."

Maria married John Eppes, and raised one son—Francis.

My father generally enjoyed excellent health. I never knew him to have but one spell of sickness, and that was caused by a visit to the Warm Springs in 1818. Till within three weeks of his death he was hale and hearty, and at the age of 83 years he walked erect and with stately tread. I am now 68, and I well remember that he was a much smarter man physically, even at that age, than I am.

When I was fourteen years old I was put to the carpenter trade under the charge of John Hemings, the youngest son of my grandmother. His father's name was Nelson, who was an Englishman. She had seven children by white men and seven by colored men—fourteen in all. My brothers, sister Harriet and myself, were used alike. They were put to some mechanical trade at the age of fourteen. Till then we were permitted to stay about the "great house," and only required to do such light work as going on errands. Harriet learned to spin and to weave in a little factory on the home plantation. We were free from the dread of having to be slaves all our lives long, and were measurably happy. We were always permitted to be with our mother, who was well used. It was her duty, all her life which I can remember, up to the time of our father's death, to take care of his chamber and wardrobe, look after us children and do such light work as sewing, &c. Provision was made in the will of our father that we should be free when we arrived at the age of 21 years. We had all passed that period when he died but Eston, and he was given the remainder of his time shortly after. He and I rented a house and took mother to live with us, till her death, which event occurred in 1835.

In 1834 I married Mary McCoy. Her grandmother was a slave, and lived with her master, Stephen Hughes, near Charlottesville, as his wife. She was manumitted by him, which made their children free born. Mary McCoy's mother was his daughter. I was about 28 and she 22 years of age when we married. We lived and labored together in Virginia till 1836, when we voluntarily left and came to Ohio. We settled in Pebble township, Pike county. We lived there four or five years and during my stay in that county I worked at my trade on and off for about four years. Joseph Sewell was my first employer. I built for him what is now known as Rizzleport No. 2 in Waverly. I afterwards worked for George Wolf Senior. and I did the carpenter work of the brick building now owned by John J. Kellison in which the Pike County Republican is printed. I worked for and with Micajab [?] Hinson. I found him to be a very clever man. I also reconstructed the building on the corner of Market and Water streets from a store to a hotel for the late Judge Jacob Row.

When we came from Virginia we brought one daughter (Sarah) with us, leaving the dust of a son in the soil near Monticello. We have born to us in this State nine children. Two are dead. The names of the living, besides Sarah, are Harriet, Mary Ann, Catharine, Jane, William Beverly, James Madison and Ellen Wales. Thomas Eston died in the Andersonville prison pen, and Julia died at home. William, James and Ellen are unmarried and live at home, in Huntington township, Ross county. All the others are married and raising families. My post office address is Pee Pee, Pike county Ohio.

[Madison Hemings died of consumption on November 28, 1877, age 72 years. His death notice in the Probate Court records of Ross County, Ohio, II, 15, lists him as "colored, male," born in Virginia, widowed, with the occupation of farmer. His personal goods, sold at public auction for $221.59, included a bedstead, a mare, wagon, and carpenter's tools. His real estate was sold for $685; his debts were listed as $963.93. Property records in Chillicothe, Ohio, show seven transactions involving Madison Hemings, and two involving Eston Hemings. Madison bought 25 acres for $150 on July 25, 1856, and sold them for $250 on December 30, 1859. On September 25, 1865, he bought 66 acres for $660; these were sold after his death for $682. Eston Hemings and his wife Julia Anne sold a lot for $590 on August 10, 1850, and another lot on August 18, 1852, for $1,000.

Madison's granddaughter, Mrs. Nellie E. Jones, of Watseka, Illinois, wrote to Stuart G. Gibboney, at the Thomas Jefferson Memorial Foundation, Monticello, on August 10, 1938, stating that she had a pair of spectacles, silver buckle, and an inkwell that had belonged to Jefferson. Her great-grandmother, Sally Hemings, had given them to her son Madison, she said, and at his death they were inherited by her mother. Mrs. Jones was the daughter of Mary A. Hemings, who, according to the Ross County Courthouse records, Chillicothe, Ohio, was married on April 25, 1864, to David Johnson.]

NOTES

From "Life Among the Lowly, No. 1," *Pike County (Ohio) Republican*, March 13, 1873.

1. James Madison.
2. Meriwether Lewis.

Index

About the Author

BYRON W. WOODSON, SR. is a son of Minnie S. Woodson, who researched the Woodson genealogy and wrote the *Woodson Source Book*. He is a sixth-generation descendant of Sally Hemings and Thomas Jefferson and a great-great-grandson of the Reverend Lewis Woodson, the father of black nationalism. Byron Woodson gave a blood sample for the Hemings/Jefferson DNA test in 1997 and with his wife, Trena, has extended research to Thomas Jefferson's papers, uncovering new findings. Woodson is a graduate of Lincoln University (Pa.) and Temple University, where he earned a MBA.